The British in Germany

Educational Reconstruction after 1945

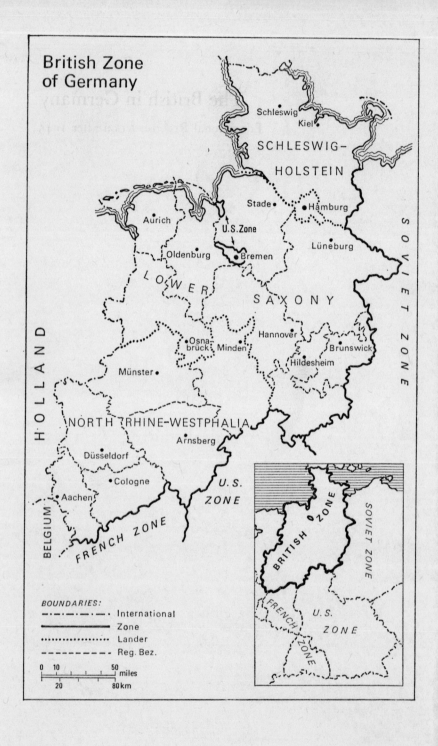

British Zone
of Germany

SCHLESWIG-HOLSTEIN

Schleswig
Kiel

Stade
Hamburg

U.S.Zone

Lüneburg

Aurich

Oldenburg
Bremen

LOWER

SAXONY

Osna-
brück
Minden
Hannover
Brunswick
Hildesheim

Münster

NORTH RHINE-WESTPHALIA

Arnsberg

Düsseldorf

Cologne

Aachen

U.S.
ZONE

FRENCH ZONE

HOLLAND

BELGIUM

SOVIET ZONE

BOUNDARIES:

- – - – - – International
———— Zone
·············· Lander
– – – – – Reg. Bez.

0   10   50   miles
    20   80 km

BRITISH ZONE

SOVIET ZONE

FRENCH ZONE

U.S.
ZONE

The British in Germany

Educational Reconstruction after 1945

Edited by
ARTHUR HEARNDEN

Hamish Hamilton · London

First published in Great Britain, 1978
by Hamish Hamilton Ltd.,
90 Great Russell Street,
London WC1B 3PT

ISBN 0 241 89637 1

Printed in Great Britain by
Bristol Typesetting Co. Ltd,
Barton Manor, St Philips, Bristol

Contents

CONTENTS Cont.

This volume was conceived as a tribute to all those, both British and German, whose privilege it was to co-operate in the daunting tasks that confronted German education in the British Zone of Germany during the years that followed the Second World War.

This book has its origins in the conference on British education policy in early post-war Germany, which was held, under the chairmanship of Sir Robert Birley, at St Edmund Hall, Oxford in January 1975. Those who participated were convinced that the papers given on that occasion formed the nucleus of a unique and valuable record. By commissioning additional contributions it has been possible to expand the material to comprehend virtually all aspects of the British involvement in educational reconstruction.

The chapters therefore fall into two major categories, those intended for delivery before an audience and those written expressly for publication. In the course of the editorial work it has seemed best to allow certain elements of conversational style in the former to stand, in the hope that this will help to convey the spirit of a gathering which succeeded remarkably well in recapturing something of the atmosphere of the period under study.

Other contrasts will be apparent to the reader. While the majority of the chapters are in the nature of memoirs of those who were personally involved, others are pieces of documented research. In view of this only a minimum of standardisation of terminology has seemed called for. Thus, for example, it can in one case be appropriate to make plentiful use of specialised German vocabulary while in another, loose translations of some of the same terms may fit the text better.

The most important acknowledgement to be made is our indebtedness to the British Council for the financial support which made the conference and this publication possible. At the time when the project was being planned I was myself by a fortunate coincidence engaged at the London University Institute of Education on the restoration of the GER archive and on more general research on the role of the British in post-war educational reconstruction in Germany. I am grateful to the

A*

Social Science Research Council for their sponsorship of this work, which provided a valuable additional incentive to see the conference launched. But the credit for the original initiative and the lion's share of the administrative arrangements involved must go to Werner Burmeister who is happily one of the authors writing in this volume.

I must acknowledge with gratitude the willing co-operation of all the contributors which greatly eased the task of assembling the material for publication. The original papers were by Jane Anderson, Sir Robert Birley, Fritz Borinski, Edith Davies, Harald Husemann, Marion Klewitz, George Murray and Ken Walsh. George Murray subsequently took the further trouble to write the chapter on teacher training and to help with the appendices. Geoffrey Bird, Werner Burmeister, Trevor Davies, Kathleen Davis and A. W. J. Edwards were all willing at short notice to add their contributions. In particular my thanks go to Jane Anderson and Judith Guilmant who translated those papers that were originally given in German, and to a number of friends and colleagues who read parts of my own manuscript and made valuable suggestions.

Finally, it is the hope of all of us associated with the book that it will do something to extend the Anglo-German friendship which permeates the text. To give practical expression to this wish we are proposing to devote our royalties to the furtherance of Anglo-German relations, setting up a fund to establish a new kind of travel scholarship.

A.H.

1. *Education in the British Zone*

Arthur Hearnden

In July 1945 the Education Branch of the British Element of the Control Commission for Germany established its headquarters in Westphalia and assumed control over German education in the British Zone and the British Sector of Berlin. In the following month its task was set out in the Potsdam Agreement: 'German education shall be so controlled as completely to eliminate Nazi and militarist doctrines and to make possible the successful development of democratic ideas.' Now, a generation later, the Federal Republic is a flourishing democracy and many of its citizens look back with appreciation to the contribution which the education officers of the British Zone made towards educational reconstruction during the Occupation.

This book is a record of that work written for the most part by those who carried it out. Their accounts of how they interpreted their task mirror the conditions of the time. Any attempt to add to what the contributors have to say about their activities would be inappropriate coming from one whose first visit to Germany was as a sixth former in the summer of 1948. Suffice it to say that the weeks spent visiting refugee camps at that time made a lasting impression and that the memory of those experiences brings a feeling of gratitude at being presented now with the opportunity to share in recording some of the achievements.

If it is impossible to add much to this record of British involvement—and this will continue to be so until the official documents have been catalogued and made available to scholars —an attempt can nevertheless be made to set it in its context. The aim of this introductory chapter is to give an account of the development of the ideas which the Germans themselves entertained about educational reconstruction and thereby to illuminate the scene in which the British education officers were operating. More specifically the concern here is largely with the school systems, because this was the sector which directly in-

volved the most people and in which feelings ran highest. There
is, however, no intention to suggest that the work in the other
sectors was any less important and it may well be that the space
devoted to them later in the book will compensate for the relative neglect they suffer in this introduction.

The Reopening and After

The conditions under which German schools and universities
were reopened after the final surrender in 1945 were so varied
and so adverse that a co-ordinated operation was impossible.
The variety derived not only from the differing approaches
adopted by the British, American, French and Soviet administrations but also from the reassertion of distinctive regional
traditions within the individual occupation Zones. This was
hardly surprising in view of the discredit attached to any impulse
towards centralisation. It was the National Socialist government
which had first established a national ministry of education in
Germany and this unhappy precedent was a sufficient admon-
ishment. To the extent that the Allies wished to encourage
fragmentation of initiative and responsibility, their approach
was broadly in harmony with the predilection on the part of the
Germans for the restoration of regional and local control over
educational development. With hindsight this variety stands out
as of fundamental significance, for one of the recurrent problems
of the post-war years, at least in West Germany, has been the
search for a formula to co-ordinate if not to unify the various
systems that were resuscitated during the Occupation.

It was however, the adversity rather than the variety that was
overwhelmingly characteristic of the early days. The precision
of statistics—for example the fact that one classroom was available for every 123 children in Schleswig-Holstein where the
pre-war figure had been thirty-seven with the result that teaching was only possible by means of a shift system—is inadequate
to convey the hardship that had to be endured. The first-hand
accounts written by former education officers who served in
Germany from 1945 onwards breathe life into figures such as
these. As they make clear, the story of the resumption of educational activity is made up of countless episodes of strenuous
endeavour; struggles to enable children to be housed, clothed

and fed before much thought could be given to their schooling. These chapters tell their own story and it would be presumptuous to elaborate on them here except in one respect. They do provide a clue in the search for what was distinctive about educational reconstruction in the British Zone of occupation, in comparison with the others.

Shortly after the end of his period of service as Educational Adviser Sir Robert Birley wrote: 'As a piece of deliberate policy the members of the Branch have been deployed as widely as possible in order that they might influence German education by personal contacts with individuals. Their main task has been to get to know those persons, teachers and officials, who have it in them to create a new and healthy education in Germany, to help and encourage them, and to put them in touch with the world outside their own country.' This informality was the hallmark of the British approach to educational reconstruction. Its effect was to distribute the collective responsibility for the regeneration of German education to all the outposts of Education Branch and thereby to create maximum scope for independent initiative on the part of individuals. By this token the qualities and attitudes of those who worked in this independent way came to be identified with British policy as a whole. And it may be that this patchwork of individual contributions gives a more authentic picture of that policy than could be gained from any analysis of headquarters decisions.

Certainly the impression of variety is reinforced by an examination of the policies adopted by the four *Länder*. To judge by the flexibility of the reactions to them in the Control Commission, the very last thing that the British authorities set out to do was to impose a rigid model. Before looking in detail at these different outcomes of the interaction between the two sides, it is useful to outline in more general terms the changing circumstances of the period of British administration.

The early months were given over to establishing some kind of working relationship between the occupying authorities and the German people. Apart from the purely material difficulties it was a period dominated by the legal and administrative problems involved in granting recognition to the residual education departments and restoring status to those teachers who had not been, in the official phraseology, 'active Nazis or ardent Nazi sympathisers'. The most formidable difficulties lay in finding the right people to fill the more senior posts. Heads of schools appointed between 1933 and 1945 were generally speaking not permitted to continue their service; it was natural that great store should be set by filling these positions with people of irreproachable credentials. Administrative appointments were also of far-reaching significance. For in view of the political vacuum in the early months, the persuasions of these 'men of the first hour'—*Männer der ersten Stunde*—were a crucial factor in determining the form in which the educational system would subsequently resume its activity.

It is difficult to generalise about the success which the occupying powers enjoyed in making these appointments. The heavy toll which had been taken of the younger generation was apparent everywhere and in consequence the field was restricted largely to men and women who were in their fifties or older. One result of this was probably a greater tendency to adopt more conservative attitudes than might be encountered in more normal circumstances. On the other hand, many of those who came to prominence were former radicals and it was perhaps no bad thing that their early predilection for change was now balanced by the wisdom of experience. There can be no doubt that even if their energies were understandably flagging as a result of advancing years and physical privations a good many of them, as the accounts that follow demonstrate, combined sound sense with vision in the way that they made their mark on postwar educational development.

That the schools were in a position to be opened at all was remarkable. The chapters that follow contain many illustrations of the difficulties and the ways in which they were surmounted. The speed and efficiency of the exercise depended not only on the resourcefulness of the Allied authorities but on the degree to which they were prepared to devolve responsibility. In North Rhine province, for example, the operation proceeded more smoothly than in Westphalia.[1] However, such variations, while they caused much frustration and resentment at the time, scarcely detract from the total achievement involved in re-establishing coherent education systems throughout Germany.

With this resumption of activity there began a vigorous debate among German educationists and teachers on the fundamental principles of an education designed to build a new healthy society. Already during 1946 ideas were beginning to crystallise and by December it was possible on general political grounds for the decision to be taken to hand over the control of education to the German authorities. The decision became effective in January 1947 and this transfer of responsibility cleared the way for the politicians to pursue their objectives in more specific ways, for though the military government retained certain powers over appointments they very rarely intervened and never exercised their right to veto legislation.[2] In fact the new advisory status of Education Branch personnel, while it denoted scarcely any real change in practice, did make it easier for them to encourage widespread discussion of educational matters in the German communities. The very existence of control instructions had been an inhibiting factor.

Gradually the debate moved on from consideration of general principles to more precise concern with their practical implication in terms of structure and curriculum in the schools sector which was the main focus of interest. Predictably enough, the political differences became more and more sharply defined as plans for legislation were formulated. The radical demands expressed in the Social Democratic Party were for a fresh start based on a reorganisation which would bring all types of school together into a fully unified system. These demands picked up some of the threads of the *Reformpädagogik* movement of the early years of the century and in practice hinged on the lengthening of primary schooling. On the conservative side there was an equally strong conviction that the salvation of Germany lay in a return to traditional values, many of which the reform movement had set out to discredit. In practical terms this meant the retention of the confessional *Volksschule* and the academic *Gymnasium*.

Viewed as a whole it was British policy to keep out of this controversy. Such official support as there was for the idea of a six-year primary school, in the policy review of the autumn of 1947, referred to by Sir Robert Birley and George Murray, was so guarded as to be almost non-committal. It is true that the nature of the organisation of Education Branch was such as to allow scope for encouragement of one side or

the other, depending on the views of the individual education officers. And they were, if anything, in broad sympathy
with the Social Democrats. But most of them would appear to
have shared the view that the political struggles were very
much subsidiary to the continued pressing problems of improving the material conditions under which the schools and
universities were operating. This sober pragmatic concern for
practical priorities was re-emphasised with the second major
turning-point of the Occupation period, the currency reform,
which brought home to the *Land* governments the fact that
they were still dealing with an emergency. Nevertheless to
the Germans the political clashes were over fundamental issues
and they give a valuable insight into the forces which were
subsequently to shape the development of education. Some
understanding of these forces is necessary in order to make
possible an evaluation of the role of the British authorities,
whether it was to further them, to inhibit them or to ignore
them.

The survey that follows is therefore an attempt to identify
the salient issues in each of these *Länder* in turn and in so doing
to provide some insight into the indigenous attitudes to education with which the British authorities had the task of coming
to terms.

North Rhine-Westphalia

North Rhine and Westphalia, formerly separate provinces of
Prussia, were combined to form a single *Land* in July 1946.
Up till then they were administered separately with variations
in the pace at which educational work was resumed.

The first officials to be given responsibility for education in
North Rhine province in the early months after the war were
Hermann Platz, Josef Schnippenkötter and Josef Esterhues. All
three were Catholics; Platz was head of the department, with
Schnippenkötter responsible for secondary education and Esterhues for the elementary schools. In both spheres the initiative
was seized early. In the elementary sector which according to
the *Technical Manual on Education and Religious Affairs*
issued by the Supreme Headquarters of the Allied Expeditionary
Force (SHAEF) was to be the first priority, the Military Govern-

ment was asked as early as August to ratify a directive on the re-establishment of denominational schools. As for the secondary sector, Schnippenkötter, a former *Gymnasium* headmaster in Essen, also had his plans for reform ready by August when the *Schulreferententagung*, the first conference of education officials of the British Zone was held. A new curriculum had been drawn up and it was possible to open 120 *Gymnasien* in the province on 1 October and at the same time announce plans for the opening of the remainder later in the same month.[3] The opening of the schools in Westphalia was by contrast a more laborious affair.[4]

An emphasis on Christianity was the theme that was common to all plans prepared by the group in North Rhine Province. It was not Christianity in the broad sense of adherence to a code of values, rather a Christianity that operated through rigid denominational channels, 'im Sinne eines geprägten und geformten Kirchentums', as Schnippenkötter put it. In addition, where the *Gymnasium* sector was concerned another central theme was classical humanism. In a broadcast in the autumn of 1945 Hermann Platz declared 'how necessary it is that having been so near to losing our humanity we and our culture should recover something, indeed a great deal of Graeco-Roman dignity and Christian devoutness, and something of the spiritual and moral attitudes which derive from them'.[5] Antiquity and Christianity were thus twin inspirations of humanism, a term which had further broadened in its connotations since Humboldt's time to embrace the whole range of academic activity that characterised the *Gymnasium*, including science. Schnippenkötter was a physicist and saw science as an alternative model through which to understand man and his relationship to God. It was Christian humanism, interpreted in these ways, that lay behind educational reconstruction in the early days in North Rhine Province.

These principles were worked out in practice in the two major sectors of the school system. In the secondary sector the *Deutsche Oberschule* which had been adopted by the Nazis as the prime model was abolished and the classical *Gymnasium* was restored to its former pre-eminence. In his plan which came to be known as the *Nordwestdeutscher Plan*, Schnippenkötter at first wanted only one other type of *Gymnasium*, the mathematics/natural science one to which he was personally very committed but he

was soon prevailed upon to add a modern languages type. Latin
was to be the first foreign language in all three cases and the
Oberprima, the top form which had been done away with by
the Nazis, was to be restored so that once again the course would
last the full nine years. The reasons for making Latin the first
foreign language were three : firstly the importance of the
classics per se, secondly the value of the early years in the learning of languages, thirdly the unity it gave to the *Gymnasium*
sector as a whole. This last reason illustrates the degree to which
the grammar schools were treated separately from the elementary
schools in which some ninety per cent of children received the
whole of their education. It was assumed that an accurate
selection could be made at the age of ten. When this was
challenged, Schnippenkötter attempted to cater for late developers by providing additional courses for able pupils in the
intermediate *Mittelschulen* and by expanding the provision
of *Aufbaugymnasien*, schools specially designed to provide an
academic education beginning at a later age for the most able
of those who had remained in the *Volksschulen* beyond the age
of ten.

The schools in North Rhine were single sex and the provision
for girls was different from that for boys. Classics and natural
sciences were not considered appropriate specialisations and the
only type of *Gymnasium* for girls was one in which English was
the first language studied, Latin being added in the third year
along with French. In view of the fundamental importance
which he accorded to classics and natural sciences as pillars of
German culture, Schnippenkötter's disdain for the female sex
in education was obvious. As well as the *Mädchengymnasium*
there was the *Lyzeum*, in which it was not possible to acquire
a qualification to enter university. Three important women
educationists, Änne Franken, Luise Bardenhewer, who later
became head of the department of secondary education, and
Christine Teusch, who became Minister of Education, held more
emancipated views about the education of girls. However, all
three were opposed to co-education and this was in practice
tantamount to a denial of opportunity. For since there was no
possibility of founding new girls' schools at this time the only
way to put the *Abitur* within their reach was to admit them to
the boys' *Gymnasien*. The lack of improvement in the provision

made for the education of girls is one further illustration of the conservative nature of the revived school system of North Rhine in the early days. In this respect Westphalia was somewhat less rigid but it was not sufficiently different to invalidate the general impression that the early period had seen a highly traditional restoration, characterised by an uncompromising aversion to innovation.

The government of the combined *Land* of North Rhine-Westphalia subsequently demonstrated its concern to meet the criticisms of this conservatism by issuing a consultative document or *Denkschrift* on the reform of school organisation. It was to some extent a response to the celebrated Directive No. 54 of the Control Commission which had among other things sought to establish elementary and secondary education as 'two consecutive levels of instruction', to be enjoyed by all. If this could be done then the *Volksschule* with its 'upper elementary' classes would no longer be the sole source of full-time education for the great majority of young people; instead it would be the primary school from which all pupils would move on to secondary education of various kinds, on the analogy of the 1944 Education Act in England and Wales. The ways in which it was proposed to achieve this end in North Rhine-Westphalia illustrate the more conservative of the approaches to educational reform during the Occupation period.[6]

The plan was presented in such a way as to suggest the general introduction of consecutive primary and secondary levels. Four years of primary schooling were to be provided for all children after which, at the age of ten, they would have a number of directions in which to proceed. For the academic path the *Denkschrift* gave firm support to the maintenance of the classical *Gymnasium* but departed from Schnippenkötter's ideas in advocating that the mathematical and modern languages types which were to run parallel to it should have English as their first foreign language. There was a clearly declared wish to keep the *Gymnasium* sector relatively small in the face of increasing pressure to expand it. Here the worry was that there would otherwise be a surplus of university graduates for whom employment prospects would be slender. Indeed this notion of an 'academic proletariat' has been a familiar spectre in the Federal Republic since the War. Above all it has haunted the feast of expanded opportunity that has been consumed since the mid-1960s. In the *Denkschrift* of the North Rhine-Westphalia government the idea was even mooted that at the end of the eighth year of the *Gymnasium* course a leaving certificate should be available which did not carry with it the right to enter university, a right which had traditionally accompanied the acquisition of the *Abitur*. The new suggestion was that only those admitted to the final year would be considered potential university students. Nothing came of this unwelcome idea.

The desire to avoid excessive expansion of the *Gymnasium* sector and the dilution of academic standards which it was feared would accompany it was a factor in shaping the other proposals, namely to build up firstly the intermediate schools and secondly the network of vocational schools and colleges, a sector which was coming to be known as the *zweiter Bildungsweg*. In this way the *Denkschrift* indicated accurately the lines along which the school system was in the event organised. Changes were contemplated with extreme cautiousness and there was no question of dismantling any of the established types of school. The most difficult thing about this approach was raising the standards of the elementary schools. For they continued to provide the only full-time education open to most children because the resources were not available for building and staffing enough separate secondary schools of a non-academic kind to realise the aims of Directive No. 54 concerning consecutive levels.

In these circumstances, to extend primary schooling to six years was perhaps fairer, especially in view of the lengthy interruptions of attendance that so many children had suffered, but here again the resources, particularly for foreign language teaching were considered inadequate. The only practical ways of mitigating the injustices of selection were to place as much emphasis as possible on facilities for transfer in general, and to create the *Aufbaugymnasien* referred to earlier. The attitude to the issue of lengthening primary schooling by two years aptly characterises the conservative position on educational change not only at this time in North Rhine-Westphalia but also increasingly throughout the Federal Republic in the two decades that followed. While a new idea might well be accepted as a desirable long-term aim, as this one was, there was no question of introducing it until the technical requirements for making it a success had been met; changes were only to be introduced after successful experiments had been carried out. This view reflected the dominance of the conservative Christian Democratic Party (CDU) in the *Landtag*. What is more it remains at the heart of the surviving disinclination in most parts of the Federal Republic to introduce comprehensive schools on a large scale.

Schleswig-Holstein

Schleswig-Holstein stands at the opposite pole from North Rhine -Westphalia in that it was the first of the *Länder* of the British Zone to introduce reformist educational legislation. The Social Democratic Party (SPD) came to power with an overall majority in the first elections in 1947; the Minister of Education was Wilhelm Kuklinski who had held this position in the provisional governments of the previous year. The law passed in 1948 was the subject of a bitter political controversy which illustrates the basis on which the SPD strove to realise the aspirations of an earlier radical tradition. In broad outline the theme was the now familiar one that democracy can only be established once all educational privileges have been abolished through the introduction of a single comprehensive school system serving the entire population. Where the previous system had reflected and reinforced differences of class and confession in the way it was structured the new approach was seen as the means of reconciling them. As its designation proclaimed, the *Einheitsschule* was to unite the people.

This broad idealism was buttressed by several arguments of greater precision and immediacy. Firstly, it was contended, ten was an unrealistically early age at which to select entrants to grammar schools, especially in view of the rarity of opportunity to correct mistakes by means of transfers at a later stage. A reorganisation was therefore sought which would order the progression from one school to the next in accordance with what was regarded as the natural development of children. The psychological and pedagogical arguments adduced at the time pointed to twelve rather than ten as the proper age of transfer.

The second argument concerned the geographical distribution

of opportunity in a *Land* which had relatively few urban areas
and where the rural communities had become greatly swollen by
the influx of refugees.[7] Educational opportunity was a much more
burning issue for this refugee element than for long settled rural
families and as a consequence the conditions for access to
academic secondary education were the object of much greater
attention than had been evident before 1945. It was only in cities
or towns large enough to provide an appropriate catchment that
grammar schools were to be found. To attend them, children
from the villages were daily obliged to travel substantial dis-
tances. One solution to the problem was for them to be boarded
out, perhaps with relatives, during the week but it was only for
very few that this could be a realistic option. The widespread
damage in the urban areas had put living accommodation at
a premium. The traditionally early start to the school day
obliged many children to leave home as early as 6 a.m. and the
uncertainty of public transport meant that they might well not
return till the evening. It was possible to claim with some justification that this was too demanding for ten and eleven year
olds and so for this reason also the SPD argued for the later
transition from primary to secondary schooling.

But even for the older children the necessity of travel was
deplored. The next stage in the SPD plan for a comprehensive
school system was a network of three year middle schools which
would be attached to centrally situated primary schools to ensure
easy access. These schools were to contain two streams, one with
an academic, the other with a practical bias. For a substantial
core of the curriculum, some twenty or so weekly periods, the
teaching was to be common to both, in order to ensure that they
were equally highly valued. Transfer between them was also
to be facilitated. It was admitted that this reorganisation entailed a certain sacrifice as far as the highly able children were
concerned but this was considered of subsidiary importance compared with the task of raising the general level of education in
the whole population. For this reason there was a general wish
to emphasise the practical orientation of the *Realschule* rather
more than the scholarly virtues of the *Gymnasium.* An old
rhyme quoted in one of the *Landtag* debates on the 1948
law—

In Athen und bei den Lappen
Da späh'n sie jeden Winkel aus,
Indem sie wie die Blinden tappen
Daheim im Vaterhaus

—conveys the deep-seated resentment against an academic education which led children to spend so much time learning in minute detail about foreign cultures that they were unable to cope with the more mundane practical demands of home life.[8]

This suspiciousness of the value of academic study was not solely the result of social prejudice. It derived also from the economic worry about an academic proletariat which has already been encountered in the context of the plans for education in North Rhine-Westphalia. In the course of the *Landtag* debates of 1947 and 1948 it was repeatedly made plain by Kuklinski and other SPD speakers that many of those who felt a powerful urge to enter higher education should be channelled away from the universities towards higher vocational education; the *Einheitsschule* had to produce the manpower required for the economic recovery. They maintained that this objective was more likely to be achieved through the raising of the general level of education in the population as a whole. It was thus for both social and economic reasons that they wished to bring about the dissolution of the selective grammar schools with their strongly academic nine-year course.

As well as the unification of the school system the SPD wished to see the unification of teacher training. The plan was that all intending teachers should study for three years at a *Pädagogische Hochschule*, followed by two years primary teaching; only then would it be possible to spend two or three years at a university in order to become qualified to teach at the secondary level. The *Referendariat*, the customary induction period for grammar school teachers, would no longer be required since the two years of primary teaching would already have given candidates the necessary practical experience. Additionally the plan laid emphasis on the importance of subsequent in-service training. The urge to introduce such radical, indeed in some eyes outlandish measures in the organisation of teacher training derived from the same resentment of the social division between the academically educated, the *Gebildeten*, and the remainder of the population as was evident in the advocacy of the *Einheitsschule*. Most primary teachers had not been to grammar schools and by this token were excluded from the possibility of teaching in them. Many were therefore very much aware of a gulf that had opened up before them at the age of ten. Now the SPD plan held out the prospect of all future teachers beginning their professional training on the same footing.

Two further objectives of the SPD, the extension by a year of compulsory full-time education and the abolition of fee-paying and of all charges for textbooks and other school materials, commanded broad general support but otherwise there was strong opposition among the conservative parties, led by the CDU, to the entire conception of a reorganised education system. The CDU contended that it was merely disruptive to embark upon a complete restructuring and defended the existing system on the grounds that it had grown up organically in response to the genuine needs of the community. The social arguments were rejected. In the CDU view, if fee-paying could be eliminated there would be no longer any justification for accusing the grammar schools of being predominantly middle-class institutions. As in North Rhine-Westphalia ten was regarded as a perfectly suitable age at which to hive off the more academically inclined children as long as special provision was made for late developers.

These arguments were perhaps predictable, illustrating the archetypal controversy between left and right over the organisation of school systems. The references to the occupying powers are, however, more interesting. In the course of putting its case in the *Landtag* the SPD had made a number. The comparisons with the United Kingdom related to the six-year duration of primary schooling since the introduction of a universal six-year *Grundschule* was the first major stage of the proposed reorganisation in Schleswig-Holstein. The United States had a fully comprehensive school system and a reorganisation along these lines had been advocated for Germany in the Zook Report, the findings of a special educational commission which the Americans set up in 1946. Among other things it urged the introduction of a six-year *Grundschule*. The Soviet Zone was quoted in this connection also, for although an eight-year *Grundschule* had been introduced there in 1946 the SPD drew attention to the desire to reduce this to six years. The provision for transition from primary to secondary school at the age of twelve was therefore claimed to be in the interests of national unity in educational policy.

To all of this the CDU took strong exception. They denied that the comparision with the United Kingdom was a true one since it was well known that a great many of the leading figures in British society were educated not in the State system, but in independent preparatory and public schools. As for the United States, they resented any suggestion that the Zook recommendation should influence the way in which German education was to develop. Indeed they were able to call attention to the opposition to the Report which was voiced inside America by thirteen émigré professors in Chicago. This group claimed that in terms of academic attainment American university students were two years behind their German counterparts and hence fuelled the resentment at the idea that responsibility for the development of German education lay in the hands of the occupying powers. Concerning policy in the Soviet Zone it was possible to go further and allege that the introduction of an eight-year *Grundschule* was a deliberate attempt to stunt the intellectual development of the German people, a demontage every bit as debilitative as that which had taken place in industry. Any delay in the age of selection in the West was seen in a similar light. It was declared that the rebuilding of Germany depended on the identification and development of high ability; conversely the lengthening of the *Grundschule* would mean a lowering of standards which the country could not afford.

Although the ideological arguments were diametrically opposed and gave rise to bitter exchanges there were two respects in which both sides had similar major aims. The first concerned the importance of economic recovery. On both sides the approach adopted was claimed to constitute the best way of making the most of the country's intellectual resources and thereby providing the kind of manpower needed to bring about an economic revival. The second concerned the importance of national unity. The SPD claimed that a six-year *Grundschule* was also envisaged in the other *Länder* and that Schleswig-Holstein would be the leader in a developing national trend. A principal argument on the CDU side was that the other *Länder* showed

every sign of retaining the status quo and that what was being
enacted in Schleswig-Holstein would have a deleterious effect
on German cultural unity. There could be no settlement of these
disputes as early as 1948 but the two issues subsequently emerged
as strong determinants of development in the 1950s; in both
cases the CDU argument prevailed. It prevailed very specifically
in Schleswig-Holstein when the SPD lost its majority in the
elections of 1950. The law was repealed in the following year.

Hamburg

The other *Land* which in the course of the Occupation period
planned a radical reorganisation of the school system was
Hamburg. In 1945 the British authorities appointed to the provisional administration Heinrich Landahl, a former headmaster
of the progressive Alfred Lichtwark school and an experienced
politician from Weimar days. In an address which he gave in
July 1945 he recalled Hamburg's pre-1933 international reputation as a centre for progressive developments in education and
he declared his concern to see the threads of this tradition picked
up again. He emphasised the importance of independent thinking, moral courage and a sense of service, qualities which he
saw as being anchored in religious conviction. In his view of
future development, therefore, religious education, though it
should not be compulsory, was to play an important part.
'Through religious instruction children will once again become
familiar with the Bible, acknowledged by Goethe as the sole
source of his own moral education. But those who opt out of
religious instruction will also be taught to understand the eternal
moral values'.[9]

This was just one of many statements of the time on the
important subject of a return to absolute values. What was perhaps specially noteworthy in this case was that it could be made
without implying a demand for the restoration of the confessional
schools which had been discontinued by Hitler. Hamburg had
had a secular system before 1933 but the city had been expanded in 1938 to incorporate Altona, Wandsbek and Har-
burg, all of which had been parts of Prussia and as such had had
confessional schools. When it was decreed in January 1946
that there were to be local referenda on the issue, it was technic-

ally necessary to conduct these in the new Hamburg districts. Landahl and his colleagues were, however, very concerned to avoid stirring up an unwelcome and unnecessary controversy which would divert energies from more important priorities and they applied for a dispensation from the obligation. The dispensation was granted, an episode which provides a good example of a timely and pragmatic decision on the part of the occupying authorities and of the sureness of political touch displayed by Landahl.[10]

This sureness of touch showed itself in other ways too: in Landahl's efforts to secure the earliest possible return of evacuees so that they could be reunited with their families without delay; in his championship of elementary school teachers whom the authorities tended to regard as a source of all-purpose labour; and in the initiative to bring into being the first education conference, the *Schulreferententagung* which first made it possible for German administrators from different *Länder* to meet and discuss problems. Landahl was concerned lest the aversion to centralisation, however justifiable, might result in wide divergences of practice between regions and thereby store up problems for the future.[11] In all of these activities he gained a reputation for energy and perceptiveness which made him one of the major personalities in educational reconstruction in the British Zone.

Landahl's tenure in Hamburg was marked by acrimonious controversy once the stage of active party politics was reached. The inflammatory issue was grammar school selection. When the SPD and the Communists obtained an overwhelming majority in the City Assembly they prepared an ambitious plan, based as in Schleswig-Holstein, on the six-year *Grundschule*. The influence of the 1944 Education Act in England and Wales was particularly to be observed in the fact that it was proposed to divide secondary education into three branches, namely grammar, technical and practical. In this connection it is worth noting that Landahl was, with Adolf Grimme, of Lower Saxony, one of the first Germans to visit the United Kingdom under the auspices of GER. That visit took place in 1946 and Landahl afterwards acknowledged how impressed he was by the English schools he visited and the discussions in which he participated. Thereafter there were numerous other contacts between Ham-

burg and various parts of the United Kingdom. The reorganisation was more carefully thought out and more con-
vincingly presented than in Schleswig-Holstein, perhaps because
the whole exercise was less precipitate. The law was not in fact
passed until after the creation of the Federal Republic.

The heart of the argument in the case that was made for the
change concerned an ancient and enduring educational controversy. Few themes could have been more apposite at the time
than the quotation from Goethe chosen by Sir Robert Birley for
a lecture in 1947 and recalled by Fritz Borinski in another
chapter, 'No amount of learning guarantees the power of
judgement'. The document setting out the proposed reform
declared that 'the question of how much a school pupil can
absorb and not how much he can think for himself still domin-
ates our general view of education'.[12] This anchored the whole
debate in a more profound educational problem than those which
were prevalent in the discussions in Schleswig-Holstein. It was
clearly calling into question traditionally fundamental assumptions of German scholarship and the preparation for it in the
schools.

The response from the University of Hamburg was presented
in a closely argued *Denkschrift*[13] which, it can scarcely be doubted,
accurately reflected the views that were more generally prevalent
in universities throughout Germany. The document met
the reformist criticism head on, denying the implied antithesis
between knowledge and judgement. Its authors maintained that
this distinction, variously presented as between achievement and
character, cognitive thinking and experience, knowledge and
'life', was purely artificial, deriving from discredited educational
theories of the reform movement of the early years of the century; these idealised models were not appropriate for the new
post-war situation and plans for structural changes could not
be founded on them. The full nine-year *Gymnasium* course was,
it was claimed, indispensable in order to guarantee the depth of
knowledge and understanding needed as a preparation for university.

The document went on to characterise the purposes of the
reform as political and argued that this was not a legitimate
aim to pursue through the schools. The view taken here was
that the will of the people towards social unity depended on

many factors outside the education system and that it was a mistake to let political considerations take precedence over educational ones. The social dimension was not entirely ignored. The authors acknowledged that there was some substance in the accusation that the grammar schools had been predominantly the preserve of the middle class, but they considered that this drawback could be averted for the future if rigorous selection procedures were adopted and if the State was prepared to give financial support to those children who needed it. Any more ambitious plans for reform were in their view likely to founder on practical inadequacies, above all the shortage of classrooms and of teachers with the appropriate qualifications. To enter upon grandiose schemes that could not be fulfilled they saw as folly which could only lead to resignation or dissimulation on the part of teachers.

The university was joined in its opposition to the legislation by the grammar school teachers. The Hamburg branch of their professional association, the *Gymnasialverein*, stated bluntly that the grammar school course should last nine years and common primary schooling four years, that the first foreign language should be Latin and that changes should only be contemplated in the case of individual schools where the teachers and parents specifically requested it. The value of Latin as the first foreign language was upheld in a series of individual statements published as addenda to the university's paper by the professors of law, medicine, education, philology, physics, astronomy, forestry, zoology, chemistry, mineralogy and ichthyology, also by the professor of English who was simultaneously chairman of the *Gymnasialverein* and in that capacity responsible for the association's denunciation of the new school law. The controversy emphasised the gulf in the teaching profession between university and grammar school teachers, on the one hand, and elementary school teachers, on the other, a gulf reflected in the political opposition between the CDU and the SPD. The mutual hostility over the issue was so marked that clearly Landahl's law had gone beyond any possible middle ground of compromise. The law was passed in 1949 but so bitter was the controversy and so strongly did it feature as a subsequent election issue that it must be regarded as an important factor in the defeat of the left-wing coalition. It was repealed in 1954.

Lower Saxony

Lower Saxony differs from the rest of the British Zone in being the one *Land* where the middle ground of compromise between right- and left-wing policies was effectively explored. Here as in Hamburg the work of reconstruction came under the influence of one of the outstanding personalities in the politics of education, Adolf Grimme, who had been a Social Democratic Minister of Education in Prussia. In another chapter Fritz Borinski recounts the fortuitous circumstances in which Grimme was recalled into service to be placed at the head of the Schools Department of the provisional administration of Hanover. On the completion of the delicate task of drawing the other states, Braunschweig, Oldenburg and Schaumburg-Lippe, into the new composite *Land* of Lower Saxony, with Hanover as the capital, Grimme became the first Education Minister. To a certain extent the readiness to compromise derived from this composite character of the *Land* and the variety of political influences that had to be reconciled. In Oldenburg, for example, conservative thinking was widespread whereas in Braunschweig there was among primary teachers a strong radical impulse which in turn was at odds with the conservatism of the secondary teachers in that province. A further complication was the residual resentment in Oldenburg, Braunschweig and Schaumburg-Lippe after Hanover was designated *Land* capital.

In the event formal party politics played no very important part in determining educational developments in the post-war period. Grimme was primarily a Christian humanist thinker rather than a politician and had a certain disdain for legislation in educational matters, preferring administration by ministerial decree. An approach of this kind puts a premium on depth of understanding of the currents of educational thinking, a capacity that is unlikely to be found in more orthodox political leaders for whom education is only one of a number of alternative pre-occupations. But it is indispensable if a Minister is to be success-ful in giving a positive lead. Grimme showed intellectual and imaginative qualities which enabled him to blend the concern to preserve traditional virtues of scholarly learning with the urge to ensure that a genuine effort was made to come to terms with the social problems that the post-war disruption had caused. Though controversies flared up in Lower Saxony as elsewhere, sensitivity in policy-making was a particular characteristic of educational reconstruction in that *Land*. For the process of evaluating his ideas and putting into practice those which looked to be practicable Grimme was fortunate in having as chief executive another prominent educationist of the time, Günther Rönnebeck. After their comparatively brief but very fruitful partnership—Grimme resigned in 1948 to become Head of North-West German Radio—Rönnebeck continued in office for some twenty years, providing a continuity that was of great value in the subsequent formulation of policy.

Grimme's plans for the reconstruction of the school system in Lower Saxony were set out in a *Denkschrift* which was circulated to all inspectors and heads of schools as well as being published in the journal *Die Schule*. This document, which was written by Rönnebeck, began with an eloquent repudiation of the materialistic aims of National Socialism and set out to replace them with a reaffirmation of the intellectual and moral values which had for thirteen years been subordinated to the cult of physical strength and the glorification of the German race. The education which would inculcate this new scale of values needed, it was declared, to bring about the reconciliation of all classes and sectors of society. It had to teach the individual to look beyond purely personal demands and expectations, to teach the nation to look beyond its own interests. These and other ideas were held together by the common theme, prevalent elsewhere in Germany too, that ultimately it was only religious conviction which could provide the foundations on which to rebuild.

The *Denkschrift* then set out to diagnose in more precise terms the failings of the traditional school system which it declared had been on the wrong track for half a century. It harked back to the warnings of great teachers like Hermann Lietz and Georg Kerschensteiner who had predicted the failure of a system that allowed enormous energy to be devoted to the task of imparting knowledge and skills but ignored the importance of fostering independent thinking and judgement according to moral criteria. It saw in a resumption of traditional pre-Nazi education the danger of overburdening young people with factual knowledge in too many different domains. 'We have all known for a long time that education is not a process of breadth but of

depth, that it is by way of thorough study in five domains that
a young person learns to think for him or herself and to act
responsibly rather than by way of a necessarily superficial preoccupation with twelve or fifteen subjects.'[14] This was an
unequivocal denunciation of the encyclopaedic *Gymnasium*
curriculum which, as can now be seen, it has taken thirty years
to change. In this respect *Zum Neubau des Schulwesens* was a
seminal piece of writing. But it was not just concerned with the
Gymnasium, declaring as it did that the same religious, social,
political and intellectual values and attitudes were to be inculcated in every part of the educational system, from the
primary school to the university.

As was also the case in Hamburg the influence of the 1944
Education Act for England and Wales is evident in the aim of
parity of esteem for the three main types of secondary education :
the academic as provided by the *Gymnasium* and to a lesser
degree the *Oberschule*; the practical as provided by the elementary school followed by apprenticeship and part-time attendance at the vocational school; and the intermediate type which
had elements of both as provided by the *Mittelschule*. A great
deal of emphasis was laid on the arrangements for lateral transfer
between the three types, a measure which depended in practice
on coordinating the sequence of languages studied. Running
through the entire scheme that was outlined was the idea of
securing a qualitative improvement in those schools which
had in the past enjoyed less prestige. Thus, for example, there
was a proposal to merge the *Mittelschule*, which lasted as far as
the tenth school year, with the *Oberschule*, which provided a
full length but less linguistically biassed alternative to the *Gymnasium*.

One further suggestion in the *Denkschrift* deserves particular
mention, the *Philosophikum*. The Nazis had done away with the
thirteenth school year in order to reduce the age at which
military service could begin and there was now a widespread
feeling in Germany that this year should be restored. The idea
of the *Philosophikum* was that it should fill this gap in a new
way, namely as a transitional phase between school and university, a counterpart to the practical experience demanded of
candidates applying to be admitted to vocational higher education. The idea was that it should be in a kind of residential

college with a tutorial system which could give those intending to go on to university an induction into a more independent type of study. This experience of life in an academic community would, it was thought, be particularly beneficial for the many young people, particularly in refugee families, whose home conditions were ill-suited for intensive study. At the end of the year the staff of the *Philosophikum* would decide on university admissions, an important matter since the shortage of capacity dictated the operation of a numerus clausus.

These were radical proposals for their time. The most delicate relationships involved in the approach to them and other matters was with the churches. The Catholic Church in particular had a continuing interest in two major educational issues, firstly whether or not confessional schools should be restored, secondly whether or not Latin should be retained as the first foreign language in the *Gymnasium* curriculum. The first question was, as pointed out elsewhere in this chapter, settled with reasonable dispatch by way of the Allied policy of local referenda. The latter issue remained intensely controversial for a longer period. The debate which eventually gave rise to the creation of the *niedersächsischer Zug* or Lower Saxony stream, the apparent contradiction in terms whereby the classical *Gymnasium* was enabled to have English as the first foreign language, exemplifies the art of compromise that was practised in Lower Saxony.

The originality about Grimme's stance in the controversy was that he dismissed many of the arguments that were advanced in favour of the abolition of Latin from the early years of the curriculum. Particularly the claim that it was premature. He pointed out that it only required the right teacher for the child to enjoy it. As for the idea that it was too far removed from children's interests, his own experience as a teacher of classics had convinced him that it was precisely the exotically unfamiliar that they found interesting. Furthermore he acknowledged and indeed enthused over the virtue of translation exercises in which the search for precision was unrelenting. At the same time he took a broader view, recognising that all options should be available to all and that ten was too early an age to make what were virtually irrevocable decisions. The child that was not sent to a classical *Gymnasium* at the age of ten had little chance of enter-

B

ing one a year or two later because of the divergence in the
pattern of languages studied. The social disruption of the time,
in particular the refugee problem, placed unusually large numbers of children in this category. On the other hand, because
of this 'now or never' feeling some children who lacked the
appropriate attitude were forced to learn Latin against the grain
in case the chance would otherwise be lost of acquiring an indispensable prerequisite for subsequent university study. Whether
or not to postpone the learning of Latin for two years was an
agonising decision. Grimme's justification for eventually rejecting
the line taken by the most uncompromising traditionalists was
an original one; he maintained that the *niedersächsischer Zug*
would ensure that in the long run more rather than fewer
children would study the subject.[15]

The Catholic Church at first recognised the force of the social
arguments in favour of making English the first foreign language
but later declared that it had accepted the changes merely as a
temporary emergency measure. The claim was that from the
spring of 1946 onwards there was steadily increasing pressure
for a return to established practices.[16] The principal argument
put forward was the need for uniform provision throughout the
British Zone. Since the classical *Gymnasium* had been restored
in its traditional form in North Rhine-Westphalia there would
be a risk of disrupting the education of children whose parents
moved from one *Land* to the other if the sequence of languages
studied were not standardised. Indeed this was subsequently to
become the most powerful disincentive to any experimenting
with structural and curricular changes in the early years of
the Federal Republic. The call for standardisation caused strong
pressure to be put on all *Länder*, particularly Schleswig-Holstein, Hamburg and Bremen, to abandon radical changes introduced in 1948 and 1949. In Lower Saxony, however, the *niedersächsischer Zug* survived.

Thus one of the major aims of the *Denkschrift*, to postpone
irrevocable differentiation by at least two years, had been
achieved. In other respects the document remained unimple-
mented. Grimme and Rönnebeck recognised the deep-rooted
opposition among parents and teachers to the more radical
innovations. The proposal to merge the *Mittelschule* and the
Oberschule was tactfully dropped. Nor did anything come of

the *Philosophikum* idea, for a number of reasons. It was an extremely difficult time to introduce any measure that involved residential accommodation for with the acute shortages of food and fuel there was always the danger of accusations of favoured treatment. But above all public opinion showed little sympathy for the idea of a voluntary college-type year as a transition to university methods of study, favouring rather the reintroduction of the sternly organised *Oberprima* with which it was familiar.[17]

This sensitivity to public opinion was one of the hallmarks of the educational work of Grimme and Rönnebeck in Lower Saxony. Inventive and forward-looking as they both were, neither of them was one to use their decrees as a way of forcing ideas and policies through. But despite the practical difficulties of the situation they were constantly attempting to find new ways of realising their overriding aim to educate responsible citizens. Perhaps one final illustration of this is appropriate, namely the attempt to encourage pupil participation, *Schülermitverwaltung*. A passage from one circular in particular seems worth quoting at length :

Since pupil participation can decisively influence the formation of character, since every sharing of responsibility in a community is also self-education, I am urgently asking teachers and administrators to devote more energy to this educational task than before. For those pupils who are prepared to contribute in this respect are dependent on the more mature judgement of an adult. Firstly they must be shown objectives which are appropriate to their stage of development. The teacher can encourage some to forge ahead, and then bit by bit involve others who are less forthcoming, he can intervene where the pupil cannot on his or her own complete the tasks that have been set. However he should always do so in such a way that the young people never lose their sense of independence; much tact is required for the teacher to remain in the background and yet not to relinquish control. The success is substantially greater if the parents, through the influence of teachers and parents' committees, can be persuaded to use the idea of shared responsibility in order to get their children to derive enjoyment from their household duties.

I have no wish to impose the idea of pupil participation 'from
above'. Responsibility can no more be decreed than freedom,
the two being the foundations of any democracy. On the
contrary, pupil participation will develop in a more healthy
fashion if the responsibility is borne by a group of young
people who are by temperament well suited to it, even if the
group is initially very small.[18]

The circular then went on to list the various practical ways
in which *Schülermitverwaltung* could be fostered. It is a document which conveys much of the spirit of the educational work
of the time, not only echoing a theme of the reform movement
of the early years of the century but also reflecting the British
conviction of the importance of the community element in
school life.

The Zonal Education Council

Two broad streams in educational thinking can therefore be
identified, the conservative which derived its inspiration from
Christianity and classical humanism, and the radical which while
often sharing the desire for a return to Christian values could
also draw some of the threads of the dissenting reform movement into the fresh campaign to bring equality of opportunity
to all social classes. The religious element in the conservative
view found its expression in the defence of denominational
Volksschulen while the classical humanist aspect required that
the nine-year *Gymnasium* should be restored with its academic
programme undiluted. The force of this latter impulse can be
judged from the opposition to the reforms introduced by
Grimme. Schnippenkötter was one of his most vigorous advers-
aries in the early days, the physicist upbraiding the classicist
for betraying his heritage. In fact Grimme's reforms were extremely modest ones, nothing like so far-reaching as the fundamental changes later enacted in Schleswig-Holstein and Hamburg.

This diversity developed in response to regional aspirations
over a period when there was little opportunity for any more
central initiative to be taken on the German side. In the early
days the only wider forum for discussion of the policies being
pursued throughout the Zone as a whole was the *Schulreferen-*

tentagung, which, following the early initiative of Landahl in
Hamburg, continued to meet intermittently in the course of the
first year of the Occupation. This body was in turn superseded
by the Zonal Educational Council or *Zonenerziehungsrat* (ZER)
which had a more clearly defined constitution drawn up by the
staff of Education Branch.

The ZER provided the machinery whereby Donald Riddy,
the Director of the Branch could ensure that British measures
had the support of the Education Ministers; indeed he gave an
undertaking to issue no military instructions concerning education without first securing their agreement.[19] In this way it was
ensured that the Council would pave the way for the handing
over of responsibility in educational matters to the Germans at
the beginning of 1947. It had a longer term significance too in
that it was one of the precursors of the Standing Conference of
Land Education Ministers which was to become the major body
charged with the co-ordination of policy in the Federal Republic.

The Council showed itself to be a remarkably united and purposeful body. Generally speaking it was at pains to avoid becoming embroiled in the more sensitive political issues of educational
reform. Much of the business conducted was of an uncontentious
administrative kind and even in some of the potentially more
controversial issues it proved possible to find a formula for
consensus. School fees are a good illustration. The British
authorities had from the outset been very much concerned that
children should not be denied the opportunity to continue their
education through the inability of parents or guardians to pay
fees. On the German side, free education was generally accepted
to be a desirable aim but the political parties disagreed over
the pace at which it was possible to introduce it. At the meeting of the Council in December 1946 the delegates reported
on their various approaches to the problem and it was then
agreed unanimously that 'in principle attendance at academic
and vocational secondary schools must not be dependent on the
payment of fees. Until the abolition of fee-paying can be accomplished there are the following possibilities (a) exemption
from the obligation to pay fees for those below certain income
levels (b) progressive abolition of fees by year groups, or annually
increasing funds to provide free places and support grants'.[20]

Thus agreement on the ultimate aim was interpreted with sufficient flexibility to accommodate various shades of political opinion. In retrospect a minimum consensus perhaps, in view of the many further years which elapsed before fee-paying was abandoned throughout the Federal Republic, it was nonetheless an achievement that in its context should not be underrated. It is an example of the fruits of everyday co-operation with the British education officers and of the collective desire among German officials to bring about an effective educational reconstruction.

But there was no escaping an eventual political confrontation over educational reform. It was precipitated by a report on the progress of the Berlin School Law which in turn was the cue for Kuklinski to advance within the Council the idea of a comprehensive educational system. Here the markedly political flavour of the approach to education in Schleswig-Holstein was in evidence. The aim of the SPD government of that *Land* was to enshrine controversial educational legislation in the constitution and thereby guarantee that a two-thirds majority would be required in order to rescind it. Both Grimme and Landahl were vigorously opposed to this encroachment of politics. To meet Kuklinski's insistence on the importance of dialogue between politicians and educationists it was agreed that a high-level conference should be held on the subject of educational reform. In preparation for it Rönnebeck was to gather together information about the various plans and prepare a comparative analysis of them.[21] But to fashion any kind of unity out of such divergent aims was far beyond the scope of the ZER. Indeed this was always tacitly accepted for the comparative analysis was never made and the conference never took place. It was not till after the creation of the Federal Republic that there was a really purposeful drive to impose some unity on the diverse developments of the Occupation period.

The British Role in Educational Reconstruction

In reviewing the role played by the British in the work of educational reconstruction there is little need to emphasise here the significance of the humanitarian motive. Elsewhere in this book there is ample testimony to the efforts that were made in an atmosphere of disruption to secure the best provision that was possible for young people. But beyond the matter of the deserved tributes is that of analysing how the task was conceived of by those who participated and of estimating its lasting influence. To what extent did the occupying powers wish to go beyond the purely humanitarian dimension and bring about fundamental changes in the education system itself, and to what extent was it possible to do so? The answers to these questions hold the key to what was distinctive about British policy in education.

On the surface at any rate the other three occupying powers would all appear to have had much clearer ideas of what they wished to achieve than the British. In terms of getting their way the Russians were the most successful for the education law passed in 1946 in the Soviet Zone introduced the kind of comprehensive school system which they had desired from the outset. In a number of ways it embodied what the other Allies were aiming at, for criticism of the hierarchical structure and authoritarian nature of the traditional system was common throughout Germany at the time. But there was one fundamental sense in which it could not be compared to developments in the West. It was adopted by the provisional administrations and was never put to the test as an election issue. It could not therefore be said to reflect the will of the German people. In the West, by contrast, the cardinal principle of the right of the Germans to determine the future of their own education was respected, at least in the long run. However much energy the Americans poured into the task of persuading them to accept the idea of a comprehensive school system as advocated in the report of the Zook Commission they stopped short of imposing it. The fact that the French did go so far as to impose certain changes only ensured that they would be largely reversed once power was handed over to the Germans.

It would therefore appear that the kind of cultural force-feeding which sought to rebuild a society by radically changing its institutions on the lines of foreign models was able to succeed only in the captive conditions under which the Germans of the Soviet Zone were denied any say. This was far removed from the highly respectable phenomenon of cultural borrowing. It is of course conceivable that the system introduced in the Soviet Zone in 1946 could initially have commanded the support

of the electorate for it was in the East that Social Democracy
was strongest. But even in that case the continuance of the
support was extremely improbable once there was full awareness of the Marxist-Leninist aims that lay behind the change
and the methods by which they were to be achieved. As for
the Western Zones, it was quite clear that German attitudes had
sufficient depth of conviction to make them proof against anything other than arbitrarily enforced change. If the Germans
themselves were to be involved, then 'restoration' was inevitable
and the ambitious plans of the Americans and the French to
transform educational structures and institutions could only
founder through their failure to take proper account of the
vitality of indigenous educational politics. The question that
this raises is whether the British were more successful in a positive
sense or merely less unsuccessful because they were less ambitious.

In the early days of complete control the British had no need,
any more than the other Allies, to pay great attention to German
politics other than in the matter of finding able personalities
who were relatively untainted by National Socialism and could
be entrusted with some degree of responsibility. A situation in
which politics was kept at arm's length was particularly welcome
in education where the British authorities were greatly concerned to avoid confrontation of any kind. This was most clearly
demonstrated over the confessional schools. The staff of Education Branch were highly aware of the passionate feelings that
could be aroused in the matter. Hence they were anxious to see
it settled quickly for otherwise it might have exacerbated tensions and soured the entire process of reconstruction. The conduct of the local referenda was thus an exercise in forestalling
intense political activity.

Indeed the view appears to have been that the longer this
political vacuum lasted, the better would be the prospects for
educational reconstruction, for it was too sensitive a time to be
conducive to rational debate and balanced judgements. This
desire to discourage political confrontation was in line with a
more general feeling prevalent at the time that educational
development should as far as possible proceed by consensus,
eliminating sharp divisions over principle and solving problems
by way of pragmatic compromises. A distaste for statements of

principle was central to the attitudes adopted by the staff of Education Branch. Their concern to put a brake on political activity derived from a conviction that a reliable democratic process could develop only in a very slow pragmatic way.

The need to come to terms more explicitly with indigenous politics came sooner than was perhaps held to be desirable for the Soviets made the running by pushing ahead a merger between the Social Democrats and the Communists to form the Socialist Unity Party. This had the effect of speeding up political activity in the West and the earlier accounts in this chapter illustrate the course of this activity as far as education was concerned. It produced a patchwork result that reflected the variety of regional traditions. Above all it evidenced the vigour of educational thinking and the strength of political involvement, with each of the four *Länder* providing an individual illustration of the momentum that was built up. Dominant personalities like Grimme and Landahl emerged and the powerful themes of Christianity, classical humanism, democracy spurred those in the education service to prodigious efforts to restore what had been lost. There was an élan about it which drew its inspiration from German history, a conviction that regeneration would come through a return to the finest educational traditions of the pre-Nazi period.

This is not to deny entirely the significance of foreign models. The 1944 Education Act for England and Wales aroused great interest. As a particular instance its influence can be traced in the Hamburg legislation of 1949. But before too much is made of this, account should be taken of the peculiar pride felt by that city in its record of educational innovation. How often did the British education officers when putting forward a new idea meet with the response: *Ach, das haben wir schon längst in Hamburg!* Indeed the cynic might well observe that in terms of the reconstruction of the school system after the War the British were simply irrelevant beyond their fulfilment of the practical tasks of ensuring that buildings were repaired, textbooks and materials provided and a teaching force employed which had survived the process of screening by *Fragebogen*. It would be possible to go further and interpret this irrelevance as a failure of purpose whereby a unique opportunity to reshape the future was let slip. Such a judgement would be facile if it

B*

gave no credit to the British for the subtlety of their approach. Some of the detailed evidence of this subtlety appears in the chapters that follow. Here consideration must be confined to a few broad propositions.

The first of these is of a somewhat negative nature, namely that the British deliberately refrained from involving themselves in anything that smacked of political controversy and by that token from making any attempt to foster in the Zone new practices such as for example the postponement of the age for grammar school selection. It would at first sight appear difficult to judge whether this was a conscious policy or merely an omission that derived from lack of interest in the school system as a system. Seen in isolation the latter interpretation is convincing. When, however, the comparison is drawn with the course of events in the US Zone where the attempt was made to persuade the Germans to accept a comprehensive school system on the American model the picture is rather different. The most vivid illustration of that situation is provided by the tussle between the American authorities and the Bavarian Minister of Education, Dr Hundhammer, a long drawn-out affair in which the Germans were the victors.[22] It must be considered a mark of the positive good sense of the British that they were able to see and prepared to accept the limitations of their position and avoid getting themselves involved in a fruitless crusade of the kind indulged in by the Americans.

In other less complex sectors the problems could more easily be comprehended within clear proposals or actions. In youth work and adult education, for example, which are documented in later chapters, it was possible for education officers to take positive steps in reorganisation without getting embroiled in political controversy. In the university sphere too it appeared to make good sense to intervene in a more explicit way and the British took the initiative by setting up the commission which is also discussed at length later in this book. At the same time this episode is an apt illustration of the limits which the British voluntarily placed on even the most carefully thought out and constructive of their policies. This scrupulousness may have had the effect of delaying changes in the German university system that were already overdue. But to impose these changes against the will of those whose task it would be to implement them was contrary to the spirit of British education policy.

For there was one feature of this self-imposed restraint which was of critical significance. The British were thereby constantly putting the destiny of the German education system in the hands of the Germans themselves. This was no thoughtless abdication of responsibility. On the contrary it was a matter of conscious choice because within the context of British policy as a whole it was not an orthodox approach. It was pointed out earlier that the policy in Education Branch was to disperse its members widely and to approach its task by way of maximum personal involvement on the part of individuals. British education officers, rarely seen at headquarters, were incorrigible fraternisers in the best sense, at a time when somewhat disreputable motives tended to attach to close contact with Germans. Elsewhere it has been said that their 'competence, integrity and idealism' were above average for the Control Commission as a whole.[23] They respected true German culture and set out to foster adherence to what was best in it, with the conviction that a new democracy could be built which genuinely reflected the will of the German people.

Looked at from the German side this approach emerges as one of remarkable vision. The dominant feeling among the Germans at the time was one of being *excluded* from, or at any rate only allowed a grudging share in the deliberations that were to shape their future. By contrast, in education they were from the earliest days *included*, positively encouraged to rebuild their confidence and to believe that they themselves were ultimately the best judges of how the post-war order should develop. Such an approach gave considerable significance to the selection of those Germans who were granted the opportunity to influence developments at an early stage, and still more to the democratic processes that needed to be re-established as the foundation of political life. Above all it meant moderating any inclination to force the pace of change. Thirty years later it is inevitable that there should be regrets at some of the missed opportunities to which Hellmut Becker refers in the concluding chapter. But while it would certainly have been possible to take a more forceful line and impose the new structures which the Germans were reluctant to accept, this would equally certainly have met with determined resistance. It can only be a matter of speculation as to the outcome of the clash of will that would have resulted, and as to which course stood to contribute more to the health of German democracy in the long term. The chapters which now follow offer a first-hand account of the collective view that the British Education Branch took in this matter, and of the commitment to a vigorous educational reconstruction that lay behind it.

NOTES

1. K-J Schulte, 'Die höheren Schulen Westfalens und ihre Verwaltung 1945 bis 1946', *Westfälische Zeitschrift,* 110, (1960), pp. 154-5.
2. See R. Birley, 'Education in the British Zone of Germany', RIIA, *International Affairs,* XXVI, No. 1, Jan. 1950, p. 32.
3. L. Kerstiens, 'Die höhere Schule in den Reformplänen der Nachkriegszeit', *Zeitschrift für Pädagogik,* 11, 1965, p. 540.
4. Schulte, op. cit., p. 154.
5. See P. Hüttenberger, *Nordrhein-Westfalen und die Entstehung seiner parlamentarischen Demokratie,* (Siegburg, 1973), pp. 365-6.
6. 'Denkschrift zur Reform der Schulorganisation', *Schule des Volkes,* ed. A. Vogt, (Gelsenkirchen, 1947), pp. 28-32.
7. The number of school pupils rose from 165,000 in 1939 to 480,000 in 1949. *Material- und Nachrichten-Dienst* ('MUND'), March 1951, p. 5.
8. 'They seek out every detail about Athens and the Laps while at home they tap their way about as though they were blind'. *Schleswig-Holsteiner Landtag, Wortprotokoll der 4. Sitzung,* (1947) p. 31.
9. Address by Heinrich Landahl: 'Wege und Ziele der Schule'. *Hamburger Nachrichten-Blatt,* 43, 4 July 1945.
10. K. Zeidler, *Der Wiederaufbau des Hamburger Schulwesens nach dem Zusammenbruch 1945.* Schulbehörde der Stadt Hamburg (mimeo). Limited circulation and undated.
11. Zeidler, p. 29.
12. Schulbehörde der Hansestadt Hamburg, *Die Neuordnung des Hamburger Schulwesens,* (Hamburg, 1949), p. 62.
13. Universität Hamburg, *Die Schule in unserer Zeit,* (Hamburg, 1949),

14. *Zum Neubau des Schulwesens,* p. 4.
15. A. Grimme, 'Lateinunterricht an den Höheren Schulen', Schola I, 1948, pp. 34-41.
16. Letter from the Bishop of Osnabrück to Ministry of Education, 7.1.1948 in the personal archive of G. Rönnebeck.
17. Der niedersächsische Kultusminister K I No 500. g/Rö Hanover 17.2.47. Niedersächsisches Hauptstaatsarchiv Regierung zu Hanover, Hann 80 Hann II e 1 No. 95 Bd 1.
18. Der niedersächsische Kultusminister III 2076/48. Hannover 9.9.1948 Niedersächsisches Hauptstaatsarchiv Regierungspräsident Hildesheim. Hann 80 Hildesheim III Acc. 25/69. No. 2971.
19. Protokoll der 3 Sitzung des Zonenerziehungsrats 10.12.1946 in Bad Pyrmont, p. 2.
20. Protokoll der 3 Sitzung, pp. 5-6.
21. Protokoll der 6. Sitzung des Zonenerziehungsrats am 5/6 Juni 1947, in Selent bei Kiel, pp. 13-14.
22. Fully documented in I. Huelsz, *Schulpolitik in Bayern zwischen Demokratisierung und Restauration in den Jahren 1945-1950,* (Hamburg, 1970).
23. M. Balfour, *Four Power Control in Germany,* ed. A. Toynbee, *Survey of International Affairs,* (RIIA/Oxford, 1956), p. 231.

2. *British Policy in Retrospect*

Robert Birley

I went out to Germany in April 1947, two years after the end
of the War, though I had spent six weeks there during the
autumn of 1946. Except, perhaps, to some extent in Berlin, the
essential lines of British policy had already been laid down and
the most difficult part of our work had been carried out. I am
therefore, in a particularly good position to pay my own tribute
to the work done by my predecessor in Germany, Professor
Donald Riddy and those who worked with him in those early
days. I hope Professor Riddy will forgive me if I make use of
a metaphor I think I employed once before on the occasion
of a discussion on educational work in Germany. It was not a
matter of my coming and finding the foundations of our educational work very well laid. What I did was to come and walk
into a fully built house, and one very well built too and very well
furnished.

'German education shall be so controlled as completely to
eliminate National Socialist and militarist doctrines and to make
possible the successful development of democratic ideas.' All
things considered, I think these words from the Potsdam Agreement were a reasonably sensible statement. At least there was
no suggestion that it is possible to teach a nation to be democratic through its schools and universities. But this is precisely
what most people in this country directly after the War believed
should be done. For this reason there was coined the horrible
word 're-education' to express our policy in Germany. What is
more, two of the occupying powers, the French and the Russians,
also believed it. But the British Education Branch did not. Its
approach was very different.

Perhaps I might say a word first on the policies of the other
three Powers. We met, of course, each month at the Educational
Committee of the Allied Control Council. There we passed
splendid resolutions about 'democratic' education which did not
matter at all as we all had different ideas about what was meant

by democracy. In fact, I can only remember one discussion on a practical question during any of the meetings I attended, whether members of youth organisations in Germany should be allowed to wear uniforms. (Perhaps I may say that there was a strange arrangement in Berlin in the period before the air lift. A bus went every Sunday afternoon to Potsdam and took members of the British Control Commission to visit it. I used to go almost every Sunday I was in Berlin and sneak off by myself to see what I could find in the town. One Sunday I came across a group of the *Freie Deutsche Jugend* wearing what was to all intents and purposes a uniform. At the next meeting of the Committee I mentioned this. At least I made my Russian opposite number rather uncomfortable.) I think we may ignore the Education Committee of the Control Council.

My impression was that, in the eyes of the French, the German school teacher with his narrow socialist outlook had been the main influence in creating the society which first accepted and then supported National Socialism. For them, therefore, the most important needs were to have as many French teachers as possible teaching in the schools of their Zone of Germany and that they should control the training of future teachers. The children who were to be the future teachers were, therefore, chosen at the age of eleven and placed in separate schools, usually boarding schools, which were very carefully controlled. The plan was that they should go on subsequently to universities, which would also be largely under French influence. The plan was impressive, but, apart from the fact that the French Zone was a small one, it depended on the Allies' complete control of German education for at least ten or fifteen years, and there was never any real possibility of this.

The Russian policy was a great deal more realistic. I do not imagine that the Russians ever regarded the German teachers as capable of being reformed. The solution of the problem could only be a political one. If they could make Germany, or at least their Zone of Germany, a communist state, all the necessary educational reforms would follow, almost automatically. This of course, they have succeeded in doing. Education in the DDR has become, in the sense of the term which the Russian representatives on the Education Committee of the Control Council had in mind, 'democratic'.

I do not think I need to elaborate on this. The situation was
well summed up for me once by a pastor who had the duty
before the building of the Berlin Wall of helping the Evangelical
Church students who came over to the West. 'You must realise,'
he said to me once, 'that these students know every movement
of the communist ritual dance.' Now, there was never any
possibility of the Americans or the British adopting this policy.

I should not say that the differences between the Americans
and ourselves were fundamental. They undoubtedly concentrated
more on the educational headquarters, whether at Zonal or
Land level, and they were rather readier to lay down the law.
It was significant that they arrived in Germany after the War
with a printed text-book on German history for use in the
Gymnasien. It was so neutral as to be hardly readable. I remember that the American *Land* Commissioner for Bavaria
suddenly declared one morning that in future no fees should be
charged at German secondary schools. It was quite impossible,
of course, in the economic circumstances of the time. I admired
greatly the very astute way in which Herr Hundhammer, the
Education Minister in Bavaria dealt with the problem, setting
up a long series of committees to consider first how the change
might be carried out—on a remarkably wide spectrum of subjects. One, I remember, was on the use of projects in secondary
schools and Herr Hundhammer said to me, 'You know, I think
two teachers from Murnau on the Committee have very little
idea what it is all about.' But I think we may claim that in Dr
Konen of North Rhine-Westphalia we had for a time an Education Minister who was just as skilful in dealing with us. I
remember it caused some difficulties that the Americans could
see no reason why confessional schools should be preserved or
why a university should have a 'numerus clausus'. But I think
our relations with the Americans were good; mine certainly were
with the Director of their Department during the second half
of my time in Germany. We used to arrange to meet informally
once a month. I remember once telling him that I thought they
were giving the German youth organisations too much money.
'Yes', he said, 'you may well be right. But do remember that
you British have been occupying countries all your life. We
have only done it once before, and then it was our own country
after the Civil War—and look what a mess we made of it.'

Perhaps it is for the Germans to decide whether there were elements of colonialism in our policy and actions.

The British Military Government fully controlled German education in their Zone for only eighteen months. In December 1946 there was issued what was known as 'Ordinance No. 57', handing over the right to legislate to the *Land* Assemblies, except on certain reserved subjects, which did not include education, the Military Government retaining the power of veto. At the same time the control of educational administration passed to the *Land* governments, except on two points, the establishment of a numerus clausus at the universities and the status of the confessional school. I should say that the three main tasks of the Education Branch at that time were, first, actually getting the schools and educational administration started again and, in the autumn of 1945, the universities; second, the choice of Education Ministers and senior officials in the administration and often of head teachers and later the first *Rektoren* of the universities; and third the process known as denazification. Of these the first two were far the most important, the third, denazification, the most difficult and irksome.

As I had no responsibilities in Germany during that period, although I was fortunate enough to be able to see some of the work there, I can speak uninhibitedly and say that I feel sure that anything we were able to achieve in the educational field in Germany after the War was mainly due to the way in which the staff of the Education Branch had set about their work at the start. We should not forget what things were like in those days. In Cologne at the end of the War ninety-two per cent of the school accommodation had been destroyed. In Schleswig-Holstein only 162 out of 1,550 primary schools were available and before long the influx of refugees doubled the population of the *Land*. I hope people in Germany now appreciate the immensely hard work and the courage shown by the German teachers and educational administrators in those days. Perhaps the difficulties helped. It meant that both sides were working together. In a very short time the members of the Education Branch succeeded in convincing the German administrators and teachers that they wanted to co-operate with them. They gained their confidence; they exerted an influence through their personal relationships rather than by using their powers

as the military rulers of a conquered nation. Their work was not
spectacular, but their influence was to be seen from the Ministries
to the smallest schools in the country. To meet an Education
Minister or a school inspector or a university *Rektor* in the house
of a British education officer—I may say that I do not believe
that a single one of them paid the least attention to the various
regulations against 'fraternisation'—and listen to them discussing
problems of educational policy or to go into a small school with
the local education officer and soon see him in earnest conversation with the head teacher about some shortage of textbooks or a
leak in the roof of the school—many would say that it was all
rather trivial, but it represented a definite policy, even if it was
largely an unconscious one.

The next period may be taken as lasting from December 1946
to August 1949, when the first elections were held in the newly
formed German Federal Republic. I should say that the British
education officers in general found that their position was very
little altered. They had been accustomed to offer advice rather
than give orders and their advice was sought as much as it had
been in the past. Moreover, the *Land* governments were feeling
their way somewhat painfully and the Education Ministers
remained in very close touch with the senior officers of the Education Branch. It was remarkable how often the Education Ministers invited British officials to attend meetings of departmental
committees which were considering educational problems. On
the British side it was regarded as natural to seek the approval
of the German educational authorities for any steps that were
taken on British initiative. I can remember, for instance, attending a meeting of the four Minister Presidents of the British Zone
to gain their agreement to our setting up a commission to consider the problem of the German universities. It was certainly
not necessary for us to do this. The four Education Ministers
of the British Zone used to meet once a month for a day or two
in my house for informal discussions. I have no doubt that this
was the most valuable time I spent each month. Until the
Blockade and the air lift began they were held in my office in
Berlin, they stayed with me in my house and we always ended
with a visit to the opera, from which they were taken to catch
a military train back to West Germany. When the awkward
question of uniforms for members of German youth organisa-

tions came up for consideration by the Education Committee of the Allied Control Council, I talked the matter over first with the four Ministers and was able to state a view which was much more that of the German Education Ministries than of the Military Government. But most of our time was taken up on purely practical problems, especially, before the currency reform, on how to provide any text-books at all for German schools, and immediately after it on how to help students to remain at the universities.

During this period the *Land* governments were all engaged in discussing the question of educational reform. It meant, in practice, the passing of legislation to set up a new educational system in each *Land*. In the autumn of 1947 the British Military Government took its one step towards controlling the kind of educational systems which would be established in its Zone. It laid down four principles and declared that it would veto any legislation which disregarded them. These principles were that the status of teacher training colleges should be raised, that secondary education should be free, that no legislation should rule out the eventual adoption of the six-year *Grundschule,* and that the private schools should not be abolished.

In addition to these principles the Military Government was anxious not to disturb the compromise reached in the early days on the vexed question of the confessional schools. Whether it was right for us to continue to enforce this compromise I am not sure. I once said to the four Education Ministers that I felt that perhaps one reason why they were cautious on educational reforms was that they were always looking over their shoulders at the problem of the confessional schools. I asked them if they thought it desirable that we should cease to take any interest in the question and hand it over to them. 'For heaven's sake, don't do that,' they said, 'We may be looking over our shoulders now, but if you did that we should turn right round.'

The declaration was first suggested to me by two of the Education Ministers and it was fully discussed with all four of them before it was issued. I cannot say that I now think it was worthwhile. In any case a year later we abandoned our veto and the declaration became invalid. It had, perhaps, a certain propaganda value and it gave some encouragement to those who advocated educational reforms. The principle about the

training colleges was probably useful. The principle about
secondary education meant nothing as it was in conflict with our
policy, adopted at the same time, of giving responsibility in the
financial sphere to the German Economic Council at Frankfurt. The question whether the *Grundschule* should last four or
six years produced in those days an extraordinary amount of
heat in Germany. The declaration gave such very guarded
support to the six-year *Grundschule* as to be almost worth-
less.

This declaration was as near as we ever came to intervening
in German educational politics, for the first three principles we
supported were those advocated by the Social Democratic
Party.

Can it be said, then, that we had no policy at all? If we
were to endeavour in the educational field to 'make possible the
successful development of democratic ideas' in Germany, and
if we were to interpret democracy as a state of society in which
the people of a country exercise their personal wills freely in
determining their form of government and in choosing the rulers
who will govern them it was quite clear that to force educational
changes on the German people would be wholly contradictory
to that aim. What then could be done?

Perhaps I might return to the problem of denazification. It
was an extraordinarily difficult, perhaps an impossible task to
decide which teachers should be forbidden to teach on account
of their previous connection with the Nazi movement. Altogether, 16,000 teachers in the British Zone were forbidden to
carry on their profession. I remember once telling a prominent
German Social Democrat newspaper editor, Willi Eichler, something of the sense of helplessness I felt when faced with this
problem, and I received some comfort from his comment, 'Don't
be too worried. After all you have probably managed this better
than the other occupying States. But you will never do it really
successfully until you obtain the services of a particular person.'
'Really,' I said, 'and who is that?' He replied, 'The Archangel
Michael.'

Denazification was all very well and I should say absolutely
necessary, but it did nothing for those who were or had been
Nazis, except to put them in positions without responsibility.
But the problem of the ex-Nazis was not entirely neglected and,

as practically nothing is known of this, I thought I might spend a moment on it.

Not long after I went out to Germany I was faced with the proposal to place all the Nazi leaders in the British Zone, not sentenced to imprisonment, on a small island in the North Sea, called Adelheide. There they were to stay for the rest of their lives with their families, free except that they could not leave the island. I was summoned to a meeting at Lübbecke to discuss this along with the other senior members of the Control Commission. I was asked to give my views on the proposal. 'Well,' I said, 'I can only deal with the question of the education of the children of the Nazis. There are two alternatives. You could build a school for them on the island to which they would all go. When they reached the age to go to a university you would have to let them leave, and then, having been brought up inevitably with Nazi ideas, they would spread them throughout Germany. Or you could send them to school on the mainland, either staying with relatives or in boarding schools, and they would go back to Adelheide for the holidays. There they would be imbued each time with Nazi ideals and they would go back with them to school each term.' At this the British Chief of Staff (Executive), as he was called, said, 'I think I am going to ask each one of you in turn whether you think we ought to go on with the proposal for Adelheide.' Each one in turn said 'no'. I have little doubt that they had made up their minds before, but I am glad that I played a part, at least, in defeating one of the most absurd proposals made while we occupied Germany.

Before I refer to the other, and more constructive effort, I might mention that it was decided early in 1947 to release from the camps all Nazis below the age of twenty-one. This was I think sensible. It did no good to keep them with older and more committed Nazis who would certainly do all they could to keep their faith alive.

The one constructive effort was the establishment, at a place called St Michael's House at Blankenese near Hamburg, of a kind of conference centre. This had nothing to do with the Education Branch of the Control Commission, nor for that matter with the Control Commission itself. It was, in fact, wholly illegal. It was paid for out of Occupation costs, although

it did not fall into any category covered by the arrangements
about them. At this place all rations between Germans and
English were shared equally, which was also illegal. We were
supposed to be neutral in religious matters; nothing less neutral
than St Michael's House could be imagined, for it was a definitely Christian institution, run by an English priest (now a bishop
of the Church of England) and a German Evangelical Church
Pastor. But let me make it clear that there was nothing emotional
or 'pentecostal' about it. Those who went found they were taking
part in really serious discussions on fundamental political questions. We invited all the young ex-Nazis, now free and, to use the
common phrase, 'category six ex-Nazis,' that is, allowed only
to do manual labour. A great many accepted the invitation
and came and I have good reason to believe that many were
deeply influenced by it. Of course, we could not talk about it.
One day the Chief of Staff in Berlin asked me to come and see
him. 'I say,' he said, 'can you tell me about a place called St
Michael's House? I have just heard of it. It seems to me wholly
illegal.' There was nothing for it and I told him all about it.
Now, this Major-General was a devout Roman Catholic. After
a moment's silence he said to me, 'Do you ever take any people
from our side of the house?' 'Well,' I said, 'you don't make it
very easy for us. But I can assure you that there is not a Catholic
bishop in West Germany who, if he knows of some ex-*Gruppenführer* who he thinks might benefit from a visit, will not send
him to us.' 'Really,' he said, 'that's very interesting. All right,
don't worry. You'll hear no more about it.' And it went on for
another six months. Then in changed conditions it was clear that
it could not be paid for out of Occupation costs any longer
and it had to be closed. But the young men who had been there,
many of them ex-Nazis got together and raised money which
they sent to us and this kept it going for another month. No
Old Boys ever paid their place of education such a tribute as
these young ex-Nazis paid to St Michael's House.

The essential problem in Germany after the War was surely
not created by the ex-Nazis. I doubt whether the Potsdam
Agreement when it referred to the complete elimination of
National Socialist doctrines went deep enough. What was really
needed in Germany after the War was the development of a
sense of personal responsibility for the affairs of the State. I

came to know a very remarkable German, Professor Kahle of Bonn University, a most courageous opponent of the Nazis who eventually escaped to England. He told me how some months after the Nazis seized power he had cause to visit the Education Ministry in Berlin. There to his surprise he met two young men, recently *Lektoren* at Bonn, whom he knew not to be Nazis. They were embarrassed and one of them said, 'Please, Herr Professor, do not think that we are Nazis. There are very few Nazis in the Ministry. Some have been forced into it by the government, but they are quite useless as administrators. It is people like us who keep the Ministry going. We are not Nazis. We call ourselves *Spezis' (Spezialisten)*. It never seemed to occur to him that he was helping to 'keep going' a régime which he professed to deplore.

To give another example. One day, I went to the University of Göttingen. We had decided to set up a German commission, quite independent of the British Control Commission, to consider the future of the German universities. I came to the conclusion that I ought to explain what we were intending to do to the Senate of the University. I did not expect a very favourable reception. When I finished I saw that they had chosen to answer me a most formidable antagonist, the philosopher Dr Nikolai Hartmann. 'Mr Birley,' he said, 'you seem to think that all the Professors at Göttingen were Nazis.' 'Not at all,' I answered. 'Of course they were not. The charge against the Professors at Göttingen is something quite different. It is that they were quite ready to accept a régime, the whole policy of which they know to be based on academic nonsense.' And to this I received the astonishingly generous reply, which I have never forgotten, 'To that charge, Mr Birley, we have no answer.'

It is now thirty years since the ending of Nazi rule. It is sometimes difficult to recall the feelings one had in those years immediately after the War when it was the one thing that seemed to matter. I think we realised that not all Germans had been Nazis, but only a minority of them. But the great majority had accepted them. One could not eliminate this lack of a sense of responsibility by ourselves changing the educational system of the country or altering the constitution of the universities or preparing anti-Nazi text books. In the end there seemed to be three lines worth pursuing.

The first was to do everything possible to give the German teachers responsibility and to avoid the temptation to tell them what to do and then expect them to do what they were told. I shall give one example, which is, I think, typical. One of the obvious problems which faced the Education Branch of the Control Commission was that of German text-books. Almost without exception those in use under the Nazis had to be forbidden, especially, as was to be expected, history books. I have already referred to the American solution of the problem. The British Education Branch issued no books of its own. Instead, it set up a Textbook Committee of German educationists, with two or three British advisers.

All scripts of new textbooks had to be sent to the committee which returned them to their authors with comments if they had passages with blatantly or narrowly nationalistic sentiments. This was, I felt—I had nothing to do with starting it—true education. It was notable that when control over education was handed over to the *Land* governments in December, 1946, the committee continued to function without any changes in its constitution or procedure.

Along with this went the splendid work of a group of teachers of history at Braunschweig, led by Dr Georg Eckert, who published little handbooks on German history, each one of which had on the title-page *Beiträge zum Geschichtsunterricht. Quellen und Unterlagen für die Hand des Lehrers.* ('Contributions to the teaching of history. Source material and documentation for the use of teachers'.) These had, I believe, a great influence. The only credit we can claim is that we supported them.

The second line that was pursued went back also to the earliest days of the Occupation, when the Education Branch had done all it could to bring forward those Germans who had not accepted the Nazis, to persuade them to accept posts of responsibility and then to support and encourage them. Opposition to the Nazis in Germany was more considerable than most people realised, though of course, it had been quite unsuccessful. When I was in Germany I worked, as I have said, with four Education Ministers. For most of the time two of these were Social Democrats who had spent years in concentration camps, Herr Grimme of Lower Saxony and Herr Kuklinski of Schleswig-Holstein. Herr Grimme was not only one of the outstanding figures in educational politics of his time; he was also a delightful companion. One was a lady, Frau Christine Teusch of North Rhine-Westphalia who had been a member of the Centre Party in the Reichstag in 1933, had then left politics and devoted herself to social work, often standing up to the Nazis. The fourth, Senator Landahl of Hamburg, had been a head teacher, but was dismissed immediately the Nazis seized power and had spent the next twelve years working as a printer. Would I, I used to think to myself, have shown the courage that they had? For me to try to preach democracy to them would have been insulting. But one came to realise that every liberal, humane and Christian German carried with him or her in those days after the War the memory of an overwhelming defeat. These people needed to feel that others were prepared to have confidence in them. This could be done only through close personal relationships. The great argument in favour of the British policy of deploying its educational forces throughout the Zone and not concentrating them largely in the obvious seats of power, the capitals of the *Länder* and the universities, as the Americans did, was that it made possible such personal relationships right through the whole educational system.

There was a third line of approach. Everything possible was done to encourage visits by German teachers abroad, especially to this country. This would have been quite impossible, of course, without the co-operation of people here. The difference in the attitude of the British after the Second World War from that adopted after the First was a remarkable phenomenon. In 1949 a professor at the University of Münster told me that a quarter of the students had been abroad since the end of the War. He himself had been one of the first party of German students to visit England after the First World War and that was in 1926, eight years after it had ended. Perhaps I might mention especially the arrangement under which young *Lektoren* from German universities went for one year to a university in Britain, not as students but as members of the staff.

Particularly helpful, I believe, was the institution in the British Zone of short courses for German secondary school teachers, held in Germany, to enable them to study the actual technique of teaching their subject—history for example, or geography or mathematics—in company with teachers from Britain. In two years, from the summer of 1947 to the middle of 1949, sixty-three of these courses were held, attended by 2,500 German secondary school teachers, or one-fifth of those in the British Zone. But it should be realised that in those years most German secondary school teachers in the British Zone under the age of forty-five took this opportunity to study the teaching of their subject along with teachers of another country, a record which must surely be unique in the history of education.

I have said nothing about the changes in the educational structure of Germany, comparable, for instance, with the arrangements made in the Soviet Zone to secure a proportion of children of workers at the universities or the French insistence that the *Abitur* should be replaced by a written examination. We made one attempt which was to set up a German commission to study the universities and propose changes in them. (There were two foreign assessors, without votes, mainly to help contacts with other countries, Lord Lindsay from England and Professor von Salis of the Technical University in Zurich.) I think their report, *Gutachten zur Hochschulreform*, was a very sensible and constructive one, but I cannot say that I think it had a great influence. Not long ago a leading German educationist asked me if I had ever heard of a report on the universities which had come out in 1949. I admitted that I had heard of it. 'If only we had followed that report,' he said, 'we might have saved ourselves many hectares of broken glass.'

The Education Branch also did not become involved in German party politics, though most of its members found themselves in sympathy with the Social Democrats. Once, however, the Youth Section did become involved. The work of this section was inevitably somewhat detached from that of the rest of the Branch. But my own impression was that it was especially valuable. The occasion on which it became political was one of its greatest successes, when it persuaded the various German youth organisations, especially the Catholic ones and the Social Democrat *Falken,* to work together. The compact was celebrated by a lunch given by the *Land* Commissioner of North Rhine -Westphalia, a Major-General, who had once been a prominent boy scout. In his speech he said that he felt sure that we were all agreed on one point, that what we really wanted of any boy, be he German or British, was that he would grow up to be a good Christian democrat. It took some time to persuade the leaders of the *Falken* after lunch that he had *not* meant what they thought he had.

On the whole, the British Army gave splendid support to the Education Branch of the Commission. I sometimes think that perhaps the most important step in the history of education in the British Zone was Field-Marshal Montgomery's order, not long after the end of the War, that in future no schools were to be taken over by the Army or the Control Commission. Once there was real trouble about this and I give this as an example of some parts of the history of Education Branch which naturally received no publicity. In 1947 it was decided to set up a boarding school for the children of members of the Control Commission and the place chosen for it was what had been during the War the headquarters of the German navy at Plön in Schleswig-Holstein. Up till then it had been occupied by the Royal Engineers of the Army, generally known as the Sappers. It was decided that they should be moved to an island in the Plöner See and this meant turning out a German boarding school which came under the Education Ministry of Schleswig-Holstein. I protested as strongly as I could, but without avail. The order for the move was issued. And then I made a discovery. As a young man the headmaster of the school had taught for a short time at an English public school called Tonbridge and the British Military Governor, Marshal of the Royal Air Force Sir Sholto Douglas, had been a boy there. So I wrote the Marshal a letter in which I stated once more all the arguments against the closing of the school and ended by saying that it was particularly unfortunate because the headmaster had been for a time a master at Tonbridge and he was proving successful in spreading the ideas he had learnt there throughout the schools of Schleswig-Holstein. (I may add that I told Herr Möhlmann of the Education Ministry in Kiel that he must support me in this.) The next thing that happened was that I was summoned to a meeting of the Chiefs of Staff at Hamburg. The Military Governor was not used, he said, to having his orders questioned after they had been issued. 'However, gentlemen,' he said, turning to his Chiefs of Staff, 'I have heard recently that this school is in the position to make a unique contribution to German education. I have decided, therefore, to change my mind. The Sappers will go to Flensburg.'

What the British educational policy could mean in those days was brought home to me most vividly by a simple incident which took place not in the British Zone but in Berlin. Practically nothing that I have said about the Allied control of education in Germany before August 1949 can be taken as applying to Berlin. For one thing until it was forcibly split by the Russians on 30 November 1948, it was a single unit. It had a City Assembly, the *Magistrat,* controlled by the Allied Kommandatura with its Education Committee. Agreement had to be reached between all four occupying powers or nothing happened at all. A School Law was passed by the *Magistrat* in 1947 and eventually accepted by the Allied Powers after a most prolonged game of diplomatic chess over the continued existence of confessional schools. Agreement was quite impossible, however, on the teaching of history, a significant issue as it was here that the ideological differences between East and West were most apparent. Another point of difference which was never resolved was that of the status of the universities in the city. The Russians insisted that the University of Berlin, now called the Humboldt University, should come under the control of the administration of their Zone not of Berlin, which they had no legal right to do under the inter-allied agreements on Berlin. In reply we kept under our control the *Technische Hochschule* of Berlin-Charlottenburg, which was in our sector and which had been renamed the *Technische Universität.* In March 1948 three students were expelled from the Humboldt University after they had written anti-communist articles in a journal. The students protested with such success that they were allowed back. But I remembered their saying that while it had been a great success it would not be so the next time and that the only answer would be a new university. They were quite right. It may be remembered that the blockade of Berlin began the day after it had been announced, in the evening of 23 June, that the new West German currency would be introduced into the three Western sectors of Berlin. That night, Ernst Reuter who had been elected *Regierende Bürgermeister* of Berlin, though the Russians had vetoed his appointment, along with three other political leaders, Herr Neumann, Dr Peters and Dr Suhr dined with Mr Creighton and myself to discuss the question of founding a new university. I suggested that we had better break off our discussions to listen to a broadcast which we knew would be critical in the history of Berlin. But they refused. 'That's all right,' they said. 'We were given copies of the announcement before we left. We haven't had time to read it yet. They are in our coats outside.' So the four leading Germans in West Berlin never heard the announcement which immediately brought on the blockade of their city. They had something more important to consider.

From that moment I had no doubt that we in West Berlin would win. It is not always appreciated that for five months after the blockade began Berlin still remained an administrative unit. Towards the end of November we became fully aware that the Russians would soon split the city. It was one evening at that time, just before six o'clock that I was rung up at my office in the Fehrbelliner Platz by a lady, Frau Dr Panzer, who was responsible for the secondary schools of Berlin. She spoke from her department's headquarters which were in the Russian sector. 'Mr Birley,' she said, 'the most dreadful things have happened today. May I see you at once?' This was awkward as at half-past six I was due to read a paper at my house to a Berlin Literary Society on the third scene of the fourth act of *Othello*. However, I suggested that we should both go straight to my house, where we might have a few minutes together before the meeting began. Unfortunately she was delayed and arrived at the same time as my guests. I still feel appalled at the thought that she had to sit through my paper, the discussions which followed it and then wait until we had refreshments. It was nearly half-past nine before the last guest left and I was able to ask her what had happened.

A few days previously we had invited to Berlin Mr Lester Smith, one of the leading figures in English educational administration, to look at the schools and then give a talk on what to do with a new school law once there was one. All the officials in the education administration of the *Magistrat* and all the school inspectors had been summoned to listen to him. When he had finished he left to catch a plane at Gatow and then, immediately after, before the meeting broke up, in stalked the Russian Deputy-Military Commandant of Berlin, with a revolver in his holster, and addressed the meeting. His speech was very violent and full of threats. He said that the Russians knew quite well that money which should have been spent on education was being used instead for the so-called *Luftbrücke*, the new air station at Tegel and the *Sturmpolizei*. He added that the Russians knew quite well who were the supporters of educational reform and who were not and that the latter could expect no mercy.

She had taken shorthand notes of the speech and as she read them to me it became quite clear what it portended. The Russians had made this violent demonstration in order to frighten the educational administration to remain with them when the split we were all expecting took place. 'And then,' she concluded, 'came the most Nazi moment I have known since the end of the War.' I asked her what she meant. 'A complete silence.' The remark was significant. What happened after that I learnt later on from others who were present. The silence was broken by Frau Dr Panzer who got up and made a reply which from all accounts was a magnificent performance. She began by telling the Russian general that he had no right, even if he was a representative of an occupying power, to bring his revolver into an educational meeting. She went on to tell him that he was lying, that he knew that he was lying, and what she said was particularly insulting was that he knew that they knew that he was lying.

The effect of her speech was to ruin completely the effect of the general's intervention. A few minutes later he left the room leaving the arguments to be continued, rather miserably, by the Communist members of the administration. It did not last long. I have no doubt at all that the future of Berlin education depended on that moment when she broke the silence and answered. If she had not done so, I do not believe that most of the educational administration and the school inspectors would have come over to the West, when the split came three days later and with them 800 of the 1100 students and all but two of the professors and lecturers of the *Pädagogische Hochschule*, which, as it was attached to the Humboldt University, was under the control of the Russians.

My first action was to summon to my house members of the Education Branch in Berlin to inform them, as we had certain prepared steps to take immediately the split took place. It was not until after midnight that I was alone with her again and able to ask her the question I had been wanting to put to her ever since I had heard her story. 'Why did you do it?' The answer was immediate and may seem surprising. 'St George's in the East, Stepney.' She was referring to a secondary modern school in a very poor part of East London, a very remarkable school under a very remarkable headmaster. We had arranged for her to spend four weeks in England a few months before. She had visited this school and been deeply impressed by it. When she had returned to Berlin, she said to me at once, 'If I could have in Berlin three schools like St. George's in the East, Stepney, I could revolutionise the education of this city.' What it meant, of course, was that at that moment of crisis she felt that she could not cut herself off—not from anything so grandiloquent as Western Civilisation or the Free World—but from a particular school in London and the friends she had made there.

I have related this incident in some detail because it seems to me to sum up well our educational policy in Germany after the War. First, this lady had been chosen by us for an important educational post because we knew that she had shown herself staunch in resistance to the Nazis. She had been caught distributing underground Social Democrat leaflets and had been condemned to a concentration camp, from which she had escaped during an air raid. At the end of the War she was in the British Zone. She had become the personal friend of members of the British Education Branch in Berlin. We had been able to bring her in touch with British schools and teachers so that she really felt that she was a member of the same family. What we had never attempted to do was to 're-educate' her, to teach her democracy. That would have been an insult.

3. *The British Contribution*

George Murray

The Aims of the Occupation

It is doubtful whether at any time in history any nation vic-
, torious in war has claimed amongst the spoils of its victory the
right to remodel the traditional attitudes of its enemy according
to its own and has deliberately set out to do so by peaceful
means and within the law. Probably the first attempt to influence
a whole nation in this way was made by the Allies at the end
of the second World War during the period 1945–49 when the
Allied Control Council was acting as the legal successor to the
German government and could therefore issue directives that
had the force of law. Although the purpose of the Occupation
was reiterated at various times from 1943 onwards, sometimes
in unilateral, sometimes in quadripartite or tripartite declarations like the Potsdam Agreement, the aim generally accepted
by all the Allies at all times was not only to eradicate Nazism
and militarism from German institutions and attitudes but also
to replace them with effective and durable safeguards against
their recrudescence. Even after the Allied Control Council had
ceased to function this remained the cornerstone of the Allies'
policy although in time the differences in interpretation and
execution in the separate Zones of occupation came to widen
considerably, especially those between the Western Allies and
the Russians.

This paper attempts to describe the contribution made by
Britain towards the realisation of these aims, with special reference to the influences deliberately exerted to this end through
the German educational system, both formal and informal,
upon German society as a whole. Although of comparatively
short duration the period under review does perhaps merit recording, not because it produced any spectacular achievement
but rather for the very uniqueness of its nature.

The failure to do anything effective of this nature in Germany after the First World War only served to strengthen the determination of those who, after yet another holocaust, were charged with the task of ensuring that this further opportunity of putting an end to the perpetual menace of war should this time be exploited to the full. But nothing of this kind had ever been attempted before. History had no advice or example to follow. One might have expected some lessons to emerge during the Second World War from the liberation and occupation of North Africa, Sicily, Italy and other European countries but it became clear at an early stage in the occupation of Germany that the revival of the civil administration in a country that has been liberated and the assumption of control in a country that has been beaten into unconditional surrender are two vastly different tasks. The occupation of Germany raised problems for which there were few, if any, precedents and which required solutions of a very special kind.

Was Occupation Justified?

That Germany should be occupied at all depended on the achievement of military victory by the Allies but the planning of the Occupation went ahead from the outset on this assumption. Military victory and civil reconstruction came to be regarded as two facets of the same process and while the military objectives were being defined in terms of 'unconditional surrender' it was becoming accepted that ultimate victory would never be complete without the deliberate re-conversion of Germany to a democratic way of life. Chamberlain's declaration at the beginning of the War that 'we are not fighting against you, the German people,' was largely submerged during the dark days of 1941 and 1942 when the nation's will and energies were focused on victory by any means.

In 1943 when belief in victory began to grow, the problem of what to do with Germany after the War, hitherto subordinated to the life-and-death struggle for survival, began to claim an ever greater share of Allied planning for victory. While there were many who had misgivings about the policy of 'unconditional surrender' on the military side there were just as many who deplored the intention to 'civilise' the Germans by a post-war occupation of the country. Nothing like it had ever

C

been attempted before and there was no reason to suppose that it had any greater prospect of success in 1945. It would be the height of arrogance to assume that victory somehow gave us the moral right to impose our way of life. Some said that it would require an occupation of at least fifty years to do the job properly, assuming that the Germans would never co-operate in any plan to alter their traditional outlook. In any case how could one educate an already civilised nation that had produced many of the greatest geniuses and bene-factors of mankind? As for the means and methods, would they not approximate to those employed by the Nazis and be there-fore equally objectionable? Would propaganda acquire a fair name because it had passed into Allied hands? The Germans would certainly be highly suspicious of it, suffering as they were from twelve years of the Nazi brand and convinced that any other variation imported from abroad by a victorious enemy was bound to be even more obnoxious. Could one, for instance, persuade the Germans of the advantages of British parlia-mentary democracy while governing them by proclamation and decree? Is it in any case possible to transplant an institution from one soil to another and expect it to flourish?—even when adapted to the new environment? And above all, could the work of reconstruction be really effective at a time when Germany would be exhausted under the burden of defeat, dis-grace, disillusion, reparations and even perhaps starvation?

These arguments were typical of the doubts, misgivings and scruples that were put forward against the policy of occupation. There were, of course, some pretty cogent arguments in favour and even in the middle of the War when the whole question was being decided there were sufficient of these to tip the scales in favour of occupation. Had the planners been able to anticipate the destruction and desolation of Germany at the end of the War there would have been no hesitation in reaching the same decision. It had by then become obvious that Germany would be incapable of survival unaided. Left on her own, she would probably have looked back to Weimar for inspiration, ignoring the social and political progress made by the western world in the intervening years and risking a re-affirmation of the mentality that made Nazism and its atrocities possible. To avoid this the Allies would have to override their doubts and scruples and fill the vacuum either by direct rule or indirect persuasion or both, pointing out the direction in which democracy lay, the obstacles to achieving it and above all bringing information about its latest manifestations in other countries from which Germany had been isolated for the whole of the Nazi period.

It was vital to ensure that Germany would set her course away from the past and to help her in doing so it was clear that the presence of the Allies in an occupied Germany would be essential for a number of years. But the Allies' motives were not entirely altruistic : apart from the desire to set Germany on her feet again and as soon as possible see her cease to be an economic burden on the Allies, as she had been after the First World War, there was a grim resolve that 'it must not happen again' and that their descendants should be freed forever from the evils of war and despotism—a desire which, in itself, would appear to justify most means to most ends.

Any lingering doubts about occupation could be finally dispelled by the memory of the deliberate deceptions practised by the German militarists in the 1920s and the failure of the Inter-Allied Control Commission of those days to tie them down within the terms of the treaties of Versailles and Locarno. By 1925 the potential of the German army had been built up far beyond the limit of 100,000 allowed by the treaty of Versailles and two years later, in January 1927, when the Allied Control Commission was withdrawn, the way to German rearmament stood open and the controls then vested in the League of Nations were never effectively applied. By 1932 the scene was set for the evil genius who was to provide the German military machine with teeth, temerity and a succession of targets. Then came the political chicaneries of the 1930s and the miseries and atrocities they brought about, both inside and outside Germany, culminating in total war.

There was really no alternative to the occupation of Germany beyond the limit required for military victory and, if necessary, beyond the limit required for disarmament, reparations, denazification and demilitarisation which it was estimated could be accomplished in less time than the more delicate constructive task of leading Germany back into the ways of democracy and the comity of nations. It was a formidable decision that required

in its execution a constant recharging of inspiration especially
in those few who had to rebuild against impossible odds and
recurrent misgivings what so many others had destroyed.

Prelude to Potsdam

Although in the end there was no doubt about the Allies' determination to solve the German problem one can trace a
distinct reluctance among them, even in 1943, to discuss the
broad outline of occupation let alone get down to planning
the details. The accent was still on winning the War. The reader
of Churchill's *The Second World War* arrives half-way through
the fifth volume before he finds any hint of a constructive intention towards post-war Germany. In his record of the Teheran
conference (November 1943) Churchill writes 'The supreme
question of the treatment to be accorded to Germany by the
victors could at this milestone only be the subject of a preliminary survey of a vast political problem . . . It must be remembered that we are in the midst of a fearful struggle with
the mighty Nazi power. All the hazards of war lay around us
and all its passions of comradeship among allies, of retribution
upon the common foe dominated our minds.'[1] Even as late
as January 1945, when the Allied armies were already on the
Rhine, Churchill wrote to Eden 'It is much too soon for us to
decide these enormous questions . . . It is a mistake to write
out on little pieces of paper what the outrages, emotions of a
vast and quivering world will be either immediately after the
struggle is over or when the inevitable cold fit follows the hot.
There is therefore wisdom in reserving one's decisions as long
as possible and until all the facts and forces that will be potent
at the moment are revealed.'[2]

Barely a month later, however, addressing the House of
Commons about the Yalta conference, Churchill made it clear
that his concern now extended beyond the political and military
problems of victory, demilitarisation, reparations and frontiers.
With one eye on public opinion at home these would continue
to claim priority but from now on any reference to them
would almost always be accompanied by mention of the more
positive tasks of revival, restoration and re-orientation. In the
same report to Parliament about the Yalta conference, having

assured the House once more that Nazism and militarism would
be finally destroyed, Churchill went on 'On the other hand it
is not the purpose of the Allies to destroy the people of Germany
or leave them without the necessary means of subsistence. Our
policy is not revenge; it is to take such measures as may be
necessary to serve the future peace and safety of the world.
There will be a place one day for Germany in the community
of nations . . .'

The increasing frequency of statements of this kind on the
Allied side from mid-1943 suggests a growing realisation of the
conditions that would face them in Germany, if the War had to
be fought to the limits of unconditional surrender. It was becoming increasingly clear that Germany would be unable to rise from
the rubble unaided, at least in the early stages. Roosevelt had
occasion to make public statements in the same vein, notably when
he repudiated the Morgenthau plan to reduce Germany to a
pastoral economy. Stalin showed less consistency in his views
but the attitudes of the three Allied leaders had enough in common to make the Potsdam Agreement possible. It was signed
on 2 August 1945 by Attlee, Truman and Stalin. The provisional French government was not represented at the conference but the Agreement provided for French participation
in the Occupation on an equal footing with the Big Three. It
was the first agreement recognised by all the Allies setting out
the broad principles governing the occupation of the whole of
Germany and it provided for rehabilitation as well as the
eradication of Nazism and militarism. It was thus the reflection
and the culmination of the development of the Allied attitudes
towards Germany during the course of the War.

The preamble includes a promise of assistance in reviving
democracy. The political purposes of the Occupation as set out
in the Agreement include preparation 'for the eventual reconstruction of German political life on a democratic basis
and for eventual peaceful co-operation in international life'.
Reform and rehabilitation were to be effected by influencing
certain sensitive areas in public life in Germany, notably by
making available comparisons with her neighbours in Europe.
Some of these areas are singled out in the Agreement, for
example the judicial system—'will be re-organised in accordance
with the principles of democracy, of justice under law and of

equal rights for all citizens without distinction of race, nationality or religion'; education—'shall be so controlled as completely
to eliminate Nazi and militarist doctrines and to make possible
the successful development of democratic ideas'; administration
—'should be directed towards the decentralisation of the political
structure and the development of local responsibility'; freedom
of the press and of speech and religion were to be guaranteed
and trade unions were to be allowed.

As far as the reform of the system or any of its institut-
tions was concerned it was clear that education would be the
main vehicle of Allied influence not only because of the large
number of people affected and the comparative ease with which
they could be reached in their schools and colleges but because
most of them were in their most impressionable years; they
were the ones most in need of guidance and, above all, they
held the key to the future in their hands. The use of the
word 'controlled' in regard to education defines accurately
enough the method of work to be adopted by Allied education
officials—indeed they were called Education Control Officers
from the very early days. That their work proved in the beginning to be to a large extent as executive in character as it was
supervisory derived from the deplorable conditions in which it
was carried out.

As far as guidance on policy was concerned the ECO could
refer to a number of orders and directives issued at various times
by various authorities before the end of hostilities but most
of them were couched in terms too general to be of much help
in the practical problems of the 'bricks and mortar period'.
Others were issued piecemeal of necessity in order to solve
immediate difficulties. The following were amongst the more
important of these :—

a) A directive dated April 1944 from the combined Chiefs
of Staff (British and American) laying down inter alia the
important principle that military government would be carried
out 'through indirect rule' and that 'the principal link for this
rule should be at *Bezirk* or *Kreis* level, controls at higher levels
to be added as appropriate'—the assumption being that the war
would end before German territory was invaded and that the
administration would still be capable of functioning under orders
from military government.

b) *The Handbook of Military Government in Germany* issued by SHAEF (Supreme Headquarters Allied Expeditionary Force) in December 1944, was written under the same erroneous assumption—that Germany would collapse before she was invaded. The *Handbook* was furthermore 'intended not for the Staff Officer or the specialist but for the general administrator, the Military Government Officer in the Detachments placed at key points of administration up and down the US/BR Zones of Western and Southern Germany'. On these two scores alone the usefulness of the *Handbook* was severely restricted. A series of technical manuals was issued as supplements to the *Handbook*, one of them for *Education and Religious Affairs*, dated February 1945. These were designed for the specialist, including the Control Officers of the Commission in whose training they played a valuable role.

c) Anticipating the dissolution of SHAEF when the Allied Commanders-in-Chief would become directly responsible to their respective governments the British War Office issued a series of directives in consultation with the divisions and branches of the Control Commission as they were then constituted (Autumn and Winter 1944-5). The subjects covered by these directives included education and religious affairs (Directive No. 8).

d) A number of orders and proclamations were issued by different authorities at different times, each affecting to a greater or lesser extent the activities of Education Branch, for example Proclamation No. 1 issued by the Supreme Commander, General Eisenhower, laid down that 'all educational institutions within the occupied territory are suspended. Re-opening will be authorised when conditions permit'. The non-fraternisation orders were intended to have an even wider impact. They stemmed originally from the directive issued by the Combined Chiefs of Staff but were gradually whittled down at different times and in different Zones until it was finally agreed at Control Council level to abolish whatever restrictions were still in force since they were in any case no longer being obeyed.

e) Next came the Potsdam Agreement, signed on 2 August 1945. It came late (Education Branch headquarters were already in Bünde) and it would have been more welcome had it been couched in more specific terms. Nevertheless it did make clear that the long-term policy of the Allies aimed at reconstruction and democratisation and it dispelled any last, lingering doubts engendered by the Morgenthau proposals and any others like them. The Agreement did not supersede or rescind any of the laws, proclamations, orders or directives which had already been issued under the authority of the Commanders-in-Chief in their respective Zones of occupation. Indeed in the proclamation issued on 30 August 1945 establishing the Allied Control Council it was expressly laid down that these should remain in force in the Zones to which they applied. In any case, the terms of the Potsdam Agreement were broad enough to assimilate most of the directives already in force in the British Zone and the Agreement itself can be regarded as a retrospective authority from all Allies for such steps as had already been taken towards the revival of German education as well as a signpost pointing the way to its future development and a framework for its implementation.

f) Between July 1945, when Education Branch Headquarters arrived in Germany, and December 1946, when the *Land* parliaments took over responsibility for educational legislation, a series of about eighty Education Control Instructions were issued by Education Branch to Military Government Detachments for implementation. They provided the long-awaited, detailed guidance on policy and its application and covered all manner of problems that ECOs had to deal with: the reopening of schools and colleges, the resumption of adult education, the approval of youth groups, the control of textbooks, the admission of students. The procedures recommended in the Instructions derived largely from the *Handbook of Military Government in Germany* and the *Technical Manual for Education and Religious Affairs* and fell within the policy framework of the Potsdam Agreement.

g) The Allied Control Council also issued a number of laws and directives affecting education. These were translated into E.C.I.s at Education Branch Headquarters and passed to lower formations for appropriate action.

Military Government

Before dealing with this subject it should be explained that the term 'Military Government', although often loosely used, really had two distinct meanings. First it denoted a function, the task of liaising with the civil administration, more often by controlling it than actually governing. As a function, Military Government began as soon as the Allied armies invaded Germany and followed in their wake as far as they went. It lasted, at least in Western Germany, until the Federal Republic was created in the autumn of 1949. As far as Berlin is concerned Military Government continues to exist even today especially with regard to education and culture, although only in a legal sense without affecting the day-to-day relationship between Germans and British.

In its second, and far commoner meaning, Military Government denoted the specially trained Army units responsible for getting the German civil authorities on their feet again with the primary aim (since they were *military* units) of facilitating the progress of the Allied armies. Their duties were therefore nothing if not diverse but tended to centre round:

a) feeding and accommodating refugees, displaced persons, prisoners-of-war and others.

b) finding, checking and appointing German officials to undertake the work of restoration.

c) restoring mains services—water, gas, electricity, drainage.

d) taking all possible precautions against cold, hunger and disease.

e) maintaining law and order.

They covered in fact every emergency that arose regardless of its nature or complexity in circumstances that could hardly have been less favourable.

Although policy dictated that the Military Government Detachments should control but not govern it became obvious at an early stage that the extent of delegation to the German authorities would be far less than anticipated not only because of the unexpected enormity of the destruction but also because of the shortage of German officials available at their posts. This was especially the case in the Rhineland in the early days of the invasion of Germany when the civilian population understandably chose to flee from the fighting to safer areas in the North. Here, however, they were halted by the stream of refugees from the East and further movement became impossible either for those already on the move or for the resident popula-

c*

tion. This meant that there were more experts (engineers, police and municipal officials of all kinds) available to co-operate with the Military Government Detachments in the initial stages of reconstruction. But many of those who had been dismissed by the Nazis were now too old and exhausted, many of those who were found at their posts were Nazis and had to be dismissed or, if their services were absolutely indispensable, employed under strict supervision. This was one of the first and trickiest of the problems raised by the process of denazification—what to do with the skilled professional who happened to have been an active Nazi.

Many of the Military Government officials were also no longer in their prime, some had been wounded earlier in the war and had returned to less active service, some were experts in particular fields and could be seconded from fighting units for specialist jobs as soon as the end of the war was in sight. But it was their initiative, their unflagging energy, their devotion to duty and, above all, their enthusiasm for reconstruction after years of destruction that raised the Germans out of their apathy and their despair to take their share of the daunting tasks of revival. The Military Government Detachments were formally taken over in September 1945 by the Control Commission (British Element) which not only assumed the work of Military Government but also took over large numbers of its staff. The Education Branch in particular was very glad of the opportunity to absorb the Military Government Officers who had been dealing with educational matters, who were by now familiar with the local educational scene and were prepared to stay on in Germany for a number of years in order to see German education on its feet again. Without them, Education Branch's task would have been impossible in view of the besetting difficulties of recruitment in the United Kingdom.

Although all schools and colleges remained closed for the first few months of the Occupation there was much to be done in the way of repairing educational establishments— bricks, glass and mortar were in high demand and short supply and priorities had to be drawn up to share them out fairly. The Military Government Detachments were, of course, en- titled to the use of army communications and army transport and in those days these were extremely valuable. There was little glory in 'liberating' enough glass to weatherproof a school if you had no transport to fetch it. More often than not it was just across the river but the nearest bridge was either twenty miles upstream or downstream.

However, if you had both glass and transport, a stove or two for warmth, some slates to write on, boots or shoes to keep out the wet and the cold and a teacher who had miraculously found his way home from the War—with these bare essentials it was possible to offer a German child, if not a very warm welcome at least a start to his schooling. For he had not been to school for the previous two years most of which had been spent in an evacuation camp in the country. Born shortly before the war he lagged behind in the basic achievements of reading, writing and counting. He was hungry, bewildered, sullen and in some ways old beyond his years. He lived in a maelstrom of nationalities and languages, some familiar and friendly, some foreign and frightening, amongst a moving population either bound for home or driven forever from it by war or politics. There were in the British Zone alone over three million children of school age, an increase of twenty per cent over the pre-war figure for the same area.

But there was no corresponding increase in the supply of buildings, teachers or textbooks. Only ten per cent of all the schools in the Cologne area were habitable and available for their proper uses, the remainder having been requisitioned for such purposes as military headquarters, hospitals, shelter for refugees or food distribution centres. The teacher situation was equally disastrous. The average age of those who were available when the schools opened was between fifty and sixty. The process of denazification, the slow release of prisoners-of-war (priority was given to the release of coal-miners and agricultural workers) and the lack of accommodation in urban areas all contributed to the restriction in the number of teachers available. Things might have been easier had it been possible to use the textbooks that were procurable. The bulk of them were useless, even dangerous. Since the policy was to get the Germans to write new textbooks and submit them to Education Branch for approval there was inevitably a hiatus before new authors began to come forward. In any case the bulk of paper pulp and chemicals needed for making paper was in the Russian Zone and unobtainable without protracted negotiation and delay. The three Rs would have made more progress had the three Ps been available—pens, pencils and paper.

In spite of all these difficulties, however, 3,000 schools were open by the end of August with about half a million pupils. By the end of the year (1945) over two and a half million children were receiving some sort of schooling in something like 11,000 schools in the British Zone; in most cases this was on a shift basis, each building being shared by two, three or even more schools, each pupil attending for a maximum of two or three hours per day. Some technical and secondary schools had also restarted by the end of the year. The least damaged of the universities (Göttingen) reopened in September and the others had all begun to function, in whole or in part, by the middle of December. By this time, too, the Military Government Detachments had completed their task of first aid and had formally handed over responsibility for education in the British Zone to the Education Branch of the Control Commission for Germany (British Element), which moved from London to Germany in July 1945.

Education Branch, Control Commission for Germany (British Element)

It will be realised from what has been said about the educational work of the Military Government Detachments that by the middle of 1945 conditions were ripe for the experts to take over the increasingly complex and long-term tasks of educational reconstruction. These had been recruited into the Education Branch of the Control Commission from early in 1944—teachers, lecturers, administrators, educationists with a wide variety of interests, all with at least some knowledge of Germany, its language and institutions and all of them now willing to specialise in some branch of German education and dedicate the next few years of their lives to its revival. At no time were people of adequate calibre easy to find.

By mid-1944 with the end of the War in sight most of those in the services were looking forward to returning to their old occupations or finishing off studies that had been interrupted

five years earlier or resuming careers in which advancement
had already been sacrificed. But by the time that I myself was
accepted, at the end of 1944, there must have been a nucleus
of about two dozen officials housed in a dusty requisitioned
mansion in Kensington, surrounded by vast books of reference
on Germany, German education, German history, German
culture, politics and life under Weimar, Nazism and the War.
The Branch comprised sections responsible for universities,
schools, teacher training, youth, textbooks and other facets of
education, each collecting the latest information about their
particular field as it trickled back from wartime Germany, each
coming to realise the enormity of the tasks that lay ahead. I remember the long-awaited arrival of the first sackful of school
textbooks, how they were pounced upon as the first contact
with the reality we would soon be facing—and the awful realisation that nearly all of them would have to be condemned and
replaced by others not yet written, let alone approved or printed.
As I recall it, that problem kept the Textbook Section out of
mischief for quite some time before they emerged with a new
policy amended to take account of the realities.

Such a process was typical of the Branch's pragmatic approach
to its problems for, although the original directives laid down
that textbooks (to quote but one example of educational problem) were to be demilitarised and denazified there was still plenty
of scope for more detailed policy as to how and how far this
was to be accomplished. Policy in education as in other subjects, was therefore an amalgam of the long-term directives
issued in the early 1940s in agreement with one or more of
the Allies and the more urgent policy guidance required to
identify a particular problem at first hand and set out a procedure
for dealing with it.

This latter type of policy guidance took the form of Education Control Instructions (ECIs), drawn up by Education
Branch and issued to the Military Government Detachments for
their guidance and action. As noted earlier, between July 1945
when Education Branch moved to Germany and the end of
1946 when it moved to Berlin, upwards of eighty of these
Instructions were issued, on all manner of subjects—the opening of the universities, the resumption of adult education, youth
activities, school meals, church administration (the full title of

the Branch was Education and Religious Affairs Branch), the
resumption of the several branches of vocational education and
so on. They varied from simple instructions for the use of rail-
way station waiting rooms for youth groups to the bewildering
complexities of denominational education, from a simple elaboration of the undesirable elements that were to be removed from
physical education (ECI No. 2 of 18 July 1945) to an even
simpler instruction (No. 26 of 20 October 1945) to move the
beginning of the school year from Autumn to Easter. In many
cases a special version of the ECI was translated into German
and sent to the German authorities for action by them—these
were called EIGAs (Educational Instructions to the German
Authorities) and had the merit of letting the Germans know not
only what the overall plan was but also the role that they had
to play in it.

Education Branch moved to Germany, to Bünde in Westphalia to be exact, in July 1945 and assumed control of education (and religious affairs) in the British Zone, acting through
the Education Control Officers in the Military Government Detachments at *Land, Regierungsbezirk* and *Kreis* level. At the
headquarters of the Control Commission for Germany (British
Element) which were also situated in Westphalia to begin with,
the Education Branch was part of the Internal Affairs and
Communications Division and acted as a Zonal Ministry of
Education with a dual loyalty to the Cultural Committee of the
Allied Control Council in Berlin and to the German Education
Department of the Foreign Office in London. At the head of
the British Element of the Control Commission for Germany
was the Military Governor whose Deputy, General Robertson,
was responsible for all aspects of Military Government and who
later as Military Governor himself and finally as British High
Commissioner ensured the continuity that made for successful
policy and planning in all fields, education included, during the
first crucial years after the War.

The missing element in this hierarchy was of course the former
German Ministry in Berlin, the so-called Reich and Prussian
Ministry of Education which disappeared in the devastation of
the capital. Parts of it were evacuated during the War and
were discovered at the Ministerial Collecting Centre near Kassel
in the American Zone. But they were judged to be of insufficient

importance to form the nucleus of a restored ministry. In any case, the policy of decentralisation meant, as far as education was concerned, that legislative power would eventually be vested in the *Länder* and that until this came about in January 1947 as a result of Ordinance No. 57, issued by the British Military Government, Education Branch would, at least as far as the British Zone was concerned, fill the gap left by the disappearance of the Berlin Ministry. To revive the central Ministry would not only have run counter to Allied policy but would also have strengthened the hand of the Federal Government after 1949 in their quarrel with the *Land* governments over educational sovereignty.

In view of the recruitment difficulties which I have already mentioned it was indeed a blessing that so many members of the Military Government Detachment had qualifications and experience in education and that so many of them were willing to return to Germany after demobilisation and continue with the activities they had been engaged in as members of Military Government. They were eventually absorbed into Education Branch on the same conditions as members of the headquarters staff. To these were added, during 1946 eight University Control Officers, one for each of the universities in the British Zone. Although they became regular members of a Military Government Detachment it was a condition of their employment that they should not be required to undertake any tasks that would interfere with their university work. The importance of youth work was also recognised by the appointment of over 200 Youth Officers attached to Detachments down to and including *Kreis* level. The peak establishment of Education Branch (250 ECOs plus 200 Youth Officers) was reached in 1947 and was thereafter subject to annual decreases in line with the handover of responsibility for education to the German authorities at the beginning of the same year. The authority for this step came from a Military Government Ordinance (No. 57) which came into effect in January 1947, and empowered the *Land* parliaments to legislate in all subjects except those deliberately placed under the jurisdiction of Military Government.

Education did not appear on the reserve list and the *Land* legislatures therefore took over responsibility for it. The protests were long and loud, not least from some German educationists

who protested that the handover had come too soon and that
British assistance would be withdrawn before their policy had
even begun to be implemented and in any case long before
the German education machine was sufficiently manned and
equipped to take over. But those who thought along these lines
were perhaps failing to appreciate the nature of the relationship that had developed between German educationists and the
British ECOs. Their working basis developed quickly from the
initial control and direction to complete co-operation in a
common task, to trust, goodwill and understanding on both
sides and to lasting friendships which have survived the intervening thirty years. On this basis those dedicated to the task
of restoring German education could afford to ignore Ordinance
No. 57 and its schedules and proceed along the paths they had
found together, untrammelled by any hard-and-fast legal restrictions. A somewhat similar situation had already arisen when
the 'non-fraternisation' rules came into force. It immediately
became clear that the work of the ECOs would be impossible
without direct contact between them and their German colleagues. It is doubtful which of the two produced more practical
results—the informal, social contacts or the formal, professional
ones, but it is safe to say that, whatever advantages accrued
from non-fraternisation, Anglo-German co-operation in the field
of education was one of the main forces that undermined it and
finally led to its withdrawal.

Even supposing Ordinance No. 57 had deprived Education
Branch of impact as well as control it would still have maintained if not increased its influence through the appointment, in
May 1947, of an Educational Adviser whose terms of reference
were :

a) to initiate and co-ordinate policy for bringing influence to
bear upon the German mind and outlook so that Germany may
become a truly democratic nation ready and fit to take her place
in the community of peace-loving nations, and

b) to supervise the work of Education Branch.
The appointment clearly confirmed that the task had been
officially recognised as a long-term one which would extend
in its practical application well beyond the formal education
system into the web of society at all levels and in all fields. The
first Adviser is still prominent in Anglo-German affairs and two

of his successors are in close support—Professor Marshall and Professor Allen. In his work the Adviser was given the power and prestige of direct access to the Deputy Military Governor and thus enjoyed a status equal to that of his Allied colleagues, the American, French and Russian Cultural Affairs Advisers. This was important in his quadripartite activities in Berlin and especially in reaching agreements on educational issues in the Cultural Committee of the Allied Control Council.

Given that quadripartite work was of its nature cumbersome and in any case came to an end when the Russians walked out of the Council in March, 1948, it was understandable that the agreements reached were drawn up in the broadest possible terms. Perhaps the most important one was Directive No. 54 of 25 June 1947, entitled 'Basic principles of the democratisation of education in Germany' which was couched in sufficiently broad terms for agreement to be possible, although in some places it rested less on identity of principles than on a semantic compromise. The result was that the agreement was subject to different interpretations in different Zones and was there coloured by the current practice—the British view was, for instance, influenced by the new principles which, after years of discussion and research, were enshrined in the 1944 Education Act.

But the quadripartite educational apparatus did not on the whole produce any inspiring guide to democracy. Many of the rules and recommendations emanating from this source were too general in their expression to call for any specific, let alone immediate action. Others tended to underline the negative side of Allied policy—the principles governing admission of students to universities or the employment of regular army officers as youth organisers were largely exercises in denazification, creating vast categories of unemployable transgressors, only to see them (or at least some of them) exonerated under the Youth Amnesty of May 1947, and many of the remainder re-employed when denazification was handed back to the German authorities in October of the same year.

Anglo-German Contacts in the British Zone

Meantime in the British Zone education was gathering strength and direction from within itself, guided and encouraged by

German and British educational officials alike. From modest and hesitant beginnings at *Kreis* level committees and societies were formed and grew steadily in number, membership and influence as they reached *Land* and Zonal level. The first meeting of the Adult Education Association for *Landkreis-springe* at the beginning of October 1945 was certainly not an isolated achievement for by the end of the year a *Land* association was either already formed or in the process of formation in every *Land* of the British Zone and a Zonal advisory committee was already active at the beginning of 1946. Other Zonal advisory committees, for example those for elementary and intermediate schools, secondary schools and for teacher training appeared later in the year (1946). Those with more practical functions tended to come to life earlier in response to the urgent demand for action in their field—the Zonal Textbook Committee for instance held its first meeting in Hanover on 14 December 1945 and settled its scope, working method, organisation and secretariat straightaway. The Committee for school broadcasting produced the first programme at Radio Hamburg on 12 November 1945. A Zonal committee for visual aids also made an early start in 1945 in response to pressure from the schools. The university *Rektoren* met regularly amongst themselves (*Rektorenkonferenz*) and, with the *Land* authorities and others from public life, in the *Hochschulkonferenz*. The university students needed no second bidding to link up with their colleagues throughout the Zone and beyond it. They too had their Zonal representation—the *Zonenstudentenrat*.

By the autumn of 1946 most of these bodies had been subordinated to the Zonal Education Council (*Zonenerziehungsrat*), an all-German committee comprising the *Land* Ministers of Education of the British Zone (or their nominees) who, in turn, met regularly with the Director of Education Branch in the Zonal Educational Advisory Committee, itself a committee of the Zonal Advisory Council of Ministers President. It was at the regular meetings of these advisory and consultative bodies that German and British educationists pooled their ideas and their expertise in the reshaping of German education. It was comparatively easy to agree about the abolition of Nazi practices and institutions but when it came to filling the gaps thus created it fell to the British ECOs to provide information and commentary on the relevant social developments and educational progress achieved in Europe, and especially in Britain, during the sterile years of the Nazi régime. British educational policy in Germany therefore inevitably included the selection and projection of certain of the principles formulated in official reports and White Papers during the period roughly from the Hadow Report on the education of the adolescent (1926) to the 1944 Education Act.

Some of these found their way into the Control Council Directive No. 54 of 25 June 1947—'Basic Principles for the Democratisation of Education in Germany'. This directive was issued to the Zone Commanders and to Allied Kommandatura in Berlin for their guidance in advising the German educational authorities on the steps they should take to reform the education system and bring it up to date. There was obviously, six months after the publication of Ordinance No. 57, no question of ordering or compelling the Germans to implement this directive but it did set up a number of desirable aims to be achieved by Allies and Germans working in partnership at a common task of equal importance to both. These aims were : —

1) There should be equal educational opportunity for all.

2) Tuition, textbooks and other necessary scholastic material should be provided free of charge in all educational institutions fully supported by public funds which cater mainly for pupils of compulsory school age; in addition, maintenance grants should be made to those who need aid. In all other educational institutions, including universities, tuition, textbooks and necessary material should be provided free of charge together with maintenance grants for those in need of assistance.

3) Compulsory full-time attendance should be required for all between the ages of six and at least fifteen—and thereafter, for those pupils not enrolled in full-time educational institutions, at least part-time compulsory attendance up to the completed age of eighteen years.

4) Schools for the compulsory periods should form a comprehensive educational system. The terms 'primary education' and 'secondary education' should mean two consecutive levels of instruction, not two types or qualities of instruction which overlap.

5) All schools should lay emphasis upon education for civic

responsibility and a democratic way of life, by means of the content of the curriculum, textbooks and materials or instruction and by the organisation of the school itself.

6) School curricula should aim to promote understanding of and respect for other nations and to this end attention should be given to the study of modern languages without prejudice to any.

7) Educational and vocational guidance should be provided for all pupils and students.

8) Health supervision and health education should be provided for all pupils and students. Instruction was also to be given in hygiene.

9) All teacher education should take place in a university or in a pedagogical institution of university rank.

10) Full provision should be made for effective participation of the people in the reform and organisation as well as in the administration of the educational system.

The ten points of this directive represent one of the more positive and helpful pieces of educational policy guidance to issue from the Allied Control Council. Certainly in the clarity, and conciseness with which the aims and principles were set out for consideration the directive contrasts sharply with the terms of numerous other orders and injunctions listing the institutions that had to be closed and the practices that had to be abandoned in the name of denazification and demilitarisation and so on. Admittedly the directive was a composite document including contributions from all of the Allies who defended their own principles and hobby-horses with the conviction born of successful practice at home, while lending varying degrees of support to the proposals of their colleagues and retaining a number of possibilities for horse-trading. A clause about religious instruction supported by the British and American delegates on the Cultural Committee of the Control Council met with determined resistance from the other two members and was only withdrawn when it threatened to nullify the whole agreement. The condition of withdrawal was, needless to say, the substitution of another of the disputed clauses. The degree of emphasis and urgency given to the various clauses of the directive also differed considerably in the four Zones of occupation, each Ally choosing to stress those that were politically and socially topical in his own country at the time and would in his view be best fitted to bring German educational practice up to date and into line with other Western countries, not least with his own.

Eight months after the publication of Directive No. 54 when legislative powers in education had been restored to the *Land* parliaments and the first school reform laws were being drafted in the British Zone the Educational Adviser undertook a review of progress already achieved. As a result, although it was recognised that the implementation of all ten points of the directive must now be the responsibility of the *Land* parliaments, it was decided to single out four of them for particular attention as being, more than all the others, the guarantors of eventual successful reform. The four essentials were :

a) All education in schools controlled by the State should be free as well as the educational material used in those schools. (This was obviously designed to pave the way for equality of opportunity).

b) The training of teachers should be carried out at universities or institutions of university rank. (The purpose was not only to raise the level of training for elementary teachers but also to gain for them some of the social prestige enjoyed by their colleagues in the grammar schools and at the same time to create one integrated teaching profession for all schools).

c) No educational legislation should preclude progress towards a six-year period at primary schools. (This was a measure aimed at social integration by keeping all pupils together at primary schools for six instead of the traditional four years before the process of selection for secondary education took place. It also facilitated selection by postponing it until the age of eleven or twelve and, by establishing a clean break between primary and all forms of secondary education, it was calculated to advance social integration at the secondary stage as well).

d) The right of existence of private schools should be preserved. (This was aimed at keeping the field open for pedagogical experimenters outside the control of the State. Germany has always been in the forefront of educational experiment and there was never more need for new ideas than in the post-war period).

These, then, were some of the principles that Education Branch believed would ensure a healthy future for German education and which they tried to get accepted under the new circumstances brought about by Ordinance No. 57 at the beginning of 1947. This can be described as one of the Branch's major tasks now that the 'bricks and mortar' period was nearing its end. Coming at the end of the 1940s and the beginning of the 1950s it coincided with a period of almost feverish activity in the *Land* parliaments in preparation for new educational legislation borne along on a vigorous wave of argument and discussion at all levels, from the village school staffroom to the higher councils of the *Land*, gathering force and substance from all those local and Zonal bodies which, as has been said, were at this time in process of redevelopment and only too eager to get their teeth into the problems of the future as a relief from the overwhelming burden of day-to-day routine.

It is probably true that this general airing of views, this wide involvement of all those most closely affected by the outcome would never have been possible had the Control Commission still been in a position to issue mandatory orders to the German authorities on educational subjects. I suspect that in this guise a copy of Directive No. 54 would have found its way into the Ministry in each *Land* capital and been put on ice on one or more of a number of possible pretexts—lack of finance, political party differences, more urgent and immediate priorities or an understandable reluctance to commit officialdom to specific reforms at a time of extreme social and political flux. As it was, school reform laws were passed in Schleswig-Holstein and Berlin in 1948 and in Hamburg in 1949 and all accepting one or more of the basic principles laid down in the directive. It is true that the measures in question had to be introduced more gradually than had been intended in the first flush of reforming zeal. Some fell foul of governmental changes once the main political parties took their stand by this or that issue, more so in those *Länder* where the majorities were small and governmental changes therefore more frequent but also where the religious communities were of comparable strength bearing in mind the effect of the influx of refugees from the East.

Without the Education Control Officers in their new role of advisers under Ordinance No. 57, the suggestions made in Directive No. 54 might well have fallen entirely on stony ground. It was due to their initiative and inspiration at the different levels where they functioned that the issues were so widely and thoroughly discussed between them and their German colleagues. It was practical proof that, if it is to be effective, the democratic process must begin at ground level and rise on a wave of popular approval on which the State will set its seal, rather than be inflicted from above on an uninformed, uninterested and possibly, in the long run, unco-operative public. The British education officials played an important perhaps even a decisive role in this process, especially in the early stages when the repair of physical damage bulked so largely in the daily round that the more fundamental issues tended to be deferred to a later date.

Anglo-German consultation and co-operation were developed to their fullest extent during this period and, although the school domain has been taken as an example of how it worked, the same technique applied in other fields—universities, youth and so on. The presence of ECOs was welcomed in German councils and committees long after responsibility for education had been returned to the Germans. The relationship became in most cases a personal rather than an official one (one of the by-products of Ordinance No. 57) and suffered for this reason from the periodic reductions in Education Branch staff. The same spirit of collaboration persisted well into the 1950s when the ghost of the Zonal Educational Advisory Committee of 1945 sat in at the informal meetings between the Educational Adviser and the *Land* Ministers of Education and retired again to Bünde scarcely believing that the preoccupation was no longer with bricks, mortar, glass and transport or even with school reform but with British Centres and international contacts.

International Contacts

This mutual consultation and exchange of views and experiences between German educationists and British ECOs was enlarged and intensified by the annual programme of sponsored visits arranged by Education Branch from 1946. These were at first for German educationists to visit Britain and for their British counterparts to visit the British Zone, but extending before long to include politicians, administrators, municipal

officials and representatives of many other professions. The purpose remained the same, to exchange points of view and experiences and, in the case of the Germans, to see British practice at
first hand. These visits were arranged and financed by
Education Branch and in the peak years of 1947 and 1948
they provided for over 2000 visitors from Germany to the
United Kingdom and over 1000 in the reverse direction each
year. In addition to these fully sponsored visits there were
others partially paid for by Education Branch, others completely
independent especially after the travel restrictions had been
raised. Among these were the town-to-town and area-to-area
links initiated by Education Branch who laid down the broad
policy for these exchanges, put the German and British organisers in touch with each other and, where necessary, provided
finance to prime the pump and secretarial expertise in arranging the details of the visits. Many of these links immediately
blossomed and continue in full vigour even today, nearly thirty
years later. Some unfortunately dried up for lack of funds but
only a very few died for lack of enthusiasm. From 1949 onwards these visits have covered all three Western Zones of Germany as well as West Berlin.

Wilton Park

Certainly the oldest and the most enduring meeting-place for
Anglo-German exchanges—and arguably the most successful—
was Wilton Park which was taken over by the War Office as an
education centre for prisoners-of-war and later developed by
the Foreign Office into an Anglo-German discussion centre to
which German visitors were invited from the British Zone and
later from all three Western Zones.[3] Since 1957 membership
of the conferences, of which there were ten each year, has been
extended to include visitors from countries in membership of
the Organisation for Economic Co-operation and Development. Between 300 and 400 visitors attend the conferences each
year, representing parliament and press, industry and trade
unions, civil service, local government, universities and other
walks of life. Every conference touches on a broad range of
world problems—political, economic, social and strategic—and
makes an intensive study of one particular aspect that may be

of overriding public interest at the time. The numerous tributes paid to the work of Wilton Park by German participants leave no doubt about the contribution it made, especially after the War, to the relief of Germany's spiritual isolation and her re-integration into the European community. The fact that Wilton Park was one of the first British projects to obtain German financial support and that there are still a number of associations of 'Old Wiltonians' in Germany who meet regularly to keep alive the traditions and the comradeship of Wilton Park leaves no doubt about the success of its methods and the force of its influence.

The British Centres

No one will ever know for certain where and when the first of the 'Information Centres' (as they were originally called) was created. It could well have been in some British Army mess when the secretary decided to offer the German staff the chance of reading old copies of British newspapers and periodicals —they had a mysterious habit of disappearing in that direction in any case, as often as not ending their career on the local black market cut up into single pages and sold for cigarettes, the number varying in direct proportion to the topicality of the articles and in inverse proportion to the amount of advertisement on the reverse side. There was obviously a widespread and insatiable hunger for news amongst the German reading public, not only for the foreign press from which they had been cut off for over twelve years but for the German press, limited as it was in scope and circulation by the lamentable shortage of newsprint. The need was recognised, however, at an early stage and, while invaluable local initiatives grew in spite of the closure of army establishments as the Occupation troops returned home, a special section was created in the Information Services Control to co-ordinate the various aspects of this new service and administer them at Zonal level.

Where adequate accommodation was available the local reading rooms expanded into something more deserving of the title of 'Information Centre', the largest of which were equipped with lending and reference libraries, film studios, display rooms and lecture rooms. A regular supply of British and German news-

papers, periodicals and magazines was distributed from the Information Centre Section of ISD together with books for the
libraries and material for displays and exhibitions collected and
mounted by a special production unit. A magazine called *Die
Brücke* was specially produced by ISD for the centres, carrying German translations of selected articles from the British and
foreign press and was always in great demand in the reading
rooms. The title *Die Brücke* (the bridge) came to be applied
to the centres themselves, but where, when or by whom is
unknown unless it was a spontaneous invention at several centres
at once.

The original plan was to open sixty centres in towns in the
British Zone with a population of over 50,000, in addition to one
in the British Sector of Berlin. They were to be divided into
three categories according to accommodation and facilities available and the relative importance of the town where they were
sited. Category A offered all necessary facilities, including a
library, a display or exhibition room and a film studio. Category
B normally lacked one or more of these but the shortcoming
could be redeemed to some extent, though never entirely satis-
factorily, by adapting the rooms to two or even three uses. It
was possible by a similar device to increase the scope of the Category C centres but, even so, some of these advanced little beyond
the original reading room until they moved to more spacious
premises.

Accommodation was, indeed, the key factor in the development of the network of centres. It was so difficult to obtain
in competition with other priorities that for a considerable time
there were only two Category A centres—in Berlin and Hamburg, the former opened in May 1946, the latter in July of the
same year. It was no easier to find premises for Category B
centres and in the early years therefore the great majority remained in Category C, including some unscheduled ones opened
in small localities at the request of the German authorities. By
the end of 1946 about forty centres were functioning and by the
middle of the following year the total had reached its peak of
over sixty. The network was maintained at this level with few
casualties over the following two years by which time accommodation was more freely available and the more important centres
were moved to larger and more suitable premises.

The new centre in Düsseldorf was one of the best : 'It is a vast window of Britain. Its spacious, dignified reading room with a seating capacity of more than 200 has an infinite variety of British newspapers, magazines, periodicals and technical journals. The lending library, which at the moment houses 7,000 British books, has a capacity of up to 20,000 whilst the reference library with more than 1,000 volumes of up-to-date reference material will prove a boon to serious students of culture and current affairs. A large well-lit exhibition hall and a small film studio with room for 150 people take up the rest of the ground floor. The upper floor with its imposing balcony which can also be used for exhibitions houses the Inter-Allied Music Lending Library as well as a radio room, offices and social rooms. But the most impressive part of this floor is the tastefully decorated concert and lecture hall with a fully equipped stage and a seating capacity of 300.'[4]

The removal of the principal centres into more suitable premises was completed by the opening of the new centre at Kiel by the UK High Commissioner in August 1950. Administration of the centres had already passed from Information Services Division to the Office of the Educational Adviser in January 1950 and at the same time the costs of running them were met from British funds and no longer from Occupation costs. The gradual process of run-down had also begun by the date of the hand-over when, more often for financial than for any other reason the total of over sixty centres had been reduced to fifty-one to the chagrin of most of those concerned of whom the local German authorities were not the least vociferous. It was partly because of these closures, however, that it was possible to rehouse more of the larger centres. The centres in Hamburg, Hanover, Braunschweig and Essen re-opened in new premises in December 1949 and Lüneburg, Oldenburg and Stade followed suit a month later.

The increasing costs of maintaining larger centres from British funds necessitated further closures and by mid-1951 the total had reached thirty-four, of which a further ten were closed by the end of the year. This was accompanied by a renewed chorus of protest from the German side from municipal authorities, cultural societies, adult education associations and others, some of which were able to save the local centre from the threat of closure. In such cases it was usually found possible to continue at least some of the services, as before, at British expense, such as newspapers and magazines, lecturers, library books and documentary films. Where the centre had to be closed completely and all services withdrawn it was normal practice for the library to be donated to the municipal library, the university or college library or to some other responsible body who would give it a safe and permanent home. The only condition attached was that the books should be available to members of the library on an 'open access' principle. In many cases, however, there was no alternative to closure in spite of the protests. The Minister of Education for North Rhine-Westphalia, Christine Teusch, went on record as saying. 'You cannot close any more centres at the present time. They are not merely valuable educational and cultural institutes, they are bulwarks for us in our struggle against communism' and another eminent authority on the German side summed it up 'A *Brücke* closed is a bridge broken.'[5]

The financial saving made by closing some of the smaller centres in the British Zone did permit the establishment of a number of centres in the French and American Zones, for example, in Freiburg, Stuttgart, Nuremberg, Munich and Mainz at the same time as the first *Amerika-Häuser* and *Maisons de France* were beginning to appear in the British Zone. Apart from the Frankfurt centre which had been active since the early post-war years these centres in the French and American Zones were comparatively short-lived. They barely had time to settle down and decide the scope and content of their appeal to the community around them when further economy plans were announced.

As a first step it was decided that the German authorities at federal, *Land* and local levels should be invited to participate in the administration of the majority of the British centres. The resultant discussions, consultations and negotiations lasted for the greater part of 1952 but by the end of the financial year 1952-3 the way ahead was clear. Of the twenty-four British centres still functioning four were to be continued as entirely British institutions (Berlin, Hamburg, Hanover and Frankfurt), and two were to be closed completely. In the case of the remaining eighteen centres the response from the local German communities was far more generous than had been expected. One had dared to hope for co-operation in perhaps fourteen centres. In fact, support in a variety of forms was undertaken by the Germans in eighteen centres (henceforth to be known as 'Anglo-German Centres') and even at the beginning of 1955 as many as ten of them were still being financed and managed on an Anglo-German basis.

The end of the Occupation in May of the same year hastened the process of hand-over. The final act came soon afterwards when the British Council took over the four British centres that remained and adapted them to their purposes within their terms of reference. Not that these were all that different for, although in the beginning the emphasis had been on the supply of news and background information about the events of the day, the educational and cultural function of the centres soon emerged and, indeed, became the dominant partner, thus easing the eventual hand-over to the British Council. The appeal of the centres was therefore twofold—to journalists and others engaged in the media who require unbiased news from countries all over the world and to teachers, authors and university staff and students who need the enlightenment of books and the spur of intellectual argument with their equals in debates and discussion groups. The facilities provided by the centres corresponded broadly to the basic requirements of these important social groups, the moulders of opinion. For the publicists there was, for example, the reading room with copies of the international press, the lending and the reference libraries and the documentary films. The others responded to the appeal of language lessons, chamber music, play and poetry readings. Both came together to listen to lectures (political or otherwise), to join a discussion group, a mock trial or election or a debate on some topical subject.

As the centres extended the scope and nature of their activities they came to play an increasingly important role in the work of Education Branch as a whole (renamed Cultural Relations Division, with effect from January 1951) and their contribution to the course and conference work, for instance, brought an additional element to the definition of their aims and purpose. They emerged as British institutions serving an international purpose which was, in the first place, Anglo-German. Their primary aim remained to bring to the German people knowledge of British thought, culture and institutions and to promote the development of Anglo-German relations on a firm basis of mutual understanding. But the ultimate and much wider aim that emerged as the centres took a bigger share of the Division's activities was the integration of Germany into Western culture. The centres therefore provided among their facilities visual material from other countries: Swiss books, French films, Commonwealth exhibitions, American lecturers and so on.

But it is the spoken word in the discussion groups and similar two-way revelations of attitude and ethic that illustrate the essential unity of European civilisation as well as the relative importance to be ascribed to national divergences and it was mainly in these groups and circles, meeting together in the centres, that a genuine demand for knowledge of other ways of life could be created and satisfied while at the same time the democratic virtues of discussion, debate, sympathetic listening and rational argument which are at the roots of the Western way of life could be demonstrated in practice. It was therefore appropriate that after the fundamental political changes brought about in 1949—the federal elections, the Basic Law, the Occupation Statute and other milestones to German sovereignty— the British contribution to Germany's cultural recovery should radiate from the centres and that to an increasing extent the staffs of the Cultural Relations Groups in the *Länder* should be based on them and be gradually divorced from the German administrative hierarchy.

NOTES

1. *The Second World War* (London, 1948-54), Vol. 5, p. 359.
2. *Ibid*, Vol. 6, p. 305.
3. See Dexter M. Keezer, *A Unique Contribution to International Relations: The Story of Wilton Park,* (London, 1973).
4. *British Zone Review*, Vol. 3, No. 1, 20 June 1949.
5. At a meeting between Foreign Office Consultative Committee on German Education and a group of German administrators, Hamburg, Autumn 1951.

British Policy and the Schools

Edith Davies

The letter inviting me to apply to join Education Branch of the British Element of the Allied Control Commission is dated September 1944. It summed up those aspects of German life which were to come under the control of the Allies when hostilities ceased. With hindsight the invitation seems somewhat premature: Arnhem was yet to come.

At an interview in London I received my first briefing from the man who was to plough the first furrow in our field of enterprise in Germany, Mr Donald Riddy, a senior member of His Majesty's Schools Inspectorate. He explained to me that one of the main planks of our policy would be to enlist as soon as possible the co-operation of those Germans who had had perforce to go underground or suffer demotion in their profession as teacher or educational administrator. It was recognised that there were two Germanies and one would be prepared, indeed eager, to work with us for the benefit of the children of Germany. Such co-operation with German educationists would be accompanied by a root-and-branch operation to make straight the way for what was in August 1945 to be enshrined as Article 7 of the Potsdam Agreement. This root-and-branch operation entailed: (i) the closure of all schools, (ii) the vetting of all teachers and the dismissal of any teacher who had been a member of the Nazi party, (iii) the impounding of textbooks pending their appraisal by Education Branch, and (iv) the examination of school syllabuses submitted by German education authorities prior to the eventual reopening of schools. I arrived in Germany on 24 August 1945 with colleagues who would have responsibility for universities, adult education, textbooks, youth, teacher training, physical education or as a young British typist headed the first letter she churned out on the latter subject—*Liebeserziehung!*

As that great German educationist, Adolf Grimme, was to observe at the opening of the first schools' education conference which took place in Braunschweig, *Wir stehen vor dem Nichts* (we stand before the void). This applied to conquerors as well as conquered. Most of the schools throughout the British Zone had been at least partially destroyed. A number of teachers had seen fit to join the Nazi party, not through acceptance of its ideology, but in the interests of their pupils, fearing that unless they did so, a dedicated Nazi would be appointed in their place. The lack of textbooks almost made a farce of any attempt to teach, especially in the grammar schools which were my particular assignment. I had in fact been appointed to cope with grammar schools for girls but the appointment for boys' grammar schools was never made. For some months I included *Volksschulen* in my tours of inspection until the arrival of a specialist officer from the United Kingdom. Our powers were very great.

For a month or so before coming to Germany those of us who were to form the headquarters of Education Branch studied a vast tome called *The Handbook of German Education*. This had been compiled by Allied Intelligence Division and gave a detailed account of German education in the Weimar and Nazi periods. It augmented the knowledge I had acquired at first hand of German schools. I had visited Germany regularly until as late as Easter 1939 when I had taken a party of senior grammar school girls to Germany. On most visits I had sought and obtained permission from the education authorities to attend lessons and talk to teachers. I now had a gap of some six years to make up. I learned in general outline of the *Napolas* and *Adolf Hitler-schulen*; of the latter I was later to have information at first hand from six of their former pupils. I learned of the fate of that valuable sector of German education, the experimental schools— Herman Lietz, Lichtwark, Rudolf Steiner and Kurt Hahn schools—which along with the Froebel kindergartens had given a lead in educational thinking to Europe and beyond.

My main task during the first two months after our arrival in Germany was to examine syllabuses submitted by the German authorities via our Education Control Officers at *Provinz* and later *Land* level. There were schools officers even at *Kreis* level and many of these, still in uniform, had been specially seconded by our military authorities, mostly from Intelligence Division. There was also an Intelligence Section at the headquarters level of Education Branch. There was, for instance, an education staff of some five officers at Kiel, the headquarters for Schleswig-

Holstein; also a schools' officer attached to the military government staff at *Kreis* Schleswig, the former capital of the *Provinz*. Hamburg, despite a full complement of British Education Control Officer staff, as always went her own way within the prescribed limits and these British schools' officers had to be on their guard lest they were persuaded into eating out of the *Schulverwaltung's* hand.

By September 1945 there was a strong team of German educationists at all capitals of the *Länder* of the British Zone— Kiel, Hamburg, Hanover, Münster and Düsseldorf; the last two were presently amalgamated as an educational unit, a surprisingly successful marriage. After all, it entailed considerable concession of authority on the part of the Westphalians and is an instance of the way in which these enlightened German authorities put the interest of their country first.

The leading school personalities with whom I had the privilege of working in close co-operation during the years under review were: *Regierungsdirektor* (later *Ministerialrat*) Carl Möhlmann in Schleswig-Holstein; *Oberschulrat* Merck and *Frau Oberschulrätin* Emmi Beckmann in Hamburg; *Frau Oberschulrätin* Dr Panzer in Berlin; *Oberschulrat* Dr Rönnebeck in Niedersachsen; *Frau Oberschulrätin* (later *Ministerialrätin*) Dr Luise Bardenhewer in North Rhine (later North Rhine-Westphalia); *Oberschulrat* Adolf Bohlen in Westphalia (in charge of the *Abwicklungsstelle*). They all became cherished friends.

An interesting fact emerges from this list: three of the number were women. Women had fared ill under the National Socialist régime when it came to leading positions in the sphere of education. In those early days I encountered none who had been heads of grammar schools let alone educational administrators under the Nazi régime. Even the girls' grammar schools had had men in the headship. It was British policy to redress this anomaly and to urge the German authorities to appoint women to the headship of girls' schools. The implementation of this policy was by no means easy. It was the women themselves who were reluctant to apply for headships. The Nazi régime had done a thorough job in conditioning the majority of the women of Germany. A case in point emerged in Schleswig-Holstein where an excellent *Studienrätin* whom we had invited to England on a study tour

D

was chosen for the headship of a school near Lübeck. Herr Möhlmann, always open to ideas for the democratisation of the schools in his charge, reported that Frau X had refused his offer. He asked me to have a word with her. Full of pioneering zeal I went to see Frau X; she had invited me to coffee. I shall always remember her panic at being asked to assume a job most teachers regard as the peak of their ambitions. I remember her exact words: 'Please don't ask me any more—I enjoy teaching English. I would be afraid of the parents, especially the fathers, but above all, I could not face the responsibility'. And this from a woman of the highest calibre, academically and morally. It was obvious to me and, what was more important, to Herr Möhlmann that Frau X was the product of conditioned thinking. If such a woman repudiated responsibility what of the able women in other walks of life in Germany?

This thought prompted us to bring leading women over from Britain to study the role of German women, not only in education but in other fields of public activity, notably women's organisations. The report of Miss Edith Deneke, a former lecturer at Oxford and a leading light in the Women's Institute and Town Women's Guild movements, led to the establishment of a Women's Affairs section in the Local Government Branch of the Internal Affairs and Communications Division of which Education was also a part.

It so happened that after the General Election of October 1945 a woman was appointed Minister of Education in Britain, the redoubtable Ellen Wilkinson. This appointment gave timely support to our policy with regard to women in responsible positions and showed that we practised what we preached. Not many of us will forget the session at Education Branch Headquarters in Bünde when Ellen Wilkinson received the heads of departments in audience. The Minister had put educational policy in Germany high on her list of priorities soon after taking office and she now demanded account of each of us as to what we had so far done in the four months we had been in Germany. She asked me why it took such a long time for all the schools to re-open in the British Zone. I explained the sheer physical difficulties: lack of classrooms, lack of fuel in the school boilers, lack of food in the children's stomachs and their hopelessly inadequate footwear to get them to school; in some areas there was only one pair of shoes for a whole family of children. The dynamic Ellen ordered her secretary to take note of all we had said and then harangued us on the importance of our work to the children of Germany. It was through Miss Wilkinson's intervention that a modest school meal was introduced. It was no more than a plate of milk soup but it was a beginning.

I have mentioned the visit of Frau X from Schleswig-Holstein to Britain and that of Miss Deneke to Germany. These visits in both directions have been one of the most vital aspects of British educational policy. The first and most significant in the sphere of school education was the visit of Adolf Grimme and Heinrich Landahl, directors of education respectively in Lower Saxony and Hamburg.

These two educationists were briefed at Education Branch headquarters by Mr Riddy and the relevant members of his staff and their visit to the United Kingdom early in 1946 included all types of schools as well as Wilton Park, the *Hochburg* of Anglo-German cultural activity in the post-war years. Few institutions have done more to acquaint German teachers with British life and customs and to break down the isolation in which so many of them had languished during the twelve years of the Hitler régime.

The Education Act of 1944 provided an effective backcloth for the policies advocated by Education Officers. The raising of the school-leaving age and the greater equality offered by the newly-established secondary modern school with its doctrine of equality of status for the less academic eleven to fifteen year old, was discussed with interest by German educationists. The British public school has always been a source of particular fascination for German people, not only educationists. The fact that I lived in Harrow, as I once mentioned to a group of teachers, but had no connection whatsoever with the school on the Hill, was received in shocked silence by my audience. 'But surely,' one of them insisted, 'Harrow is the School!' That it contained a quarter of a million people beside seemed irrelevant or perhaps irreverent. How timely, therefore, Mr Birley's arrival hotfoot from Charterhouse!

That the public school had a great deal to offer in our work in Germany soon became very clear. The fact that such schools —and this applies equally to State grammar schools—drew up their own syllabus of work as well as their timetable, was a source of amazement as was the considerably greater authority enjoyed by the principals of the British schools. They were indeed captains of their ships, not, as was the case in most German schools, *primus inter pares.*

The fact that German schools worked on *Land*-centralised syllabus *Richtlinien,* which were pretty detailed in their directions, made life a good deal easier for me whose job it was to examine these syllabuses. As it was, I had only five sets to cope with, the *Länder* of the British Zone, four in number, and the British Sector of Berlin.

The first grammar school to reopen in the British Zone was the Graf Spee-Oberschule in Kiel. It is now called the Humboldtgymnasium. I still have a copy of that historic meeting of British and German officials. Herr Möhlmann, *Regierungsdirektor* at the time, was determined to beat Hamburg to the post and he achieved his objective by a short head. The school building was relatively undamaged, the teachers had been vetted and only the syllabus needed approval. Mr. Walker, the Regional Officer at headquarters' level, and I had spent several hours studying the syllabuses of the various subjects and consulting colleagues who were specialists in those subjects which the school was equipped to offer. These were: German, English, Latin, mathematics, physics, chemistry, biology, history, music, gymnastics, games and art. No textbooks were permitted. Subject teachers would be asked to submit sources of all their notes, even for dictations, songs, hymns and recitations (prose and verse).

The problem of religious instruction was a thorny one. The subject had been actively discouraged by the Nazi régime, though, curiously, never actually forbidden. It was British, American and French policy that religious instruction should be catered for in all schools—primary and secondary—and to this end an Education Control Instruction was duly issued. Here at last was a subject for which the basic textbook was beyond reproach.

As regards English as a subject of the curriculum, it was laid down by the British representatives at this conference that undue stress should not be laid on the political aspect of the subject. The pupils should not be shown the British Empire as a unique historical achievement. The cultural side of the subject should receive most attention. It was felt that the political aspect of the subject in the present circumstances was open to misinterpretation.

In biology it was felt that the undue emphasis on heredity which had been the case in the syllabus of the late régime, was unsuitable. The statement in the proposed syllabus : 'Biologically correct thinking may lead cultural development along the right path', was deemed objectionable and was to be deleted.

History was, without doubt, the most controversial subject of all. Prussia had, by order of the Allies, been deleted from the map of Europe whereas it had always loomed large in the history of Germany in the previous hundred years. The name had been synonymous with Germany as a whole in the eyes of the world. The word 'bolshevism' had also figured prominently in the syllabus of the Hitler period. In the minds of German children it was synonymous with all things odious about Russia. This too was considered to be *ein heisses Eisen* and teachers were advised to keep off the subject. Colonial expansion, whether of Britain or any other country, was similarly taboo. The military achievements of Frederick the Great, much extolled under the late régime, were not to be over-emphasised. When the *Lehrbuch-prüfungsstelle* was established in Braunschweig under the dedicated guidance of Professor Eckert, the difficulties encountered in trying to compile a history textbook unbiassed as regards the traditional history teaching of any nation, proved well-nigh insuperable. In one of the meetings I attended feelings ran high even regarding the nationality of Copernicus. Was he German or Polish? Neither, proclaimed the Italian representative, his spiritual home was Italy.

The gymnastic and games syllabus came in for a measure of criticism; in this instance it had been copied almost word for word from the official syllabus of the years 1937-41 which should have been impounded. On the subject of sport, we were chiefly concerned about the *Turn- und Sportvereine*. These had come under strong influence from the Nazi party—Baldur von Schirach had made a dead set at these organisations and very subtly indeed the ideology of the National Socialist movement had found expression in the gymnasium and on the sports ground. It was urged by the representatives of Education Branch that it should be the ultimate aim of all schools to keep gymnastics and sport under the aegis of the schools.

The geography syllabus was criticised for too much emphasis on navigation and map reading and *Auslandsdeutsche*. In short, there is much in this list of criticisms embodied in the report which, viewed thirty years on, strikes one as niggling and merely chipping at the central problem. Our policy, however, was that if there was any doubt whatever in our minds concerning the subject matter to be transmitted to the rising generation of young Germans, we had to question and where necessary, eradicate it from the syllabus, even if it meant making decisions bordering on the trivial. We had to bear in mind that every aspect of the school syllabus had, during the twelve years of National Socialism, been impregnated with the doctrines of that party. Even the textbooks for mathematics contained problems which spread the insidious gospel: 'If it takes 50,000 members of the *Wehrmacht* 3 days to conquer Holland [area of the country stated], how many days will it take 80,000 men to conquer England [area stated]?' Such problems were admittedly more realistic than those most British children were having to contend with in those days. These seemed forever to have to cope with plumbers filling plugless baths with water.

The curriculum which was finally approved at the end of this marathon Anglo-German session in Kiel was to be regarded as temporary until Easter 1946. Its general outline served as emergency guidelines for the syllabuses applicable to the whole British Zone.

Meanwhile there was the problem of teacher shortage. In a special article in *The Times* of 7 October 1947, the figure of 72,000 was quoted for the Russian Zone alone at that time. In 1946 an Education Control Instruction in respect of an Emergency Teacher Training Scheme was issued. This was designed to enable men and women up to the age of thirty-five who had seen war service and who had certain basic qualifications, to undergo a shortened teacher training course at colleges specially devoted to the purpose. At the end of this course they would be qualified to teach in *Volksschulen*.

The scheme worked very well and it was generally agreed that these more mature men and women educated in the university of life rather than in the groves of Academe, had much to offer their young charges. It should be mentioned that it was at the suggestion of the Allies that German script was replaced by Latin script *(Normalschrift),* a move which had the full agreement of the German authorities.

In December 1946 the Headquarters of Education Branch moved from the Zone to Berlin, mainly to facilitate contact with the Allies. During the eighteen months we spent in the former German capital, I attended a number of Schools Committee meetings of the Allied Kommandatura. These took place in turn in each of the four sectors of the city. All these meetings were jovial on a social basis but the differences in approach to school policy soon emerged, especially between the three Western allies and the Russians. We soon realised that Four Power collaboration on an inter-Zonal level would be uphill work. The most significant area of agreement was that to differ, which was not altogether a bad prospect for German education when one considers the uniformity in the system up to that period. Only in the case of Berlin itself the *Einheitsschule* was surprisingly accepted.

The Americans, in their Re-orientation of Teachers Program, introduced throughout their Zone a series of Study Workshops; one of these I attended. Eminent educationists were brought over from the States to lecture to some 200 German teachers gathered together during a holiday period in a teacher training college or university hostel. After the lectures the participants were sub-divided into groups of about fifty for discussion on the lectures. The main feature I recall from the sessions I attended was the amount of paper churned out at the end of each day—synopses and verbatim records of lectures, even minutes of discussions.

The French spearhead in their schools' policy was the appoint-ment of a fully-qualified French teacher at every single secondary grammar school in their Zone, not necessarily a teacher of the French language but a bi-linguist qualified to teach certain specialist subjects of the curriculum. This innovation was not altogether welcomed by the staffs of the schools concerned who regarded their French colleague with some suspicion. However, the method did ensure contact at the grass roots. The policy of selecting certain pupils at the age of eleven and training them as future teachers in accordance with French educational principles was, as far as I know, not implemented to any great extent.

The Russians were soon going their own way with a rigid system of control at all levels. It was difficult for us to acquaint

ourselves at all with the syllabuses in use in their Zone. One
single instance will serve to show how difficult it became to have
any co-operation between the Western Allies and the Russians. I
had suggested that a Christmas concert might be arranged at
which German and Allied schoolchildren from each Zone could
sing, act and dance for each other's entertainment. By this time
—December 1947—the families of Control Commission staff
and Army personnel had arrived in Germany. The Russians were
particularly enthusiastic about the whole idea and immediately
undertook the responsibility of hiring the hall, the Admiralitäts-
palast in the Friedrichsstrasse. The programmes were printed,
each sector rehearsed its contribution in the various schools and
very heartening it was to experience the brave efforts of so many
keen young people in rehearsal. There were to be carols, too,
which could be sung by all participants, the highlight being 'O,
come all ye faithful' with a verse in each language plus Latin.
The tickets had been sold long before the date of the concert; the
Allied commanders and the dignitaries of the City of Berlin had
all agreed to be present. Then the blow fell. Through a trivial
breakdown in communication, an official in the American Control Commission spotted that the Russians had invited Professor
Mauersberger and his famous Kreuzchor from Dresden to per-
form at the concert. Professor Mauersberger had, at this point,
not been cleared by the American panel of the Allied Denazification Board and had ventured into the American Sector where
he had been an organist before the War. He was bluntly told by
this minion that he was persona non grata, whereupon he
naturally appealed to the Russian Authorities who took
immediate umbrage and despite appeals from Mr Birley, our
Educational Adviser, and the American Commander, cancelled
the concert four days before it was due to take place. The whole
episode, which had been intended to strengthen goodwill between
several nations, did only harm and was profoundly discouraging
to those of us working in Germany.

Most of us were glad to leave in May 1948. The climate of
work had become claustrophobic as a result of the enforced
airlift and our work could henceforth only be carried out from
the Zone.

In the previous autumn we had invited three British teachers
of history, by common consent the most controversial subject of

the curriculum, to come to the British Zone to conduct a week's course for thirty German teachers of history. The period chosen was the Napoleonic era. We thought this safe ground as Britain and Germany had then been allies. No less than fifty teachers from Hamburg and Schleswig-Holstein had applied to attend the course which took place in Barsbüttel. Food was sparse, accommodation spartan, the *Briketts* were carefully rationed out for the stove round which we huddled. But no one seemed conscious of these privations. The spiritual isolation of the last twelve years was being broken down. The British teachers—they were, of course, handpicked and represented state, public and direct grant schools—made immediate contact with their German colleagues. The German participants revelled in the freedom of open discussion and the opportunity the course provided for contact with each other.

Education Branch soon realised that such courses should be continued and extended in their scope. They became the main plank of our schools' policy, welcomed by German and British educationists alike. In the summer of 1948 one course was held in each *Land* of the British Zone and in Berlin. In the year 1950 no less than fifty-two British teachers came during their holidays to conduct fourteen courses. These courses were attended by some 420 German teachers who likewise gave up a week of their holidays.

The courses covered several subjects: English, history, religious instruction, geography, science, mathematics, even Latin. With the passage of time, these subjects have, by the nature of this Anglo-German enterprise, been reduced to one, English, but since Zonal barriers have fallen in the West of Germany, the courses now take place in almost every *Land* of the Federal Republic and are the responsibility of the British Council on which organisation the mantle of Anglo-German cultural relations fell in 1959. In 1974 the British Council in co-operation with the German *Land* education authorities organised twenty-nine courses. The emphasis of these was on applied linguistics and special aspects of English language teaching, British life, literature and institutions.

One of my most vivid and pleasant recollections is a series of children's concerts which the schools department of Education Branch was audacious enough to organise throughout the British

D*

Zone in 1949. I have stressed that one of our main aims was to break down cultural isolation in post-war Germany. This endeavour applied to schoolchildren as well as their teachers. Examination of the school music syllabuses of the *Länder* had shown a preoccupation with German music to the almost total exclusion of the music of other nations. It was in no way our aim to detract from the great German tradition in all things musical, rather to extend the frontiers of the children's musical experience and show them the achievements of other nations in this sphere. Many German children had at this time little or no experience of concerts; most concert halls were in fact damaged.

As a child I had attended the Robert Mayer Concerts for Children in London. These had been conducted by Malcolm Sargent whose illuminating comments and explanations on the works to be performed had given me my first insight into great German as well as European music. Malcolm Sargent was unable to come over to Germany himself but at his suggestion another conductor, Trevor Harvey, came in his place. Mr Harvey spoke quite good German and made an immediate impact on the children. We had invited Sir Robert Mayer to organise the concerts which took place in Kiel, Hamburg, Hanover, Braunschweig, Recklinghausen, Gelsenkirchen and the British Sector of Berlin. The orchestras of the German cities made a noble gesture by giving their services free. The Berlin and Hamburg concerts were telerecorded. As we had discovered that the children had little or no knowledge of British, French or Russian music, we included works by Elgar, Benjamin Britten, Ravel and Borodin. The two British works were new even to the orchestras. The concerts were a considerable success and their pattern appealed to municipal concert organisers.

An Anglo-German project which had been disrupted by the War was the Assistant Scheme whereby young German *Referendare* came over to Britain for a year to help mainly with the teaching of oral German while young British people who had completed at least two years at the university were employed in German secondary grammar schools. This scheme was re-started in 1948. There is no doubt in my mind that the German schools had the worst of this deal. The German *Referendare* were older and thus better qualified for their assignment: I know from experience with the assistants I had when I taught in a grammar school in Kent. They did a better job than those who taught English in German schools. Many of these young British people, now reinforced by Australians, New Zealanders, Canadians and Americans, lacked the maturity of their German opposite numbers. There was, for one thing, a bewildering variety of English pronunciation. We did what we could to persuade the British Ministry of Education which have always been responsible for the organisation of the English teaching side of the scheme, to change its policy regarding the age of the assistants it recruited, but without avail. The German education authorities have always accepted the uneven deal with grace and tolerance. Despite these shortcomings the Assistant Scheme makes a useful contribution to international contact in a vital field of educational activity.

It may be fairly said that there was consistency in the schools' policy. I mentioned at the beginning of this paper that the first Director of Education Branch emphasised the great importance of early co-operation with the educational leaders of the real Germany. That was the guiding light we all tried to keep before us and not only those in Education Branch: a very important visitor to the British Zone in 1947 remarked that as far as he could see, the Control Commission consisted of a collection of British people all fighting with each other on behalf of their own particular Germans. I recall a colleague using Machiavellian methods to obtain a supply of penicillin for some *Oberschulrat* in Hanover whose survival was deemed essential to educational reorganisation in that area.

This close co-operation has engendered great mutual respect and the readiness to learn from each other but the final assessment of the value of our policy from 1945 to 1950 must lie with those whose task it is now to guide the educational fortunes of the young people of Germany. Those of us appointed to work in Germany had one thing particularly in common: we cared deeply about Germany and its relations with Britain. Whatever mistakes we made, however trivial some of our decisions, we approached our work with one great goal before us: as far as lay in our power to render as remote as possible any future war between Germany and Britain.

5. The Problem of Textbooks
Kathleen Southwell Davis

Work on textbooks for schools began in London in 1944 as part of the preparation for the denazification and reconstruction of education in Germany after the War. Existing German textbooks were examined in the hope that at least some of the pre-Nazi editions could be reintroduced into schools to tide them over the initial period of material shortages until a new range could be produced. While Education Branch was waiting for captured material, the American education authorities lent it 227 microfilms and seventy-six photostats of pre-1933 German textbooks belonging to the Teachers' College of Columbia University. These were read in London by the officer appointed as textbook specialist and constituted the first step in the assault on the textbook problem. The selection covered the main fields of elementary, intermediate and grammar schools.

In addition to this, seventeen specially selected books were sent in microfilm form from the Stockholm State Library, and at what was then the Board of Education Library sixty books—chiefly history, geography and civics—were examined by the textbook officer.

The result of this research, from October 1944 to July 1945, was that only eight books for the primary classes of the *Volksschule* were judged to be suitable. The books dating from the Weimar period revealed varying degrees of nationalistic and militaristic trends which had been exploited in National Socialist propaganda and incorporated in post-1933 textbooks. This applied not only to the more obvious subjects such as history, but to other fields over the whole range of the curriculum.

Textbook Section and the Central Textbook Committee

In July 1945 Textbook Section, Education Branch, was established at Bünde in Germany with a staff of four officers working for the first five months on the same lines of examination and censorship as in the preliminary London stage. However, it was now the German education authorities who were to submit books from stocks which had survived the holocaust and were available in schools. About 1000 single copies of these books were received by the section but in the main proved as unsuitable as their predecessors.

By December 1945 the German authorities were sufficiently stabilised for the section to call together a German Central Textbook Committee. This body consisted of educational representatives, ministerial, administrative and teaching, from the various *Länder* of the British Zone and the Berlin Sector. Its consultative and co-ordinating work with Textbook Section at joint conferences in Bünde was to become the mainspring of function and reform in new textbook production.

By September 1946, the good relationships it had established enabled Textbook Section to fulfil the plan for handing over the responsibility of vetting the remaining stocks and future submissions to the German authorities themselves through their own appointed *Land* Textbook Committees. Officially, the section would remain as final arbiter in cases of doubt, and its licence would still be imprinted on all books; but from this time on, in spite of accusations of being the admonishing finger (*der mahnende Finger*), it could largely relinquish the role of censorship and develop scope and dimensions of quite a different order.

Production and Publishing

Problems of supply were acute. It was felt that a Central Conference of Educational Publishers should be called. Under the Nazi régime, all school books had been subject to centralised control. This meant that all educational publishers who were not prepared to go out of business altogether were forced to publish standard Nazi books. After 1945 all publishers had to be relicensed. In this somewhat ambiguous situation there were visible degrees of co-operation with Nazism, ranging from forced conformity to enthusiastic collaboration, which regulated the relicensing process. A good number of experienced publishers remained in business.

In January 1947, the first meeting of the Association of

Schoolbook Publishers (*Arbeitsgemeinschaft der Schulbuchver-leger*) took place in Bünde, followed by the first joint consulta-tive conference with the Central Textbook Committee in April of that year. This established regular liaison on policy and pro-duction with Textbook Section as convener and mediator. Deci-sions were made on three main points: the co-ordination of paper requirements; priority lists based on *Land* and Zonal needs, having regard to types of schools and to subjects; and publishers' programmes to fit these requirements.

Supplies of paper and binding materials were crucial in all this, and were so desperately short that the publishers, with Textbook Section collaboration, set up their own Central Paper Office (*Wirtschaftsstelle für Papier*) in Bünde in 1947 under the direction of a former leading German paper agent. This helped considerably in increasing the paper allocation for educational purposes, seeking out new sources of supply and encouraging technical experiments, for example with the use of newsprint, to offset shortages.

Thus the final pattern of procedure emerges. With the return to a regional system *Land* Ministries were responsible for issuing directives (*Richtlinien*) to schools on curriculum content and syllabuses. Their book requirements were further conditioned by these directives. The detailed work of selection and discussion of new textbooks now took place within the German *Land* Committees, set up in implementation of the policy of Ordinance No. 57, which made each *Land* free to select the books it wished to have. Each *Land* was informed what its share of paper was from the total available each month in the Zone— '*Land*' includes the British Sector of Berlin—based on school-child population. Thus, North Rhine-Westphalia, for instance, received forty-nine per cent. The German *Land* Committees drew up 'priority lists', and the paper for them was directed from the Paper Office, Bünde. The Central Textbook Com-mittee continued to meet every two months. While the question of large-edition elementary schoolbooks was left to the *Land* Committees, demands for the more selective secondary and technical schoolbooks had to be co-ordinated through the Central Textbook Committee. But its chief task was more and more to act as a clearing-house for the exchange of ideas between the *Länder*, the educational publishers and Education Branch.

Peripheral Material

German education authorities were concerned at the amount of
bad juvenile literature that was beginning to appear on the market.
It became clear that Textbook Section should also be concerned
with this, but the problem was tricky. Some juvenile books were
produced by members of the Schoolbook Publishers' Association
but many by general publishers. This work had therefore to be
done in collaboration with Book Section, Public Relations/
Information Services Control, who were responsible for general
licensing; and in March 1947 a conference on juvenile literature
was held in Bünde, bringing together officers of both sections
and German librarians, education officials and teachers. The
conference sought ways and means of eliminating trashy literature and encouraging good books; and reputable publishers
asked for advisory committees to be set up in each *Land*.

Such committees were established—an announcement to this
effect was made in the *Frankfurter Börsenblatt* of 5 November
1947—but in principle the submission of juvenile manuscripts
to the respective *Land* committees had to remain voluntary.
Any publisher could bring out a book in an edition of up to
5000 without any such reference, liable only to post-censorship
by Public Relations/Information Services Control. However, in
view of the paper shortage, it was ruled that any edition above
5000 must be submitted to the German *Land* Youth Literature
Committee, which then forwarded its comments and recommendations to Textbook Section, who in turn advised Book
Section, Public Relations/Information Services Control whether
a larger edition was considered advisable. Meanwhile the German *Land* committees kept a note of books not submitted and
of persistent publishers of 'trash'. In extreme cases they would
recommend withdrawal of licences; otherwise the allocation
of paper for further editions of such books could be refused,
thus releasing paper for long-run editions of books they judged to
be worthwhile.

Further collaboration with Public Relations/Information Services Control was also undertaken in educational film and radio
scripts which had been used as integrated supplementary teaching material during the Nazi period and reflected similar lines
to the range of textbooks as a whole. The office concerned was

centred in Hamburg, where the *Nordwestdeutsche Rundfunk* (North-West German Radio) was now functioning. It was hoped that, by rewriting scripts and redubbing commentaries, some of the material still to hand could be used to bridge the gap.

So far, this account must seem to have presented a picture of increasingly tedious bureaucracy. It is time to move on to the real substance of the work of Textbook Section. The figures given in the accompanying table, however, may make clearer the material reasons why, in the earlier stages, such a highly-organised framework became necessary.

TEXTBOOK PRODUCTION IN THE BRITISH ZONE
Children in school

(Initial figures which later increased)

Primary schools	3,400,000
Secondary schools	300,000
Vocational schools	700,000

Paper supplies

(From October 1945, in tons)

	Allotted	Delivered
1st six months	1,286.0	956.0
2nd six months	903.5	217.0
3rd six months	554.4	427.9

Texbooks published

(From July 1945 to March 1947)

A. *Elementary School Books*

Emergency reprints of pre-1933 books :	1,857,000
New books :	2,581,000
Reprints :	55,600
TOTAL :	4,493,600

B. *Secondary School Books*

Reprints :	2,789,100
New books :	807,400
TOTAL :	3,596,500

C. *Technical Books*
TOTAL: 359,000

D. *Religious Books*
TOTAL: 1,491,000

GRAND TOTAL: 9,940,000
                                          (c. 2¼ per child)

Scope of Textbook Study

At this point it is appropriate to comment on the significance
of the German term *Schulbuchwesen*. It has so far been translated as range of textbooks but has the literal meaning of 'textbook body'. In an educational system where textbooks are
prescribed and produced in accordance with centralised directives covering all subjects or areas of study, a 'body' of teaching
material is produced which incorporates the ideology of the
society from which it springs, the aims of education and their
expression in content, curriculum and method. The work of
Textbook Section therefore provided a unique opportunity for
research into German education as a whole; but it was essential
that its work should be related to what was currently going on
in the schools, teacher training colleges and universities. This
entailed conferences with other sections of Education Branch at
headquarters, and with officers in the field in different areas of
the Zone and in the British Sector.

These officers and Ministry teaching members of the German
Central Textbook Committee co-operated in arranging periodic
visits to schools and teacher training institutions. The specialist
officer concerned could observe Geman teaching in practice and
study the effectiveness or otherwise of the material available. All
aspects could be discussed on the spot with inspectors, heads and
teachers and with Education Branch officers on the British
side. The Germans could give first-hand opinions on textbooks
already produced and were encouraged to make their criticisms
known and to write textbooks themselves.

Here was the crux of the matter. Material shortages could be
explained, though statistics were not always accepted by people

desperately in need of books. But there were also strong suspicions that reprints were being held up deliberately and that
unnecessary difficulties were being raised which prevented new
books being written. It was found that maldistribution had
heightened these suspicions. The two main factors here were
transport difficulties, especially in rural or badly damaged areas,
and lack of contact with the authorities responsible. These visits
had to become two-way information exercises.

To make the basic position clearer, Textbook Section issued
a report for Education Branch officers entitled 'German Textbook Literature: An Analysis of Tendencies'. It quoted the
clauses drawn up by the British Element, Military Government,
following the very general terms of the Potsdam Agreement on
denazification and the redevelopment of democratic ideas. These
clauses were as follows:

No book may be approved which:
a Glorifies nationalism.
b Seeks to propagate, revive or justify the doctrines of National Socialism or to exalt the achievements of National
Socialist leaders.
c Favours a policy of discrimination on ground of race, colour,
political opinion or religion.
d Is hostile to any of the United Nations, or tends to sow
discord among them.
e Expounds the practice of war of mobilisation or preparation
for war, whether in the scientific, economic or industrial
fields, or promotes the study of military geography or military
history.
f Encourages cruelty and morbidity.
g Encourages extreme nationalism.

(Clause f had been inserted at the request of Textbook Section, whose subsequent attitude, especially to the more grisly
tales and legends so widely in use, has been considered unduly
soft and rather silly. With the stench of Belsen—and bombed
German cities—still in the air, it was perhaps more vital than
is now supposed. Even present-day proponents of unexpurgated
Grimm might have flinched at certain new manuscripts coming
in, such as the Christmas Play for schools in which the Man in
the Moon has captured the Christ Child and put him in a

hutch to fatten him up for eating on the Feast of Christmas. In several scenes, this ogre describes in detail how he will prepare and eat him. Two children finally rescue the Christ Child, who takes revenge on the Man in the Moon and his assistant by fastening them down in a trunk to suffocate.)

The Textbook Section Report urged that, as German educational autonomy was restored, some vestige of sanctions against tendencies implied in these formulae should be retained by the occupation forces as long as they remained in Germany. German colleagues in the Central Textbook Committee and elsewhere had also urged this, and later asked Textbook Section to retain its licence imprint when in fact its official authority no longer held, as a kind of subterfuge to bridge the period needed for really new-line books to appear.

This plea to retain sanctions might well seem paradoxical and obstructive. The analysis which followed sought to make clear that it was not. German teachers had by long tradition accepted directives from the education authorities on prescribed books. In imposing State textbook totalitarianism, National Socialism had simply carried on this tradition in its own way. It had effectively exploited or revived older lines, traceable through the Wilhelmine and Weimar periods, in evolving its newer cults such as *Deutschtum,* (German identity) *Ahnenkunde* (ancestor studies), *Rassenkunde* (race studies), and *Geopolitik* (geopolitics). All new books were, of course, written and controlled by National Socialists. Complete control of textbooks and complementary material was achieved by suppression and tendentious activation. In the first case all books whose approach contradicted or disarmed National Socialist ideology were eliminated; in the second case neutral books which did not directly foster a national-socialist outlook were withdrawn, and rewritten or re-edited in that sense.

It was emphasised that the same double process had been used for more than a quarter of a century by Russian communist totalitarianism which had now extended to East Germany. The East German education authorities and teachers, familiar with the system and technique, were now producing a new range of textbooks based on Marxist communism, centrally controlled and channelled through the publishing house Volk und Wissen. Better paper supplies than in the West might well

leave them with a marketable surplus of schoolbooks; but any
hope that this 'new ideology' might mean a healthy counter-
balance to what went before was not borne out. On the
contrary, Russian-controlled books were full of (i) militarism,
descriptions of war, fighting, militant heroes; (ii) traditionalism,
folk-conscious nationalism (fostered to increase the demand for
one united Germany, from the East); (iii) the defamation of
other countries or the system they represented and the inculca-
tion of hatred and scorn of them, especially the three other
occupying powers, the United Kingdom, the USA and France.
Several lines, especially under (iii) continued those followed by
Nazism itself.

The Report then gave a short 'General Analysis' of pre-Nazi
and Nazi tendencies in German textbooks which were contrary to
the interest and policy of Great Britain and which had recurred
in manuscripts submitted for publication *since* 1945. The broad
grouping was under (i) militarism; (ii) nationalistic trends (including regionalism and racism; (iii) morbidity and sadism.

All this was introductory to the main body of the Report, a
fairly monumental 'Specific Analysis' of extracts from German
manuscripts, textbooks, teacher training publications and so on,
from 1896 to the present time, concluding with an appendix
from Soviet Zone books.

No adequate selection of examples can be given in so short
a paper as this, but perhaps the following quotations, illustrating German racial-nationalistic lines, may throw a little more
light on the problem.

Post-1945:

'There can be no doubt that the old Indo-Germanic ruling
class was completely Nordic. Thus Homer describes far the
greatest number of his heroes as tall, blond and blue-eyed,
whereas Thersites, to whom, by the way, he refuses to give the
title of honour "Achaer", is by his description, typically non-
Nordic.' (from a proposed new Greek Grammar, Kaegi's
Griechische Schulgrammatik).

'Wherever the Hellenic spirit was absorbed by the great racial
groups of Nordic origin, it did not destroy, but had a strengthening effect on the Roman spirit . . .' (from the Teachers' hand-

book to a Latin Course, *Gens Cornelia,* proposed for reissue).

'It is from the converted German tribes'—converted 'of their own free will'—'and under the leadership of the German Nation . . . welded together by the Christian faith . . . that the community of Western civilisation was formed. It comprised the areas settled by Germanic tribes, Romance lands whose population of ancient tribes had lived through Roman civilisation and had been rejuvenated by Germanic invasions, and lands of Slav settlers. This second phase covers nearly 1000 years . . . In the Crusades the Teutonic knights were fighting for *Reich* and Church on the Eastern borders of German national territory (*Volksraum*)'. (from a proposed new Primer for Religious Instruction, *Christenfibel,* Peiper-Rasko. *Reich* refers to the Holy Roman Empire of the German nation—*das Heilige Römische Reich Deutscher Nation*—as it is always called in German.)

'King Alfred defeated the Danes in many battles . . . King Alfred was by far the greatest of the Anglo-Saxon Kings . . . The Anglo-Saxons came over the sea from the land that we now call Germany . . . etc.' (Three of twenty-six similar examples *for language manipulation* about Alfred and his ex-German people as conquerors and civilisers of Britain, scattered through Schad's English Language Course, *Lehrbuch der Englischen Sprache,* proposed for reissue. Other examples deal with Baron von Steuben, who went to North America to 'help the young American nation gain her freedom'. Some forty other sentences deal with Anglo-French colonialism.)

'I am sitting before the map of Germany. Germany is the land of our dreams. Germany is the height of all glory! My schoolmate Jürgen Wieben went to Hamburg once with his father; his boot had trod on ground where Denmark had no say. Jürgen Wieben's boot was a hallowed boot'. (from a Schleswig-Holstein source in a proposed new Reader, *Lesebuch,* for Lower Saxony).

'Never since the world began was a race so prolific in crime.' (said of the Jews, in a proposed History of the Church, *Kirchengschichte,* for schools, by Karl Kastner.)

For comparison:

Examples of trends such as these, however much readers may

now agree or disagree with them as factual statements or justifiable expressions of feeling, had to be set against their immediate
background. Below are a few quotations from Nazi and pre-
Nazi sources.

'*Of Race and Nation (Volk)* . . . When the Ice-Age came
to an end, the Nordic peoples poured westwards into the areas
of what we now call Europe . . . the German Nation (*Volk*) is
basically sixty per cent Nordic . . . Nordic blood—present in
every German, even if his outward appearance does not reveal
it!—determines the resolute character and the unity of German
life. That is why National Socialism has a mission and an
obligation to wage the fight against the Jewish people.' (Werner
May, *German National Catechism for the Young German in
School and at Work,* Breslau, 1935).

'Germans who do not live in the German Reich are called
Auslandsdeutsche (ex-patriate Germans) . . . Every third German today is an *Auslandsdeutscher*! . . . Germans who belong
to the German-speaking area but have been cut off by the
Treaty of Versailles, imposed upon us by force, are called
Grenzlandsdeutsche (Border Germans) . . . The Dutch are of
German blood . . . The changing course of our history has
meant that not all the fellow-members of our nation (*Volks-
genossen*) in Central Europe are united . . . If one counts the
Dutch, the Flemish, the German-Swiss, as well as the Germans
in Hungary, Siebenbürgen and other lands in the East, the
number of Germans living in Europe amounts to 80 million.'
(from Teubner's *Geography for Secondary Modern Schools*,
Part 5, 2nd. edition, 1930, Weimar period. The terms italicised
and the pan-Germanism implicit here are commonly attributed
to the Nazis. They preceded the régime, but were increasingly
emphasised over the twelve years of its rule.)

'For years after the war, foreign troops dominated German territory on the Rhine—they occupied towns and villages,
filled barracks with black soldiers, took over dwelling-houses,
interfered with shipping, spied on friends of the fatherland . . .
women were importuned, monuments desecrated . . .' (from a
German Grammar Course, 8th. school year, 1930, Weimar
period. *The passage is meant for grammatical analysis.*)

'The French take over barracks, schools, dwellings, occupy
factories and mines, drive men and women out of theatres with

horsewhips, shoot innocent workers in Essen . . . take coal, steal
money, incite coloured soldiers against defenceless Germans . . .'
(from *My Mother Tongue, Meine Muttersprache,* a German
Grammar Course for Senior and Middle Schools, Nazi period.
The section is headed 'From the Period of German Shame'. The
pupil is required to *rewrite the passage a) in the Active, b) in
the Passive Voice.*)

Source Libraries

Even if this Textbook Section Report presented a convincing
argument for continued caution, the outcome only seemed to
aggravate the problem of getting new books written. Who was to
write them? German teachers and academics had been brought
up on traditional lines. Expatriates who had been in contact
with other systems and ideas, for instance in the USA or the
United Kingdom, were regarded with suspicion by many of
the Germans who had remained at home. Older teachers looked
back to Weimar books; young teachers had had nothing but
Nazi indoctrination from the age of ten or so. Most had been
cut off from comparative sources, either internally or abroad, for
twelve years. New and more acceptable sources had to be found.

The establishment of a 'source library' in Education Branch,
proposed by the Foreign Office Working Party in the spring of
1945, had been accepted and a grant was obtained from the
Treasury for this purpose. This was intended as a reference
library for British education officers. Textbook Section saw in it
the germ of an idea for the provision of source references for
German writers. At first this would consist of British books, but
the scope would be extended and adapted to German needs. In
July, 1946, the Control Office approved the expenditure of a
Treasury grant of £5,000 for 1946-7 for the establishment of
what were now to be officially called 'source libraries', *Quellen-
büchereien.* The system was centred in Texbook Section at Bünde
at what was then Education Branch Headquarters, and administered from there. Six regional source libraries were set
up in the Zone at Düsseldorf, Münster, Hanover, Kiel, Hamburg and Berlin (British Sector). These were put under German management, wherever possible in German premises, with
regional Education Branch supervision.

Textbook Section maintained a facsimile source library in Bünde. The section had, in the nature of its work, received copies of all new German schoolbook publications in the British Zone as they appeared. They were added to the source library and publishers were asked to supply a copy or copies of their new books to the regional source libraries.

The first consignments of English books, selected and ordered from Bünde, arrived in April 1947 and were distributed to the regions. In October 1947, the Deputy Director of Books, British Council, who was a professional librarian, made a visit as consultant to all the source libraries and a number of his suggestions were adopted. The most important of these was the appointment of a qualified German university librarian who took over the executive organisation in Bünde. To improve access facilities, the regional source libraries also set up branch libraries in their respective areas. With a second expenditure grant of up to £6,000 made by the Treasury for the financial year ending March 31 1948, plans could go ahead to increase the scope of the libraries.

The composition of the source libraries was as follows: (i) school textbooks in all subjects; (ii) theory and practice of education; (iii) standard reference and new works in fields of special importance—history, sociology, politics, philosophy, religion, psychology, etc; (iv) literature (*belles-lettres*); (v) new English publications presenting modern and topical life in Britain; (vi) juvenile literature; (vii) specialist periodicals. The aim was to present 'the utmost variety of viewpoint', so that German readers should have 'the opportunity long denied them of drawing from many sources irrespective of race, creed and politics'.

If that aim was to be achieved, it was clear that sources must be extended. Contacts and mutual visits were made between Textbook Section and their equivalent officers of Education Branch in the American Zone of Germany. Thanks to this collaboration, the section was able to arrange the exchange of British for American schoolbooks and other publications as between the British source libraries and the American 'curriculum centres'. From May 1947, an important American section was built up in the main source libraries.

In the early days, Swiss books in the German language had

been sent in to help alleviate the dearth left by the War. Further consignments of Swiss schoolbooks were now sent through the *Schweizer Bücherhilfe Zürich*, to add to the German language section of the source libraries, though some of these seemed old-fashioned where method was concerned.

The French occupation authorities were also approached. Textbook Section officers visited the French Zone and had talks with French education officials. The French system was different from the British and American. The schools were working with some imported Swiss books and with French textbooks in German editions. A 'Pedagogic Commission' of French professors, experts on German and Germany, had been set up to write textbooks. There was no equivalent of the source libraries. Nevertheless, Textbook Section was able to acquire some books of French origin for the source libraries. There were objections in the British Zone to some aspects, mainly to a bias towards military historical presentation, but they were useful comparative material.

The fourth source was, logically, East Germany through the Soviet authorities. Personal contacts proved too difficult, but liaison was made through correspondence and at first there seemed a readiness to co-operate on an exchange of publications. The few books and publications received at Textbook Section made a valuable addition to comparative studies and sources, but, despite their vehement anti-Nazi line, they contravened the principles to which Education Branch was committed.

The Russians and their German collaborators disapproved of what they considered the 'bourgeois', 'capitalist', 'imperialist' approach in the Western Zones, and their disapproval and hatred were incorporated methodically in their schoolbooks. After protests had been received, in particular from a regional education officer on the nature of material from the Soviet Zone sent to the teacher training college in his area, efforts to continue exchanges and collaboration were finally abandoned. It was a sorry check in the attempt to represent 'the utmost variety of viewpoint'. However, studies including Marxist and other revolutionary views were still available in source library references.

After the winding-up of Textbook Section in 1950, the source library network was housed in the *Brücken*, the British

Cultural Centres finally taken over by the British Council. The transfer, though inevitable in the changed climate, was not welcomed by the German source librarians who had housed and run the service, nor by the Central Textbook Committee and retiring Textbook Section officers, who feared that, once housed in British Centres, the libraries would be stigmatised as propaganda.

Overcoming Stumbling-blocks in the Writing of New Textbooks

This psychological aspect had always been very important. In the earlier days, potential writers were mostly as ill-nourished, ill-housed, ill-equipped and non-mobile as anyone else, over-worked, teaching in shifts, disillusioned and often understand-ably resentful and suspicious. The mere existence of source libraries was not enough.

The most baffling problems were in history, in *Heimatkunde* (home regional studies), and in the *Lesebuch*, the German 'Reader'. History books had been completely banned in all four Zones. In the British Zone, two major efforts, very different in themselves, set the ball slowly rolling again. The first was the creation of a new comprehensive history for secondary schools, *Geschichte unserer Welt* (History of Our World), edited by Fritz Karsen at the head of a group of German academic émigrés living in the United States of America. They had begun work on it before the end of the War and Bermann-Fischer was to pub-lish it. In the British Zone, there had been official insistence that new books, to be acceptable, must be written by teachers and authors living in Germany. But Textbook Section, to whom the first volumes were submitted in October 1945 and who studied the book critically as its parts appeared, urged its introduction, and the ban was waived by the summer of 1946. Herr Suhrkamp, who had the publishing right for Fischer in Berlin, appointed a team of German experts—historians and teachers—who made revisions and amendments, in consultation with Textbook Section. There were difficulties in interpretation, dramatic delays in produc-tion, but in early 1947, Part I of Volume II (732-1660) ap-peared. Part II of Volume II (1660-1890) was ready for print-ing by July, when the edition of 50,000 of II/I was completed. The sheer size of the work—480 pages of II/I, 360 pages of

II/II—shows the scale and ambition of the project, and
perhaps a certain lack of realism about conditions and shortages
in a ruined country immediately after the War.

The second group of pioneers had no illusions and approached
the problem from the opposite end. In Braunschweig, in December 1946, a History Working Party was set up by Herr Turn,
a school inspector and member of the Central Textbook Committee, and Professor Eckert, Professor of History at the Kant
Hochschule. This group produced the first curricula for the
re-introduction of history in schools, taught on new lines. They
held innumerable meetings and discussion groups with teachers
at all levels, and they realised that the first necessity was to produce material for the teacher and teacher-in-training, based on
'actual sources of history', providing 'objective historical data'.
At their own expense they set about publishing small booklets
on specific subjects to form a series : *Contributions to the teaching of History, Beiträge zum Geschichtsunterricht.* The first, Dr
Eckert's *Der Bauernkrieg* was printed on scrap paper discarded
by the local newspaper, in an edition of 2,000. This remarkable
enterprise, strongly supported by Textbook Section, gained
attention and influence throughout the Zone and beyond. By the
end of 1948 the following titles had been published :

No. 1 : Georg Eckert, *Der Bauernkrieg* (The Peasants' Re-
volt)

No. 2 : Georg Eckert, *Die Revolution von 1848/49*

No. 3 : Karl Mielcke, *Der Vormärz* (Prelude to the March
Revolution, 1848)

No. 4 : Georg Eckert, *Arbeiterleben in der Frühzeit des Indus-
triekapitalismus* (Life of the Workers in the Early Period of
Industrial Capitalism)

No. 5 : Georg Eckert, *Freiherr vom Stein und die preußischen
Reformen*

No. 6 : Karl Mielcke, *Städtewesen und Frühkapitalismus*
(Urban Life and Early Capitalism)

No. 7 : Karl Mielcke, *Das Zeitalter der Entdeckungen* (the
Age of Discoveries)

No. 8 : Georg Eckert, *Vom Bismarckreich zur Republik*

No. 9 : Hermann Trimborn, *Das Menschliche ist gleich im*

Urgrund aller Kulturen (Humanity is the Common Element
in all Civilisations)

No. 10 : Fritz Wenzel, *Der junge Luther*

No. 11 : Karl Mielcke, *Das deutsche Bürgertum im Zeitalter
der Reichsgründung* (The German Middle Classes and the
Founding of the Empire)

No. 12 : Georg Eckert, *Das junge Deutschland und die Revo-
lutionsdichtung des Vormärz* ('Young Germany' and Revolutionary Poetry to 1848)

These titles suggest a Socialist approach as opposed to a
National-Socialist, but the aim was to avoid 'isms' and to deal
with key subjects traditional to German history teaching, the
treatment of which was under controversial scrutiny.

All proceeds from the sale of the booklets were used to support new writing, lectures, research travel; and the first books
for school class use were beginning to be written as a result, with
history teachers gaining more confidence. They ranged from
revised approaches on traditional lines, such as Witte and
König's *Deutsche Geschichte im Europäischen Zusammenhang*
(German History in its European Context) to an experiment
with cheap booklets in a series counteracting the cult of the
military hero called *Helden des Friedens* (Heroes of Peace).

In January 1949 Mr Robert Birley, as Educational Adviser
to the Military Governor, sent a memorandum to the Director
of Education Branch stressing the importance of the work that
Textbook Section had been doing and urging that this approach
to the textbook problem should be made permanent, beginning
with 'the most important, namely, History textbooks.' He
suggested the setting up of an International History Textbook
Committee open to any country, and listed possible procedures
and difficulties. This elicited a number of suggestions from Education Branch, including Textbook Section, beginning with an
immediate short-term arrangement on an Anglo-German footing,
using 'two experienced and proven bodies', the Historical Association in England and the Braunschweig History Institute under
the aegis of Dr Eckert in Germany. Textbook Section could act
as intermediary and could suggest criteria based on its experience within the whole context of textbook literature. Collaboration could gradually be extended to other Zones and countries.

From such beginnings, international co-operation in the teaching of history, which had been tried, and foundered, in the 1930s, was renewed. In 1949, the first Anglo-German Conference of History Teachers took place. In August, 1950, a Franco-German History Rally was held at Freiburg. Although to go beyond 1950 is to overstep the period with which this paper deals, it is worth calling attention to the subsequent work published in the volumes of the *Internationales Jahrbuch für Geschichtsunterricht* (International Yearbook for History Teaching) produced in Braunschweig. These show the extraordinarily rapid development in co-operation between nation after nation in the early 1950s, and the boldness with which controversial subjects were tackled.

Heimatkunde represented a method of integrated study from the child's earliest years. It drew on history, geography, literature, arts and crafts, industry, commerce. The basic principle was to advance from the known to the unknown by relating life in the child's home environment to a gradually widening world. This concentric circle method had been universally accepted in Germany for many decades. But *Heimatkunde* had always been treated emotively. The emotional attachment to *Blut und Boden*, blood and soil, had been frenetically heightened by the Nazis, from *Heimat* to *Vaterland* to the *Thousand-Year-Reich*, from family and ancestor-study to the Nordic Master-Race theory and so on. Paradoxically, decentralising authority after the War had re-emphasised regional and local cults.

Reports from school, and many new manuscripts, showed that the whole circle was starting up again. The problem was now exacerbated and confused by the redeployment of population within the *Länder* and the influx of refugees. One or two examples may help to explain this.

A new *Heimatkunde* by Josef Dietz entitled *Teure Heimat, sei gegrüßt* (1948) (Greetings to Thee, Beloved Homeland). The author writes: 'Yes, our *Heimat* is like a good mother. She cares for us from our cradle; shares sorrow and joy with us; and after death gathers us into her cool lap. This little book is to tell you about her, so that she shall grow ever closer to your heart, yours and your dear ones!' All the facts and figures that follow are thus conditioned. Probably up to half the children studying from this book, which is written for young people of the

Bonn region, were not born and brought up in that area. When
an attempt is made to reform the method on more universal
lines, it can founder on the same emotional reef. The preface
to Hüls' *Heimatkunde Westfalen* (1949) has the stirring title :
'Let us build bridges'—bridges of peace from nation to nation.
You will do this by learning to love your homeland, it says,
because every one of the two thousand million people on earth
loves his homeland. The first chapter begins : 'You are a child
of your homeland; and you love your homeland as a child
loves its mother. You love your village, your town and its
people. You belong to each other in sorrow and joy.' It is certain
that Herr Dietz and Herr Hüls did not collaborate; both were
echoing Arndt and all the traditional quotations of their own
schooldays. But Herr Hüls does try to encourage the refugees.
'Perhaps,' he says, 'you will learn to love your new homeland,
you who have lost your old one.'

Great arguments arose between proponents of the method
and its critics, who included Textbook Section. The members
of the German Central Textbook Committee began to find
themselves in some sympathy with Textbook Section. This cul-
minated in a special Conference at Bünde in March, 1949 on
'Home Studies—World Studies' (*Heimatkunde—Weltkunde*)
convened by Textbook Section and attended by a number of
influential members of the German Central Textbook Committee. This led to a further Conference on geography and
home studies. As a result of these discussions, the Germans
planned meetings and discussions with teachers and authors, the
publishing of articles in relevant journals, and pressure to
revise curriculum directives on broader lines. Textbook Section
prepared and circulated an analytical Report on 'Home Studies
—World Studies' similar to the 'German Textbook Literature'
mentioned earlier and added a bibliography with quotations,
mainly where these illustrated common human elements world-
wide as a basis for teaching, that is, a parallel method in contrast
to the concentric circle method. It had to be conceded that no
immediate and radical reform could be expected against the
historical, geographical and political background in Germany;
but the connection between this emotional tradition and what
had happened in the 1930s and 1940s was recognised by a
number of Germans, foremost among them Regierungsdirektor

Müller of Arnsberg, a member of the Central Textbook Committee, who propagated ideas for a more factual approach on broader lines.

The *Lesebuch*, the general German Reader, extended the problem posed by integrated *Heimatkunde* throughout the whole school age range. It had traditionally been regionally based, incorporating local literature, poetry, history and so on into the general anthology, and had evolved as a kind of cultural vade-mecum. To give an example, and show the connection with *Heimatkunde* : a middle-school Reader for ninth to tenth school years, published in 1926 (Weimar period) is entitled *Heimat und Vaterland* (Homeland and Fatherland). Its fly-leaf introduction is a quotation from Arndt which begins : 'How glorious for all with any feeling in their hearts is the sound of those words : This is my Homeland, that is, this is the place where my forbears and parents lived, fought and died . . . What a wealth of blessings and strength lies in those two words : Fatherland and Homeland.' Another example to complement this is a typical Index of Contents, of which we give a few section-titles here from *Leben*, (Life) a Reader for Westphalian Middle Schools (Part 5, 1928) : Homeland/Hearth and Home/To the Youth of Germany/Fatherland and Foreign Lands/From German *Gauen*/Spring Greetings to the Fatherland/From our German Heritage/ . . . Ode to the Prussian Army/The Watch on the Rhine/ . . . Die and be born again/ . . . Faith and Consolation/German Consolation/Germany/Of German People/ German Men/Where Bismarck is to lie/German Women/ . . . Poets of the Westphalian Homeland.

It was from such elements that the National-Socialist Reader was welded together as a *Deutsches Lesebuch*. By 1939, but still before the outbreak of the Second World War, Book 4 for Primary Schools throughout Germany (published by Crüwell) looked like this :

Contents:

Volk wird (a Nation emerges)—seventy pages of extracts, etc., from the Nibelungen to Clausewitz, almost all dealing with patriotism and military/political subjects.

Volk arbeitet (a Nation works)—sixty-nine pages of varied

items showing all kinds of occupations, first devoted to work on the land. It finally leads into Germans' adventures overseas, ending with 'Homesickness', *'Die Auslandsdeutschen'* and Hebbel's 'Exhortation' to the Fatherland about its 'Children far away'.

Volk Kämpft (a Nation fights)—the longest section, ninety pages of extracts drawn entirely from war and military-political themes. It begins with a poem *Vaterland*, contains a number of extracts from Hitler's writings and speeches and those of Nazi authors alongside traditional extracts from World War I, and ends with a verse: 'It's up to you' . . . 'Horst Wessel is watching you: do your duty'.

Volk feiert (a Nation commemorates)—seventy-one pages, mainly poems traditional to the *Lesebuch* and consistent with the preceding sections, including regional elements. An interesting use of the latter is Weinheber's 'Through the farmlands of the *Ostmark* (Austria)', followed by Franke's poem about Hitler's (Austrian-born) ancestors, entitled: 'Where the Leader's ancestor stood on farming land', which ends: 'German and tough, true and hard as granite are the kind of people in his ancestral *Gau*.' The section ends with Sayings of Hitler, a poem about him by Baldur von Schirach and two nineteenth-century patriotic poems.

At the upper end of the school course, *Hirt's* huge *Deutsches Lesebuch*, published in 1940 shows how this treatment can be carried further into a general German anthology. Each of its six sections begins with a quotation from Hitler, and the book ends with a prayer by him. Every aspect of Nazi ideology and propaganda seems to be presented here; 365 pages draw on the great treasury of German literature and culture—for *Volk und Führer*.

To break away from the traditional *Lesebuch*, Textbook Section and its German colleagues suggested short 'whole texts' (*Ganzschriften*) each based on some familiar section-theme, but avoiding stock titles that might only evoke stock attitudes again. Such booklets would also have the advantage of being quicker to write and easier to produce while paper shortages lasted. There was, however, no doubt that the educational idea behind the *Lesebuch* had been basically a good one. Correspondence and discussion about it were therefore infused with idealism and often passionate conviction on both sides. All this needed wider airing.

The Textbook Exhibition

The use of comparative sources and the need to give them wider publicity inspired Textbook Section to devise a mobile exhibition, drawing on the now considerable research and resources of the section archives and the Source Library. It was called 'The Textbook in Great Britain and America' (*Das Schulbuch in Grossbritannien und Amerika*). Mounted by Public Relations/Information Services Control, it consisted of some 1000 books: key exhibits fixed on stands, with their duplicates and others, including teachers' books, in an attached reference library. Alongside English and American books were German books as comparative material. It was divided into the following sections:

1 *Curriculum and Content:*
   Language and Literature
   Man in his environment and development
   Mathematics and Science
   Arts and Music
   Practical and technical work
2 *Method and Presentation:* Special Exhibits
   The Reader
   Man in his environment and development
   Drama in education
   English as a foreign language
3 *Illustration* in school books and auxiliary material
4 *Comparative Reference Library*

The method of presentation was analytical and critical. Quotations and observations were placarded alongside exhibits and an explanatory guide was issued. The whole formed a distillation of the work which has been outlined in the main part of this paper.

The exhibition was supported and publicised by Education Branch and by German Central Textbook Committee members and their colleagues in the various *Länder*. It was opened at Bielefeld on 22 June 1948 by Lord Lindsay, then Master of

E

Balliol, and was subsequently shown in Osnabrück, Hanover, Oldenburg, Kiel, Düsseldorf, Cologne, Essen, Berlin, Münster, Braunschweig, Hamburg, Lüneburg, Göttingen, Gelsenkirchen and Dortmund, introduced by various distinguished people. It ran for thirteen months and was estimated to have had some 24,000 visitors. At first received with suspicion and outright hostility by many Germans, it gradually began to arouse positive interest. It served as a basis for lectures, seminars and discussions with teachers. The Textbook Section officers who produced it visited a number of the exhibition centres for that purpose.

In 1950, the United Nations Educational, Scientific and Cultural Organisation, which had been sponsoring the international study and reform of textbooks since 1945, became interested in the exhibition. It was adapted, and finally moved to Brussels for international exhibition under the aegis of UNESCO. To those who had worked in Textbook Section this was a happy epilogue.

6. *The Training of Teachers*

George Murray

It was recognised at a very early stage in the existence of Education Branch that, if education were to play its full part in Germany's return to democracy, the role of the teacher training colleges would be crucial. It has always been the case that their products have represented a potential for good or evil in social or political developments, all the more effective because of the number of young captive minds that can be influenced in either direction within the four walls of a teacher's classroom. The Nazis had unfortunately come to the same conclusion about the importance of education in attaining social or political ends and had for nearly twelve years assiduously and with considerable success grafted their theories onto the German teaching profession through their own particular form of teacher training college. They found considerable support amongst the radical ranks of the elementary teachers—who are said to have provided about twenty-five per cent of all Nazi party officials whereas the secondary school teachers were able to entrench themselves behind their more conservative outlook, their more comfortable mode of life and their much greater social prestige. It is difficult to say which was in the end the more demanding of the two tasks—to get rid of the insidious influence of Nazism spread, in some cases quite unwittingly, by so many of the elementary school teachers or deliberately to bring back on to the right lines the teaching of such politically sensitive subjects as history and biology in the secondary schools. Both were long-term problems and each had its own method of approach. But as was the case with other aspects of educational reform the most urgent problems were of a more physical nature—staff, students and buildings.

The denazification process acted particularly severely on the staffing of the training colleges for elementary school teachers. The intention of Education Branch was (at least in the beginning) to apply the normal rules even more strictly than to others holding positions of influence in public life. But this was, of course, of little help in restocking a profession sorely depleted by desperate mobilisation in the latter years of the War and now lacking those who would never return from it and those who were held in prisoner-of-war camps abroad. The choice was either to keep the colleges closed for lack of reliable staff and so delay the start of a process that was officially designated urgent or else employ staff whose reliability was not entirely beyond doubt. A further, and rather more peda- gogical obstacle to the immediate production of new teachers, was the determination of Education Branch that the training of the new generation of elementary teachers would not be skimped but would be extended to a full three-year course with a wider educational content that would eventually give them an enhanced status comparable with their graduate col- leagues in the secondary schools.

This policy was in line with similar developments in other European countries, notably Great Britain, and there was little difficulty in reaching agreement in the Allied Control Council to the addition of a clause to the same effect in their Directive No. 54 of 25 June, 1947: 'All teacher education should take place in a university or in a pedagogical institution of university rank'. The point was particularly relevant to the more conserva- tive areas of Germany where there was a lingering adherence to the out-moded system of training elementary teachers at special colleges in six-year courses following immediately after the elementary school period. At the same time it was clear that, if the teaching profession as a whole was to be integrated into a single service, the system of training secondary teachers would have to undergo corresponding adjustments affecting especially the theoretical training of the students. The narrow academic path leading via the *Abitur* to the university and after graduation back to the secondary school as a probationary teacher, attending periodic seminars run by other, more ex- perienced teachers, would have to be opened to admit a much wider curriculum and a more intensive professional training in the theory and practice of pedagogy. Helped by its favour- able geographical position Hamburg was in the forefront of teacher training reform at an early stage. The authorities wasted no time in making the Institute of Education an integral part of the university (in 1947) and centralising all forms of teacher training on it, even introducing would-be secondary teachers to teaching practice in their first year at the university and giving them a basic training at the Institute after graduation. A comparable experiment was made in Lower Saxony where students were offered a basic course in pedagogy at a teacher training college before going on to university.

As far as the internal reform of teacher training was concerned it was generally agreed by the Allies and German authorities that the curriculum of all types of training had to be enlarged and liberalised if it was to acquire a role in social progress as a recognised social service and at the same time provide students with a wider knowledge and experience not only of the child mind and its learning processes but also of the part that the school plays in the community and its relationships with other social institutions. To this end social studies, civics and other cognate subjects were introduced into the curriculum and under such headings students were able to take part in youth and social activities outside the colleges and, during the vacations, even take a responsible rôle in vocational guidance, youth employment and other branches of the social services. More emphasis was laid on applied psychology at the expense of philosophy as a basic subject. The compulsory hours of attendance were reduced to give the student more time for individual study for the development of his particular interests and for participation in social activities. A wider range of optional subjects was introduced and greater recognition given to art, music and handicrafts. The students were encouraged to elect their own councils, clubs and committees and to develop them as far as is possible where colleges are non-residential. Finally, amongst the longer-term objectives was the establishment of a model school either integral with the college or within easy reach of it.

These then were the main objectives, both political and pedagogical, both long and short-term, that both British and German authorities were agreed upon. It was hoped that they would re-establish teacher training on a firm and up-to-date basis and, most important of all and perhaps the only criterion of success, bring in their train the fundamental change without which the others would be of no avail, the one that could not be ordered or legislated for—a complete change of spirit. But even here there was evidence of a desire to make a practical beginning. In those days fumigation of public buildings was the order of the day and was strictly enforced as a protection against epidemics. But, as far as some of the Nazi colleges were concerned it was possible to detect in this process as much preoccupation with exorcism as with hygiene. In some cases, indeed, the college was moved to a completely new building and became a new creation with, one would like to think, a new spirit to watch over its fortunes.

But the main job of the training colleges was to train teachers and it was obvious that all these plans and policies were of little avail in supplying the immediate need. The order had gone out for the schools to open on 1 October 1945, barely five months after the end of hostilities. About that time the number of schoolchildren divided by the number of teachers available would have given a teacher/pupil ratio nearer 1 : 70 than 1 : 60. The only teachers available, for reasons already mentioned, were those already in service who had survived the process of denazification. Very few of those in training at the *Lehrerbildungsanstalten,* resurrected by the Nazis as an emergency measure midway through the War, were acceptable not only because of their political indoctrination but also because of their youth (these colleges offered the old-fashioned six-year course for pupil teachers already mentioned). The policy of re-introducing the basic two-year (eventually three-year) course for elementary teachers was not exactly calculated to solve the immediate problem. Nevertheless the task of reopening the colleges went ahead and the first students were admitted to the full-length courses as soon as the conditions laid down by Education Branch in respect of staff, students, curriculum and so on had been fulfilled. By the beginning of December 1945, two two-year courses (in Detmold and in Braunschweig) had started while Hamburg was already running courses for teachers in intermediate and secondary schools as well as a three-year course for elementary teachers. One month later, the colleges at Hanover, Celle, and Alfeld had reopened and Aachen, Bonn, Essen and Kettwig were ready to function. At about the same time courses were being arranged in various places in the British Zone for teachers in technical, special and nursery schools. Reference will be made later to the plethora of re-training and rehabilitation courses for teachers already in service.

The training facilities already in operation during the first few months of Occupation were enumerated in Education Control Instruction No. 24, dated as early as 20 October 1945. The preamble acted as a reminder to all Education Control Officers that all administrative decisions would ultimately be subject to German political control— 'The whole question of teacher training is closely bound up with the broader issue of the status of the teachers in the community as a whole. This is a long-term matter which only competent German authorities themselves can settle, and fully competent in this sense can be only an administrative body of not less than *Land* or *Provinz* status responsible for its decisions to elected representatives of the people. Such authorities do not yet exist. It is therefore important that the emergency plans produced by authorities to meet the present scarcity of teachers should not unnecessarily complicate the final settlement.' There followed a list of the responsible German authorities who were required to submit their plans for teacher training in their areas, bearing in mind that no college or course could be started without the written permission of Education Branch and that, as far as denazification was concerned, the rules were to be even more strictly applied to staff and students than in the case of universities and colleges of similar status.

The plans would include an estimate of each authority's requirements and details of what they proposed in the way of courses of different types. They had a choice between :

a) normal full-length courses of at least two years' duration for students beginning at the normal age (that is, not below the age of eighteen years);

b) emergency shortened courses of a stated duration for students desiring to enter the teaching profession at a more advanced age;

or c) courses for pupil teachers or school helpers if these are regarded as absolutely essential to meet the immediate situation.

Authorities were also required to show how they proposed to solve the problem of student grants and to suggest how a teacher qualified after a shortened course could eventually overtake, in status as well as in salary, those who completed a full-length course. The German organisers were also directed to consider what to do with any worthwhile material thrown up by the closure of the Nazi colleges (Education Branch was in favour of transferring them to normal secondary schools and postponing a decision on admission to teacher training until they had completed a normal secondary curriculum). As each college or course got under way full details had to be submitted about the buildings, the staff, the students, the curriculum, the syllabus for every subject and the textbooks to be used. And finally there was a requirement that all major organisational changes should be notified to Education Branch in advance, including those that became necessary when the responsible German authorities already referred to were finally created. As in other aspects of education Education Branch retained the right of control and supervision over all teacher training at this time (October 1945) and until January 1947. Such was the policy, the organisation and the machinery for the provision of teachers for the schools immediately after the War.

But the colleges, like the schools, also had staffing difficulties and it soon became obvious that within the terms of E.C.I. No. 24 alone the process of producing fully trained teachers was going to be slow and inadequate even if, in the end, they would have received a thorough theoretical and practical grounding in their craft. Ultimately the whole basis of teacher training had to be extended and amplified in order to produce more teachers more quickly. But in the meantime it was also essential as well as extremely urgent to provide in-service training for the teachers who were already in the schools, including those who had suffered from the abuses and limitations of the Nazi system, especially the political slant given to the curriculum in the training colleges. Although the shortage of teachers made it extremely difficult to release any of them for these courses, the German authorities were nevertheless required by E.C.I. No. 51, issued in February 1946, to 'organise teachers' refresher courses, both cultural and professional, subject and general, and teachers' conferences within relatively small areas as well as large. These courses and conferences should be devised for teachers in all types of schools, either separately or together according to the nature of the individual course or conference'. Special encouragement was, in fact, given to the holding of conferences not limited to teachers from one type of school, since this would foster consultation between different sections of the administration and make some contribution to the integration of the teaching profession and the widening of the individual teacher's world. Full details of these courses and conferences had to be submitted to Education Branch for approval before they could be started and were supervised by them as far as manpower permitted. Although they were originally conceived as part of the general teacher training emergency they eventually acquired a permanent role in the regular provision of in-service training. Education Control Instruction No. 51 unleashed a wide variety of training schemes of different purpose, content and duration. There were supplementary courses for ex-members of the armed forces whose training had been interrupted by call-up. There were six-month courses for women teachers (including many war widows) whose training was held to be inadequate and politically tainted. Special subject courses were organised mainly for teachers in intermediate and secondary schools aimed either at the denazification of vulnerable subjects like history, geography and biology or the assimilation into the curriculum of new subjects of general interest like civics, social services, civil law or European history. Short courses were arranged for teachers who had held some minor Nazi party office but felt confident that they would eventually win their appeals and be acceptable for further employment, even if it meant demotion. Weekend conferences on political education were organised to bring together all teachers in a given area, attendance being compulsory in spite of the exhausting rigours of the teacher's daily routine in those early days. Preliminary courses were also arranged for large numbers of students who, although accepted by a college, could not be admitted immediately because of the restricted intake.

By Easter 1946, after nearly one year of Occupation, twenty-eight colleges for elementary and technical teacher trainees were functioning in the British Zone with a total of about 4,000 students of whom 1,500 were attending a normal two-year (in Hamburg three-year) course, the remainder an emerg-

E*

ency one-year course. There were, in addition, eight seminars for secondary teachers and, as already mentioned, a welter of courses for existing and would-be teachers. The total output from all these sources, however, was barely sufficient to cover normal wastage, let alone make good the abnormal wartime depredations. It was clear that the teacher provision already organised would have to be redoubled, especially with an eye on the not-so-distant future when over half of the teaching body, as it then existed, would have to be replaced in the space of ten years—it was estimated that the average age of teachers in the British Zone in 1945-46 was nearer sixty than fifty, which by itself meant that a disproportionately large number of teachers had to be found in the younger age brackets, not only in order to offset the heavy losses inevitable when such a crowded upper age bracket came to retirement but also to make a start with the restocking of the depleted middle generation of twenty-five- to forty-five-year-olds.

Similar difficulties were being experienced in the other three Zones of Occupation, so much so that the problem finally came before the Allied Control Commission who issued a directive on 'measures to be taken to fill teachers' posts with democratic elements'. Each of the Allies had his own interpretation of the significance of the directive, each proceeded with the plans and policies he had already implemented, applying his own interpretation of the word 'democratic'. In the British Zone an Education Control Instruction (No. 66 of 23 May 1946) was issued with the following preamble—'Present estimates show the shortage of teachers to be in the neighbourhood of 15,000. It is impossible to rely on the output of teachers from the normal training colleges to make good this deficiency. It has accordingly been decided that German education authorities shall establish Special Emergency Teacher Training Courses. Full instructions to this effect are therefore being issued in the accompanying EIGA No. 6'. The EIGA (Education Instruction to German Authorities) was an amplified version of the E.C.I. making clear to the German administrators what action they had to take in organising these new courses. Each of the *Länder*, including Hamburg and Berlin, was required to produce a stipulated quota of teachers in a series of one-year special courses spread over three years. In order not to conflict with the essential demands of the labour market the age of the candidate had to lie between twenty-eight and forty but this at least ensured that a breath of wider living would enter the traditionally narrow corridors of the teaching profession and at the same time fill the ranks of the missing middle generation in the same way that the normal training courses would provide the new youth bracket.

The difficulties in finding staff and students for these special courses were enormous but, in spite of this, the denazification rules were stringently applied to both—at least in the beginning, although even then it was considered justifiable to accept former officers in the armed forces as staff, provided they had not been regular officers, in an attempt to ease the staff recruitment problem. Even so, it took some time before the scheme really got under way but there is no doubt that, in the end, it did attract a worthwhile number of recruits into the teaching profession before the middle of 1948 when the currency was reformed and economic recovery brought with it many more attractive openings in industry and commerce—a process only partially counterbalanced by the gradual return of some denazified teachers, prisoners-of-war and by a fair proportion of war widows.

Adherence to the principle that training should be as thorough as possible in the circumstances meant that, in spite of all the courses already in train—normal, emergency, special emergency and various forms of continuation and refresher—not one new teacher had been trained by the beginning of the Autumn term of 1946. The situation in the schools was still being described as 'urgent', 'desperate' and 'crucial' and it was clear that any further emergency measures would have to be focused, not on the colleges but directly on the schools themselves, primarily by regularising the employment of *Schulhelfer* (unqualified teachers); this was rapidly becoming recognised as the only means of getting teachers into the classrooms without undue delay. The relevant ECI (No. 74 of 17 September 1946) was entitled 'Temporary employment, as *Schulhelfer* under supervision, of students accepted for normal and special emergency teacher training'. The preamble read— 'It has become clear that the situation created in the schools by the shortage is such that immediate measures must be taken to relieve the pressure.

Nevertheless it is important that the standard of training given to intending teachers, their position in the profession and the equating of supply to demand should not be prejudiced by any steps taken for the alleviation of an acute situation. The following measures which have been designed to meet this situation take account of the principles outlined above. They have already met with acceptance in various Regions and it is recommended that they should be adopted by all German education authorities.' The latter were required to recruit and employ *Schulhelfer* to meet the most pressing needs of the schools but within the limits of the budget provision for teachers' salaries in the *Land* concerned. The conditions laid down for selection and employment envisaged eventual merging with normal and emergency courses. The eighteen to twenty-seven-year-old group could not exceed in numbers a single year's output from a two-year normal training course and their selection would be based on the same denazification rules as the candidates accepted for the two-year course, whereas the twenty-eight-forty-year-olds would be employable up to the *Land*'s quota for the Special Emergency Courses for 1947-8 and the standard of selection, both political and pedagogical, would guarantee entry into these courses. The idea was to send the *Schulhelfer* direct to the schools as soon as they were found (in many cases even the denazification process was carried out retrospectively) without any training since the doubtful advantage of inadequate training could without great loss be sacrificed in favour of giving immediate practical help in the classroom. At the same time, however, the German authorities were made responsible for seeing that :

a) they are placed under the supervision of reliable and experienced teachers in the schools and

b) they are given instruction in practical teaching and matters of general interest during their period of employment.

It was never intended that this temporary expedient should in any way undermine the standard of entry to the teaching profession. All *Schulhelfer* were recruited on the understanding that, if they were found acceptable, they would eventually take either the normal or the special emergency course and become fully qualified teachers. The maximum length of employment as a *Schulhelfer* was fixed at one year by which time he had to be enrolled in a full-length course. This meant that the number of *Schulhelfer* accepted in any one year would depend on the number of places available for them the following year on the type of course appropriate to their age-group. Thus the colleges would be assured of a steady flow of recruits with at least some experience of the classroom and the schools, in their turn, would benefit from the immediate presence of a welcome reinforcement to the hard-pressed staff, some of them capable of teaching a subject but all prepared to add their enthusiasm to the running of the school, even to organising school meals, gathering fire-wood and other extra-mural activities which in those days were as important as classroom teaching. As the E.C.I. stipulated 'the first essential is to achieve such an allocation of children to teachers in school classes as will make working conditions in the schools possible'. Although the employment of *Schulhelfer* meant the partial abandonment of a principle jealously guarded by the profession there is no doubt that it did ease the situation in the classrooms as well as the task of recruitment to the full-length courses. Unlike the latter, whose impact on the schools was delayed for anything up to three years, the *Schulhelfer* scheme had an immediate effect where it was most needed and, in addition, by being dovetailed into the full-length courses it contributed to the foundation of a permanent teacher training system.

What has been said above about the various training schemes applied mostly to teachers in elementary and secondary grammar schools. The training of teachers for vocational schools was beset with problems, some of a similar nature and complexity, others peculiar to the vocational schools. There were losses in buildings, equipment and manpower to be made good. Being based traditionally on one large central Institute per *Land* the training of vocational school teachers suffered disproportionately from the loss of or damage to even only one or two of the Institutes. The problem of finding staff and students for them so as to make good normal wastage as well as abnormal war losses was acute enough. But the training of additional teachers for the tradesmen and skilled workmen required for the re-covery and expansion of the economy also fell to the Institutes as well as the task of coping with the high intake resulting from the increased birth-rate of the mid-Thirties.

Pending a solution to these immediate, practical problems there were also several questions of principle to be considered, for example should the basic training course be extended to three years as had been the case in some of the Institutes before the War and was now being pressed upon the German authorities as the appropriate period for the training of elementary school teachers; should the training, or at least the liberal studies and the pedagogy, be taken over by the universities as recommended by Education Branch? Cologne University followed the example of Hamburg at the end of 1947 except that the technical aspects of the training remained close to industry in Solingen and the training as a whole therefore lacked integration. On the other hand, the academic content of the curriculum grew in scope and depth as a result of the university's interest and came gradually to include social studies, history, a foreign language (usually English) as well as education, psychology (preferred more and more to philosophy) and teaching method.

As far as the kindergartens were concerned most problems derived from the fact that they were sometimes provided and/ or maintained by the Churches, by welfare organisations or by central and local government departments other than Education. The task of integrating them into the education service and obtaining for their teachers the same prestige and conditions of service as teachers in other types of schools was therefore largely an administrative one.

The main aim in regard to schools for physically and mentally handicapped children was to ensure that their neglect by the Nazis should be made good and that, in the training of their teachers, close contact should be maintained with new or re-surrected social welfare institutions like child guidance clinics so that they could see at first hand the application of psychology, psychiatry and kindred subjects in the education of handicapped children.

In these few paragraphs an attempt has been made to enumerate the chief aspects of teacher training that appeared to be in need of reform, not only by eliminating undesirable elements but also by bringing the system up to date and in line with progress in other European countries. There are inevitable echoes of ideas that were current in the United Kingdom at the time but few of them were tried out in Germany without close consultation with the German authorities nor were they put into practice without their approval and support.

It can safely be said that, by the end of the period 1945-9, teacher training had made truly remarkable progress. Not only had the pupil-teacher ratios recovered some of their respectability and teaching some of its attraction but the supply of teachers had been launched on a steady course and with time would overtake its former standards both of quantity and quality. The 'economic miracle' was still to come and, in the early 1950s, attract many teachers to the world of industry and commerce, especially male teachers. As a result, in 1951, for the first time, more women were admitted to the training colleges than men and two years later two-thirds of the intake of elementary teacher trainees in Hamburg and in North Rhine/Westphalia were women. But no doubt this phenomenon was accelerated by the general scarcity of funds for education and by the fact that, since women taught fewer hours than men, their salaries were lower and therefore more teachers could be employed if they were women than if they were men. At a time of such drastic shortage every extra teacher was worth her weight in gold.

Schools need teachers but the new type of schools that Germany had promised herself in the post-war era demanded a new strain of teachers altogether if they were to fulfil their obligations towards the new generation of children. It fell to the training colleges to cast the new teacher in an entirely fresh mould, stressing his development as an individual rather than as a teacher of a given subject, however much this conflicted with the traditional German love of exact scholarship. The administrative and organisational reforms already mentioned could hardly be expected to produce the required personal qualities except perhaps as fortuitous by-products. The extension of the curriculum in the colleges helped considerably by introducing subjects that had to be lived rather than learned. Life in the colleges and in the community around them was, however, the most fertile agent. By the time a trainee had finished his course he had had experience of the college's role in the community where it belonged and practice in discharging his responsibilities towards the communal life of the college itself. Every intake of students was encouraged to join in the running of college activities and to find scope for personal development within them. Students' Representative Councils were formed for the education of the students and not only for the protection of their interests. Perhaps as a result of this, when the interests of the whole college were at stake it came to be accepted that the S.R.C.s had a voice worth listening to and a useful part to play in consultation with the staff of the college.

In the post-war period when the colleges were being given a new character and a new role to play in German society the contribution made by international contacts was of supreme importance. Education Branch devoted the maximum time, effort and finance to the arrangement of visits to and from the United Kingdom by British and German experts active in the field of teacher training and, in doing so, enjoyed the fullest and most generous support from the Ministry of Education, the local education authorities, the teacher training colleges and innumerable associations, societies and individuals in Britain. Visits to Britain were arranged for individuals or for groups from German colleges, lasting from a fortnight to a term or even a whole academic year. The students were able to attend lectures and join in the life of the colleges and the German staffs met their English opposite numbers and compared notes on current problems and practices. Attendance at international conferences, summer school and vacation courses was made possible and provided opportunities for German and British teacher training experts to consult with one another. The groups varied considerably in size, the student groups being understandably much larger than those composed of staff lecturers or administrators. At first, costs were borne entirely by Education Branch but later they were shared with the German educational authorities and with many other generous sources in Britain.

These conferences, courses and visits varied considerably in length, scope and purpose but they all had one common element, the meeting of minds and the sharing of problems and points of view. Of all these visits and contacts there are two that deserve to be singled out for special mention not only because they were unique of their kind but because there was an element of permanence in both of them. The Berlin teacher training college had been restarted in the Russian sector of the city after the War and, although it was administered on a quadripartite basis, the political influence exerted by the Soviet authorities became eventually intolerable. When the split in the city came, the staff and students, with the support of the Allied authorities, decided to pay a permanent visit to the West. The new Pädagogische Hochschule which was opened in the American Sector, three days after their move, had all bar about ten per cent of the staff and students and, as a bonus, several of the schools used for teaching practice. The second example worth quoting was the Wilkinson Foundation, created by the students of Lüdenscheid teacher training college in memory of the Education Control Officer responsible for teacher training in Westphalia. He was killed in a car accident in December 1948. The students of the college agreed to contribute to a fund to enable foreign students to attend the college free of charge for a term or even a whole year.

These then were some of the ideas that were brought to bear on the recasting of teacher training in Germany after the War and some of the means that were employed in the hope that a new spirit would arise answering to the demands of the post-war period—a spirit attractive enough to inspire the new strain of teachers and, in time, all those others who share the responsibility for understanding and guiding a dazed and difficult generation of youth in desperate need of new ideals.

When the Military Government took over the German universities in 1945 a University Control Office (UCO) was appointed at each university[1] in the British Zone with the task of helping the process of material and academic reconstruction and, in the words of Mr Robert Birley, of 'calling forth a body of men, dedicated to the task of rousing once more the love of freedom, and the readiness to accept personal responsibility for the actions of the community'. The University Control Officers were all fluent in German and well acquainted with German history, institutions and traditions.

The first period of reconstruction lasted until the beginning of 1947; before this the UCO, later designated University Education Control Officer (UECO), had absolute power over the university to which he or she was attached, subject to instructions from the Military Governor through his Educational Adviser, Mr Donald Riddy, a senior member of H.M. Schools Inspectorate, who was succeeded in 1947 by Mr Birley and in 1949 by Professor T. H. Marshall, who had been Head of the German Section of the Research Department of the Foreign Office.

Having been demobilised after six years in the army I arrived in Göttingen in December 1945 to 'take charge' of the university at which I had been an exchange student and later *Lektor* some fifteen years earlier. My posting to Göttingen was pure coincidence, but it made things easier for me as I was familiar with its systems and traditions and still knew some of the teaching staff by reputation if not personally. The university had suffered only little material damage compared with others in the British Zone, and I was therefore spared many of the formidable difficulties of material reconstruction with which my colleagues elsewhere had to contend, and was able to concentrate my efforts mainly on the rehabilitation of the academic and administrative staff, the admission of students, and the encouragement of a return to normal university activities. This was, of course, only possible with German co-operation and so it was necessary to build up an amicable relationship first with the *Rektor* and the *Kurator* and then with reliable members of the teaching and administrative staff, and later with students.

The *Rektor* is the approximate equivalent of a Vice-Chancellor at a British university but elected from and by the professoriate for a period of one, or in some cases two years. The *Kurator*, for whom there is no equivalent in the United Kingdom, is a permanent government official representing the Education Minister of the *Land* Government to ensure that the educational policy of the *Land* is being adhered to and through whom staff appointments proposed by the university have to be confirmed.[2] This system varied at the different universities but the principle of *Land* control applied throughout the Zone. It was thus essential to have the co-operation of both the *Rektor* and the *Kurator* if we were to succeed in finding that 'body of men . . . ready to accept personal responsibility for the actions of the community'.

I worked closely with the first *Rektor* and the *Kurator*. They were certainly not Nazis, and the only slight opposition the *Rektor* occasionally showed towards our policy was, I felt, motivated by the well-founded suspicion that we were aiming to break the traditional system of oligarchic government of the universities and to make possible the development of democratic ideas. He was therefore inclined to be highly suspicious of the appointment of young progressive lecturers. By and large the *Rektoren* of all the universities in the British Zone co-operated well with the UECOs, and as far as I know only two were removed from office for alleged obstructive tactics.

The task of finding reliable members of the staff was made no easier by the considerable amount of conflicting evidence and the denunciations which were forthcoming from a few professors about some of their colleagues. Sometimes these denunciations proved correct, while a few, less reliable, were inspired by personal jealousies and grudges, and it was not always easy to elicit the facts.

Before we approved the appointment of a member of staff he had to fill in a *Fragebogen* (questionnaire) giving full details

of his past activities, particularly membership of or positions held
in Nazi organisations. The withholding of information or the
making of false statements carried very heavy penalties. After
reading through the *Fragebogen,* interviewing some of the applicants and making discreet enquiries, I would pass all relevant
documents, with my comments, on to the Public Safety Branch,
which consisted mainly of police officers seconded from the
United Kingdom, whose knowledge of Germany and the German
language was limited and who sometimes found it difficult to
appreciate the significance of the difference between active and
passive membership of Nazi organisations. They were inclined
to oppose the appointment of professors who I felt were, in spite
of previous technical membership of such organisations, genuine
in their desire to co-operate in rebuilding the university as a
democratic and socially responsible and influential institution.
If the appointment of everyone who had been technically a
member of a Nazi organisation had been disallowed there would
have been very few qualified university teachers left. The Public
Safety officers with whom I had to deal were, however, without exception co-operative and helpful, ready to consider any
extenuating circumstances which were brought to their notice
concerning a particular person.

Actions by some of the occupying forces due to ignorance
about Germany would occasionally cause resentment amongst
the Germans and hinder our efforts to gain co-operation. An
outstanding example of this occurred in 1946 when a British
army sergeant ordered Professor Max Planck, the eighty-eight-
year-old physicist and Nobel Prize holder, who had given no
support whatsoever to the Nazis, to vacate his house at short
notice on the grounds that it was required by the army. News of
this rapidly reached the Prime Minister, Mr Attlee, who
promptly sent a telegram requesting immediate information
on the incident and an assurance that Professor Planck was not
being disturbed. The sergeant apologised and withdrew his
order.

In the early post-war period the *Rektor* and the *Kurator*
would call to see me in my office daily and discuss questions
concerning appointments and the shortage of materials and
equipment, and to consult me regarding the attitude of the
Military Government towards the policies they and their col-

leagues wished to pursue. I also attended the Senate[3] meetings, where I endeavoured to clarify our policy and answer questions. I was occasionally asked to express my views on differences among themselves over questions of internal academic policy which were not the concern of the Military Government. These meetings were amicable though the members did not always regard our policy with favour. Their criticisms were nevertheless of value in enabling us in Education Branch to understand the views prevailing among the German staff and could help us in forming our attitude. At no time did I experience or sense any feeling of hostility and any criticisms were always expressed with the utmost courtesy.

The same system of *Fragebogen* applied to the admission of students, but here we were faced with enormous numbers of applicants, mostly ex-servicemen still in tattered field grey uniforms and worn-out boots. Many were still dazed by disillusionment, a few were arrogant and unfriendly, but all were keen to get down to their studies. Theoretically they had to be politically vetted, but the task was too formidable even for the officers of Public Safety Branch and most admissions were approved without the *Fragebogen* having been passed on to them.

The university authorities, overwhelmed with applications, found it well nigh impossible to check academic qualifications and would admit more students than they could really fit in, realising that a large number would fail to complete their courses. Living accommodation was extremely difficult to find, particularly in the more heavily destroyed towns, and students were forced to live in primitive conditions, often without heat or light and with the minimum of food. The situation was further complicated by the German system which allows students to move around to various universities during their course of study, and by the influx of thousands of refugees from the East entering the Zone through the nearby reception centre at Friedland. In several universities students were admitted only on condition that they had worked for a period clearing bombed sites or building huts for temporary accommodation. In Göttingen thousands of books from the university library had been stored for safety miles away in some salt mines and after being transported back to the university were replaced in some sort of order on the shelves by groups of men and women students who

spent several weeks acting as 'chain gangs' passing them up
from temporary huts in which they had been dumped. There
were no student grants, but with the help of Education Branch
some were able to find jobs to enable them to earn enough
for food and rent, attending what lectures they could find time
for but getting very little sleep.

There was an almost complete lack of teaching materials,
books, stationery and equipment. It was quite common for one
student among a group of friends to take notes at lectures on a
scrap of paper with the one available pencil and pass them round
later on loan to the others. Education Branch did its best to alleviate the situation but our resources were also strictly limited. When
Lord Pakenham, now the Earl of Longford, who as Chancellor of
the Duchy of Lancaster in 1947 was responsible for German
affairs, came out on a fact-finding tour, and after addressing
groups of students on policy in the British Zone asked for questions, it was significant that nearly all the questions concerned the
urgent need for the simplest of materials, such as pens, pencils,
paper, blankets and articles of clothing. He made detailed notes of
their requirements and his promise to do everything possible to
remedy the shortages certainly raised their morale and reassured
them as to our intentions. But conditions remained extremely difficult until the middle of 1948 when the currency reform changed
the situation almost overnight.

When the appointment of staff and admission of students had
been more or less completed our efforts were concentrated on
getting to know as many of them as possible and finding and
encouraging those with a genuine belief in the possibility of a
democratic future for Germany who were at the same time prepared to put their belief into practice. I think we had more
success with the students than with the staff, as many of the latter
were seldom willing to risk the disfavour of their own particular
head of department and so jeopardise their academic future,
unless they knew he shared their views. I am not suggesting that
the majority of the professors did not want a democratic Germany, but that many were not keenly in favour of democracy in
the universities.

I had many informal discussions with students on all sorts of
questions, often long into the night. They wanted to know
everything possible about the outside world—what had happened

before and during the War, how much we considered them responsible for events, why everyone had 'turned against them' and what they could themselves do to help to restore democratic government and build up a peaceful and prosperous state. They felt strongly the need for the universities to regain the respect of the general public and to play a leading role in public discussion on social and political issues, and they were very interested in the British tradition whereby such issues could be influenced by letters from academics to papers like *The Times*. Their questions were startling in the implication of the state of mind behind them, as when a student asked a visiting British MP in 1946 why we had not yet launched an offensive against the Russians in order to rescue the many thousands of German prisoners of war, whether we intended to do so, and if not why not. The question met with applause from the audience, but not the reply!

Students were much preoccupied in their minds with the question of individual responsibility during the war years and the ethics of breaking the *Fahneneid* (oath of allegiance) by plotting to overthrow the Nazi régime. When word got round that a leading ex-officer student, Axel von dem Bussche, who had taken part in the plot against Hitler's life, was to speak publicly justifying his position, many hundreds turned up and a long and at times heated discussion ensued. I was present only as an observer, but it was occasions like that which helped us in our understanding of the German mind and therefore in our work in trying to influence it.

The students needed much advice and encouragement in organising their own affairs, such as the formation of a student union, *Allgemeiner Studentenausschuss* (ASTA). They needed guidance in simple democratic procedures, such as electing their officers and committee, setting up committees dealing with problems of accommodation and student welfare, and how to chair a meeting. They were inclined to wait for orders from someone.

On the German side valuable assistance was given by Professor Erich Boehringer (an eminent archaeologist, whose obituary appeared in *The Times* recently). As *Geschäftsführer* (chairman) of the *Akademisches Hilfswerk* (Academic Welfare Organisation) he was untiring in his determination to improve the students' lot and to encourage them to think and act for themselves. It was his initiative also which led to the foundation of the first student hostel *(Die Börse)* in Göttingen on the lines of a British hall of residence. His enthusiasm for this project inspired him to launch a campaign among industrialists and public bodies to raise the necessary funds and he persuaded many student volunteers to work on the site. He had to overcome tremendous difficulties in obtaining tools and materials from every conceivable source. We helped where possible, mainly in assuring various authorities of his integrity! He frequently called in for advice. In the early days of the project when the only transport at his disposal was an ancient truck, he managed to acquire four urgently needed tyres (items almost unobtainable by the Germans at that time) which were only too obviously of British army origin, which meant he was liable to be stopped and arrested by the Military Police. Fortunately I was able to give him a carefully worded document with an official *Stempel* (stamp) testifying that he was entitled to the use of the tyres as he was on official business carrying out a project strongly supported by Education Branch. I was also able to supply him with documents confirming that he needed various materials and items of equipment, not for disposal on the black market, which was a favourite German pursuit, but for use in furtherance of educational reconstruction. He even managed to smuggle materials from the Russian Zone, at considerable personal risk. *Die Börse* still exists as a very fine student residence.

When at the beginning of 1947 the conduct of educational affairs in the British Zone was handed over to German authorities we were no longer officially 'in control' and were there only 'to help and advise.' We now became 'University Education Officers' (UEOs), dropping the word 'control'. This made very little difference at first; we had, after all, been working in an atmosphere of co-operation and mutual understanding for several months and there seemed to be no general desire on the part of the universities for us to desert them. They still needed advice and encouragement. I continued to have frequent informal talks with the *Rektor* and the *Kurator* and was invited to continue to attend the meetings of Senate. The informal talks were most helpful—the 'advice' was by no means one-sided as we too had much to learn about German problems in general, and to this end we from time to time attended meetings of the zonal *Rektorenkonferenz* and also inter-Zonal ones with our opposite numbers in the American and French Zones, including one at Halle with the Russians[4].

During the period 1948-50 I was extremely fortunate in having Professor Ludwig Raiser, an eminent lawyer, as *Rektor*. His contribution to the development of the universities was outstanding and he had a full appreciation of the problems ahead of them. He later became President of the *Deutsche Forschungs-gemeinschaft*, 1952-55, and of the *Deutscher Wissenschaftsrat*, 1961-65.

With the German authorities now in control of education the emphasis of our work shifted from reconstruction to encouraging as much contact with the outside world as possible. Through Education Branch large numbers of university staff and students were enabled to visit the United Kingdom, where they were given opportunities of meeting university teachers and students, and a scheme organised by the British Council in co-operation with Education Branch provided for twenty carefully selected university teachers each year to spend a year at a British University. Candidates for these visits were selected not only for their academic qualities but also for their personalities, in the hope that they would later play an influential part in the development of democratic ideas both in the universities and in German social and political life.

We also arranged, with the help of the Foreign Office, for a series of visits to the British Zone by university teachers, writers, scientists, politicians and theatre groups. These visitors gave public lectures, sometimes in German, or in English through an interpreter, held discussions with leading Germans and talked with groups of staff and students. The lectures were nearly always crowded, particularly when they were in English, as the Germans would seize every opportunity to improve their English and would attend even when they had little interest in the subject. Discussions following the lectures were often greatly enlivened by the enthusiasm of the German audience, but the interest aroused in the subject would continue long after the visitor had left.

A notable occasion was the tour of the Zone by Lord Beveridge. Everyone seemed to have heard of the Beveridge Plan and his lectures were so crowded that they had to be relayed to other rooms and even into the streets nearby. Another memorable visit was by T. S. Eliot, who talked about and read extracts from his works, and held discussions with large groups of enthusiastic students, some of whom had come from other Zones specially to hear him. They not only asked a great many questions but also expressed their own views on his writings, and towards the end of his tour he remarked to me that after three weeks in Germany he had learnt more about what he meant in his works than he had dreamt of.

The first International Vacation Course in Göttingen was held in 1949 under Education Branch auspices. The effect of this and the atmosphere prevailing at the time is probably best illustrated by the following extract from a letter I recently received from the senior British student on the Course, Roger Henderson from Edinburgh University. He wrote :

It was the first time since before the War that British students had been in Germany (as civilians) and I remember the sense of trepidation we had on crossing the frontier (after some hilarious experiences, missing connections in Holland because our crossing was delayed—we eventually reached the frontier by taxi and crossed on foot, to the astonishment and considerable mistrust of the Dutch and also the occupying forces' frontier guards!) In Aachen we stayed overnight in the evocatively named Bunker Hotel, and in our innocence did not realise what it was or had been until we started to descend to our little cells (exactly what they were!) in the bowels of the earth. I slept rather fitfully . . . The intention of the Course was I feel fundamentally academic but my memories are entirely of getting to know, and therefore losing my inhibitions about, people of my own age, generation and to a large degree experience (i.e. post-military service) in a country which for all my adult life (from the age of thirteen) had been 'enemies'. We went to the theatre together—in the gods to a performance of Tasso, we went to have a look at a film studio (a large empty barn with a few floodlights)[5], walked and talked in the garden in the sunshine and ate sticky cakes. And we talked over beer and 'acorn' coffee in the evening and well into the night. I remember sitting on a second floor balcony in the moonlight listening to the final chorus of the St

Matthew Passion on old 78 gramophone records with some German and English friends and Susanna the German girl who translated (or perhaps corrected) the draft of my speech for the closing ceremony in the Aula of the university, and realising in that music the underlying waste of the previous ten years. The music was new to me then, and always, when I hear it now it evokes a very strong emotional reaction.

In the early days of the Occupation it was customary that we should make any public statements in English through an interpreter. This could have its hazards. At the reopening of the Mining Academy at Clausthal-Zellerfeld I had to make a short speech to the assembled staff and students. The staff and civic dignitaries in their magnificent robes occupied the front seats in the Aula, with several hundred students in the rows behind. In the course of my speech I said :

'I am sure you students will fully appreciate the difficulties which the staff here had to face in reopening this Academy.'

Concentrating on my next few words I failed to listen to the German interpreter, but suddenly became aware of loud and enthusiastic applause from the students and hostile glares from the staff. After the ceremony the *Rektor*, who was a good friend of mine, explained to me that the interpreter had said :

'*Angesichts dieses Lehrkörpers werden Sie die Schwierigkeiten gut vertsehen, die wir bei der Wiedereröffnung dieser Akademie hatten.*'

('In face of this staff here you will fully understand the difficulties we had in reopening this Academy').

Fortunately the *Rektor* understood English well and was able to reassure his colleagues that I had praised them, not insulted them. Nevertheless I was conscious for some weeks afterwards of a slight reserve towards me on the part of some of the staff and an extremely friendly attitude from some of the students. It transpired that some of the staff were convinced that the *Rektor* was merely trying to gloss over the insult implied by my words.

By 1949 Education Branch had begun to set up British centres throughout the Zone rather on the lines of British Council Centres in other countries, their aim being to further interest in and knowledge of British institutions and the British way of life. The centres (each centre was called *Die Brücke*) were either in existing buildings, suitably adapted, or in new purpose-built buildings. They comprised lecture rooms, reading rooms with English journals and newspapers, discussion rooms, libraries, exhibition rooms and facilities for providing refreshments and entertaining visitors. In some cases the buildings were extended to include a small cinema or concert hall. The libraries were well stocked with English books on a wide variety of subjects.

Each centre was under the supervision of a British Director who in the university towns would usually be the UEO, who had to arrange a monthly programme of meetings—lectures, discussions, films, exhibitions, and visits from prominent personalities from the United Kingdom. The centres were used extensively and no doubt made a lasting contribution to Anglo-German understanding. Unfortunately the smaller ones had later to be closed for economic reasons, but the larger ones were taken over by the British Council and still exist.

By about 1951 our work as University Education Officers virtually ceased with the Germans having by now taken over all responsibility for their educational affairs, but we left with the feeling that we had helped in forming a permanent link with the Germans, with mutual ideals of friendship and co-operation, a link which has grown stronger with the years.

NOTES

1. Kiel, Hamburg, Göttingen with the Mining Academy at Clausthal-Zellerfeld, Münster, Cologne, Bonn, and the Technical Universities at Hanover and Aachen.
2. This could lead to considerable delays in the confirmation of staff appointments either due to pressure of work at *Land* level or in the absence of the official responsible for dealing with applications from the university. In one instance, after the Germans had taken over full responsibility for educational affairs, nearly a year elapsed before decisions were made.
3. The Senate at that time comprised only the *Rektor, Prorektor,*

the Deans of faculties, the *Rektor* designate and a small number of elected members of the professoriate.

4. This conference was attended by representatives of the Education Branches of the four occupying powers and not by Germans. The only common language however proved to be German and the proceedings were therefore held in German.

5. This was given much encouragement by the British authorities and was the forerunner of what has now become the *Institut für den wissenschaftlichen Film.*

The reforms of Oxford University during the 1850s received their main impetus from former pupils of Thomas Arnold's Rugby School who had gone on to become students of Balliol College, Oxford under its most famous and Germanophile Master Benjamin Jowett. A. C. Tait (later Archbishop of Canterbury) had taught at Rugby and had succeeded Thomas Arnold as headmaster of the school in 1850, a year in which he also became a member of the Oxford Commission set up by the Government to suggest reforms of Oxford University. A. P. Stanley, later Dean of Westminster, was the Secretary of the Oxford Commission.

In *The Life and Correspondence of Thomas Arnold* Stanley describes Arnold's admiration of Germany: '[A] new intellectual world dawned upon him, not only in the subject to which it related, but in the disclosure to him of the depth and research of German literature which from that moment he learned more and more to appreciate, and as far as his own occupation would allow him, to emulate'.[1] The Oxford reformers admired the State-supported Prussian universities, free from religious entrance qualifications, and their professors, appointed by the State and dedicated to research.

The classical statement of mid-nineteenth century admiration for the continental education system is to be found in Matthew Arnold's *Schools and Universities on the Continent* of 1868: 'Our university system is a routine . . . but it is our want of science, not our want of liberty, which makes it a routine. It is in science that we have most need to borrow from the German universities. The French university has no liberty, and the English universities have no science; the German universities have both'.[2] Matthew Arnold shared his father's belief that it was the task of the State to educate the new middle classes for political power.[3] At the turn of the century the editor of Friedrich Paulsen's works on German education commended the State's restraint in education but commented on the paradox of the university's intellectual independence and political subordination to State control.[4]

In England and America admiration for the German university survived into the Thirties of this century. Abraham Flexner's standard work *Universities, American, English, German* said of the German university: 'It has stimulated university development in Great Britain; from it has sprung the graduate school of the new world; to it industry and health . . . are infinitely indebted'. A delegation of the English Association of University Teachers reported equally favourably on the German universities in 1931.[5]

By 1946 the pendulum had swung the other way. S. D. Stirk's influential *German Universities Through English Eyes* opened with Palmerston's dictum, 'Germany is a country of damned professors'. Sir Walter Moberly, then Chairman of the University Grants Committee quoted Ortega y Gasset's exclamation, 'How brutal, how stupid, and yet how aggressive is the man learned in one thing and fundamentally ignorant in all else' and continued 'Such an abdication of responsibility was the fatal error of the German universities during the Hitler régime . . .'[6] Just after the War Ortega y Gasset's *Mission of the University*, written in 1930 but not published in England until 1946, added the Spanish thinker's authority to the negative view of the German university in England. His condemnation of the German academic's pedantry masquerading as research, and his call 'to rid contemporary science of its purely German excrescences, its rituals and mere whims, in order to save its essential parts uncontaminated' carried all the more weight because he concluded that he owed four-fifths of his intellectual endowment to Germany.[7]

As late as 1960 Karl Jaspers, *Idee der Universität* evoked in its English editor and commentator 'the memory of the thousands of students who had forsaken the books of Kant for the loudspeakers of Goebbels and the jackboots of the élite guards, the professors who had eagerly believed the nationalistic and racial propaganda, forsaking their standards of critical thinking; and those other professors who, while not believing the doctrines of the Third Reich, yet found it prudent to pretend belief, and not deceived, yet aided the deceivers'.[8] Before the

War it had already been argued in England that '. . . we are witnessing something more than merely "Nazi" or "Fascist" education. We have in effect a new form of the belief that environment can be all-powerful in the moulding of the young of the future'.[9]

The Post-War Role of the University

In the event, Hitler's system opened new sinister perspectives in mass indoctrination through education. German exiles like Adolph Loewe and Karl Mannheim heightened English educationists' awareness of the tacit assumptions on which their social and educational systems were based. Under the significant subtitle 'The New Society' Loewe explained the necessity of allocating to the universities the key role in educating the enlightened expert, who needed to have social, political and moral commitment in addition to his academic or technical expertise.[10] Mannheim and Loewe stressed the need for a planned democracy. Their ideas were widely taken up and their works were quoted by Sir Fred Clarke, then Director of London University Institute of Education and Lord Lindsay, Master of Balliol, former Vice-Chancellor of Oxford, later founder of Keele, the first post-war English university.[11]

The definition of the university as primarily an institution devoted to research and the pursuit of knowledge or as a centre of cultural progress were both rejected as 'strangely and dangerously German'. Sir Walter Moberly exclaimed: 'For God's sake, stop researching for a while and begin to think'. With a side-glance at Germany he added, 'If the "intellectuals", in large part trained in universities, decline to interest themselves in public affairs, the practical alternative is abandonment to the adventurer, the spell-binder and the mob'.[12] In England renewed emphasis was placed on the educational aspect of the university. This emphasis was, of course, rooted in the faith in the educability of man and in the effectiveness of planning for his moral and political improvement: 'If we could solve the problem of general education, we could confidently strike any third world war off the calendar. General education means the whole development of an individual, apart from his occupational training. It includes the civilising of his life purpose . . .

and the maturing of his understanding about the nature of things according to the best knowledge of our time'.[13]

Faced with the rise of the middle classes, Thomas and Matthew Arnold had felt it their duty 'to educate our masters'.[14] Twentieth-century English educators felt: '. . . today it is the turn of what we compendiously call "the masses", and government of the people, for the people, is in sight, if not here'.[15] Even during the Second World War Sir Fred Clarke and Sir Richard Livingstone had warned against the smug attitude of 'It can never happen here', pointing out that the forces at work were not just Communist or Fascist, that they were, in the ultimate resort, historical. At the height of the War Lord Lindsay had written in a preface to Amy Buller's very sympathetic account of *Darkness over Germany*: 'The most alarming obstacle to our hopes for Europe is the state of mind of the German youth. If we are going to have the least chance of bringing young Germans back to sanity after Germany is beaten, we had better understand what made them insane'.[16]

England emerged from the War weakened but victorious and with the consciousness of enormous moral prestige in Europe.[17] This was as much an asset as an obligation. 'If the next generation of Germans finds that democracy is not a reality in the countries that profess it, no educational or personal methods will make Germany democratic'.[18] From 1947 on the British Zone had an Educational Adviser who was directly responsible to the Deputy Military Governor. The first of those Educational Advisers was Sir Robert Birley who had been educated at Rugby and Balliol and from 1935 to 1937 had been Headmaster of Charterhouse.

Sir Robert Birley resembled Thomas and Matthew Arnold in his profound knowledge of German history, literature and culture. In his various lectures and addresses during his term of office, in later addresses to the Deutsch-Englische Gesellschaft, and in lectures delivered in South Africa and England he made reference to St Boniface, Ludger (first bishop of Münster, educated at York), the German influence on the English Common Prayer Book, Goethe, Nietzsche, Albert Schweizer, Max Weber, Pater Delp, Kardinal Graf von Galen. In other words, he spoke to Germans in terms of their own history, philosophy and literature at a time when their recent past pre-

F

vented a backward glance at their national identity in terms of
history. He consciously defined the tasks ahead with reference to
Germany's recent past :

> . . . to all who are now called or will soon be called to posi-
> tions of leadership and guidance, one can only say remorse-
> lessly : 'Mindful of the fearful disaster that followed the
> élite-less so-called "Weimar period", your business is to look
> to your successors, to create a mechanism of élite-making
> in which personalities of intellectual eminence with a bent for
> politics can come to the top, every bit as much as to see that
> the poor shattered German people somehow get work and
> bread . . . and are trained up in self-government in the
> mass.[19]

Birley insisted that Germany's future élite needed to be a serving
meritocracy rather than one founded on inherited privileges, and
explained :

> The main duty which lies before the British in Germany
> who deal with German education . . . is to help to call forth
> this body of men, dedicated to the task of rousing once more
> in the Germans through education the love of freedom, the
> readiness to accept personal responsibility for the actions of
> the community, which seem to have been lost to the nation.[20]

Birley deliberately proclaimed his faith in Germany's regeneration although he had not minced his words on her previous
failures :

> For there is no escape from the fact that the Germans, at the
> time of the Nazis' rise to power, failed to show that almost
> primitive and unconscious reaction, which is the basis of social
> morality of ordinary people, of exclaiming that there are some
> actions which are beyond the pale.[20a]

Birley did not spare the German university the reproach of
having failed politically. He said of the German professors :
'They display the worst failings of a subservient civil service. The
universities are entirely cut off from a large part of German
society, by which they are despised and hated.' At the same time
he pointed out the glorious past of the German universities and
their challenging future : 'The future of German civilisation

largely depends on them and it is, perhaps, our first duty to try to help them.'[21]

At first, reconstructing the German universities was literally a matter of bricks and mortar, plus fiddling an extra supply of gas for the Bunsen burners, at which ragged students could warm their hands prior to taking notes in discarded exercise books donated by English schools.

The AUT Delegation

A year after they had been reopened a delegation of the English Association of University Teachers (AUT) was invited to tour German universities and to offer advice on the question 'What measures are necessary to enable the German universities to play their part in a new democratic Germany?'

In order to introduce democratic methods which would ensure consultation and publicity the AUT delegation suggested the creation of University Councils. They were to bridge the gulf between the universities and the world at large, to give the representatives of the Ministry of Education, of other branches of education, political parties, Churches, chambers of commerce, and trade unions on the Council some influence in framing the outlook of the universities. A previous attempt by the British authorities at bringing trade unions, parties, and universities into closer contact had been 'noteworthy for the abyss it revealed between the attitudes of the Rectors and the Trade Union and Party representatives'.

Proposals for the creation of a body of full-time lecturers were modelled on the English example, as were proposals for an association of university teachers as a collective representative body; for the university's annual budget to be allocated as a block grant; for strengthening the Rector's position by extending his term of office; for enlarging the power and scope of Senate to make it the governing body of the university at the expense of all-powerful faculties or individual professors; for advertising vacancies; for submitting higher degree papers to external examiners; for broadening the social composition of the student body, relating admissions to capacities by introducing university entrance examinations with a view to ascertaining suitability of character as well as academic promise.

The 1931 AUT delegation to Germany had commented favourably on the post of *Kurator* (the representative of the Ministry in the university), on the professorial system, and on the principle of *Lehrfreiheit* and *Lernfreiheit*. 'We were left with the impression that this basic principle is, in general, operated with every endeavour to secure justice to both the advancement of knowledge and the satisfaction of those to whom it is imparted'.[22] Under the impression of recent events the AUT delegation eventually came to the conclusion that no lasting reform was likely to come about on the sole initiative of the universities and recorded its distrust of the 'conservative, nationalistic and even reactionary attitudes noticeable in many of the German universities today' and of 'this particularist and individualist spirit in the German universities [which] is a result of the special interpretation of academic freedom known as *Lehr- und Lernfreiheit*, which can in practice become perverted into a state of anarchy tempered by professional tyranny'.[23] Such criticism from outside and foreigners, on the basis of what they had seen in a fortnight, together with their proposals for international inspection of German universities, secured the report a very unfavourable reception in Germany and debarred any likelihood of measures being taken on its recommendations. Robert Birley later considered the appointment of foreign arbiters on the German university a tactical mistake.

The German Commission on University Reform

Another attempt was made in 1948 when Birley obtained the consent of the four German Ministers of Education for the appointment of a German Commission to investigate a reform of the German universities. It was a radically new departure to have only four professors on the new commission, which comprised representatives of many other political and social bodies. To put the all-German Commission in touch with foreign universities Professor von Salis of the Technical University of Zürich, and Lord Lindsay, then Master of Balliol, were appointed. The Commission was left to work out its recommendations independently, to the extent that the Educational Adviser refused to attend its meetings. Nevertheless, from sheer force of argument and weight of personality Lord Lindsay influenced the findings of the Commission so much that it was later said that parts of the report read like 'pure Lindsay', and that in its day it was widely known as the Lindsay Report and that the Commission was then and is to the present day mistakenly called the Lindsay Commission.[24]

In the history of English adult education A. D. Lindsay[25] ranks among the great university teachers like T. H. Green, Arnold Toynbee, R. H. Tawney, who felt that their privileges as academics imposed upon them special duties as citizens. They made their mark as teachers of the Workers' Educational Association, conducting evening classes in industrial centres for those whose school training, social origin, or employment had prevented them from going on to higher education.

The WEA movement was a manifestation of the social and political conscience of the English universities and derived a great deal of its impetus from Jowett's and Lindsay's Balliol College. It is worth noting that Balliol provided the first Vice-Chancellors (Lord Lindsay, Lord Fulton) of the first English post-war universities of Keele and Sussex and that many key figures in the Anglo-German dialogue—George Allen, Heinz Koeppler, T. H. Marshall, Werner Burmeister—were leading figures in WEA work, which requires a great deal of social commitment, dedication and enthusiasm.

Before the War Lindsay had arranged conferences with leading German academics and politicians; during the War he received intelligence about the activities of the German opposition to Hitler as well as an account of conditions in a concentration camp. He was deeply concerned about the causes that had made young Germans accept Hitler. An enquiry into the state of mind of young unemployed men between eighteen and twenty-five in South Wales, Liverpool and Glasgow prompted him to reflect on their cynicism, fatalism and disillusionment in 1942 : 'To produce young men like that is to prepare for another Hitler.' He went on to argue the State's responsibility for the education of all young people, not just the gifted ones, up to the age of eighteen. 'We have to see that at the end of their training our young men and women are fit for citizenship'.[26] On the commission he argued fiercely against the view of some of its German members that the university, called to serve the

idea of *Wissenschaft,* was to educate the intellectual aristocracy of the nation, while lesser bodies were to train the less
well-endowed. He called a German member's conception of an
academic aristocracy sinful and evil, maintaining that the middle
classes could well look after themselves and that it was the lower
classes which deserved the greatest educational effort.[27]

It was this view which prompted Lindsay to take a particular
interest in the role German universities played in adult education. Among his papers is a heavily scored and annotated report
on Adult Education in the British Zone, submitted by three
HM Inspectors and a delegation of nine educationists who had
travelled through Germany in 1946 and 1947. The report quoted
a British *Directive on Education* of November 1945, which
charged all institutions of adult education to educate adults 'to
develop the capacity for independent thought . . . and to encourage a feeling of deep responsibility towards the community
in which they live'. The report expressed concern at the tendency
of German educationists to accept the formula that education
begins with the individual and at the fact that to most Germans
the idea of democracy was associated with military and political
defeats and the failure of the Weimar Republic.

To bring German adult education into closer touch with
reality and to introduce a more democratic element, Lindsay
worked hard to get the German trade unions and co-operative
societies to co-operate on worker's education on the lines of
what had happened in Britain some forty years earlier. Here was
the socialist and ardent advocate of the Workers' Educational
Association hoping for a democratisation of the German university through the influence of independent Workers' Educational
Associations of university standard, arguing that 'this independence of a working class organisation from either universities or
political parties is even more important in Germany than it was
in England'.[28] He argued on these lines at an Anglo-German
Trade Unionists' Conference on Adult Education in May
1949, which he had instigated because the Commission on
University Reform had agreed that the German university was
totally isolated from society, which caused mutual distrust
between the workers and the university. The British delegates
felt that this could best be overcome by educating all adults
for civic responsibility and by inducing a strong German

Workers' Educational Movement to influence the universities. Lindsay proposed the establishment of Extra-Mural Departments of Adult Education at all German universities on the English model to give the university greater educational responsibility for the community in which it was situated.[29]

The *Report of University Reform in Germany* of 1948 started from the basic assumption that the German universities had not kept in step with the social changes of the times, that they trained the specialist intellectual, not the whole man, and that universities which did not teach the students to fulfil their duty within the social body 'must be faced one day not with constructive proposals for their reform but with indiscriminate revolution'.[30] The *Report* suggested setting aside the first year at university for a compulsory comprehensive programme of general education to be arranged in a *studium generale*. The Commission recommended the linking of basic studies and student halls of residence. There were proposals for tutorials to discuss the lectures of the *studium generale* and tutorial essays to help assess the students' work. Emphasis was placed on the university's educational task towards those students who do not feel called to research, on the practice of democratic forms in the community life of students, and on the diffusion of the scientific spirit beyond the university.

Throughout his working life Lindsay had placed his duties as a teacher above those as a researcher. He had said in the House of Lords in 1947, 'We talk quite lightly about the indispensability of research, but I do not consider that knowledge which reaches nobody but its discoverer is worth very much . . . I really do not think knowledge is much good unless you manage to spread it through the people and use it in the population'.[31] The *Report on University Reform in Germany* said, 'We dissociate ourselves from those conceptions which put, not man, but research in the foremost place. We believe that university activity is justified only in so far as it renders service to man'.[32] Birley's successor as Educational Adviser, T. H. Marshall continued Birley's and Lindsay's argument about the social and political responsibility of the university. The German Commission had argued similarly that the German university must become the training ground for politically responsible leaders who were more than research specialists nurtured in an ivory tower.[33]

The university's independence from the State and its corporate sense of responsibility for the community was to be strengthened by the establishment of a University Advisory Council. In addition to representatives of the university and of the Minister of Education, it was to be composed of representatives of organisations and corporations interested in university education. The Council's composition and function of receiving annual reports point to the Court in English universities as its model. A University Council, consisting of six honorary members, was suggested as the chief organ of self-government. Its President, modelled on the English Vice-Chancellor, in the independent position of a High Court Judge, was to replace the *Kurator,* the government official, in the university and to set the *Rektor* free for his academic responsibilities. To strengthen corporate self-government, university matters were no longer to be negotiated between the Faculties or the Heads of Departments and the Ministry, but between the Council, headed by the President, and the Ministry. The University Council's budgeting powers and the allocation of funds as a block grant were to serve the same purpose.

The proposed University Council, elected, one third each, by University Council, Senate, and the *Land* Government, and the university's autonomy in managing its finances were obviously influenced by the example of English universities, as were the proposals for creating a substantial body of salaried lecturers. Proposals for the creation of 'Tutor Lecturers' and 'Professor Tutors' with research qualifications, but with greater emphasis on teaching took account of conditions peculiar to the German universities. Recommendations for the extension of the Senate to include representatives of the non-established members of staff were made because '. . . if there is *one* place where democracy should be realised and practised, that place is in the universities. They are large enough to form a state in miniature, and yet small enough to create within themselves social forms not merely organised but also organic'.[34]

In accordance with Robert Birley's principle of teaching the Germans democracy by example rather than by precept while, at the same time, offering a maximum of help and information, the German Commission had been left to reach its own conclusions. The accidental fact that Lord Lindsay had led it to accept the English university as a model in many respects secured the *Report* a particularly favourable reception in England.

In reporting on the German Commission's findings the British press emphasised the novel departure by pointing out that the Commission had resembled a British Royal Commission. Commentators attached great hopes to the fact that the recommendations represented a great co-operative effort of so many groups of German society, with the universities represented by only three professors and the head of a teachers' training college alongside representatives of the Churches, the trade unions, the co-operative societies and the Ministries of Education. The proposals most commented upon were those for changes likely to bring the German university nearer the English system.

The German press was unanimous in its enthusiastic reception of the *Report*. It likened the *Report's* ninety-five proposals to those of Luther.

In the autumn of 1948 Adolph Loewe, then professor at the Institute of World Affairs, New York, wrote: 'I still feel that the intellectuals are the least promising part of the German population particularly since all three Occupation authorities have done rather a poor job in weeding out the universities'.[35] One month previously Lindsay's son had written to his father: 'Several people have come to me and said "Do please tell your Herr Vater that if these proposals are just submitted for the consideration of the universities, the Professors will build a solid front of reaction and fight tooth and nail to have them turned down. And they will succeed!"'[36]

Official German reaction came from a conference of Ministers of Education with the Rectors of the universities in January 1949. The Rectors and representatives of university senates reasserted the university's primary obligation to the perpetuation of knowledge through research, largely rejecting the Commission's emphasis on the university's pragmatic links with society. Arguing from the primacy of scholarship and research, six out of ten speakers rejected the introduction of 'Tutor Lecturers' and 'Professor Tutors', whose emphasis on teaching would introduce a school element into the university. Besides, they were likely to divert the student's allegiance away from his professor. While an increase in staff was welcomed, provided that teaching

F*

was not divorced from scholarship, the Anglo-Saxon tutorial system was deemed inapplicable to the German university, which lacked the English university's tradition of communal living.

The University Court received modified approval as a link between the university and the public. The administrative University Council was rejected by the majority on the grounds that non-salaried part-time members of the Council would determine the fate of an institution with which most of them were not familiar. A Council President, elected for life and potentially elected by a non-academic majority, was feared likely to steer the university into controversial political issues.

The proposals for a *studium generale* received most support and there were accounts of measures taken at various universities to bridge the gap between the disciplines. There were objections to introducing it at the expense of the thirteenth school year and little mention was made of education for citizenship.[37]

British administrators took heart from the fact that the only speeches—by Professor Raiser of Göttingen and Professor Litt of Bonn—to be applauded were those in favour of the *Report*. There was also general satisfaction that nobody had considered the *Report* a foreign importation, that it had been greeted as a historic document and that there had been a great air of freedom and readiness to say unpalatable things at this first gathering of Rectors and Ministers of Education.[38]

Why was the acclaim for the *Report* not matched by action?

1. After the holocaust of war Germany went through a period of restoration in a dual sense of the word : largely at the expense of reforms, every effort had to go into the absorption of 17 million refugees and into restoring at least minimum conditions of living and education.

2. In re-activating Germany's political life the Allies naturally called on personalities who had made their mark during the Weimar Republic and whose time in the wilderness during Germany's recent past put them above suspicion. Faced with the tremendous task of reconstruction, these men in late middle age could not be expected to depart radically from what they had been brought up to.

3. As far as university reform was concerned, there was also a fair amount of vested interest. In a letter to Lord Lindsay Professor Drenkhahn, a member of the German Commission, pointed out that, by way of reform, very little could be expected from the Rectors, backed by their Senates, because they feared that the proposed reforms would deprive the universities of their pseudo-aristocratic privileged positions in society.

4. Under the influence of Lord Lindsay and in a general frame of mind to produce radical blueprints for new departures, the German Commission on University Reform had attempted to replace the State by society as the guardian of the university, asking the latter to produce good members of society rather than efficient administrators of the State. This, of course, presupposed the existence of a homogeneous society, as analysed by Adolph Loewe for Britain. It is for the sociologist to examine how far the absence of a structural society on Loewe's pattern is to blame for the post-war German university's slowness in responding to appeals for reform.

NOTES

1. Arthur P. Stanley, *The Life and Correspondence of Thomas Arnold,* 2 vols., (London, 1881), vol. 1, pp. 39-40.
2. Matthew Arnold, *The Works of M. Arnold* in 15 vols.; vol. 12, *Higher Schools and Universities in France; Higher Schools and Universities in Germany,* (London, 1904), p. 384.
3. W. F. Connell, *The Educational Thought and Influence of Matthew Arnold,* (London, 1950), p. 75.
4. Friedrich Paulsen, *The German University and University Study.* Foreword by M. E. Sadler, (London, 1906), p. VII.
5. Abraham Flexner, *Universities, American, English, German,* (Oxford, 1930 and 1968), p. 315; Association of University Teachers, *The German University System,* (London, 1931).
6. Walter Moberly, *The Universities and Cultural Leadership,* (Oxford, 1951), p. 23.
7. José Ortega y Gasset, *Mission of the University,* (London, 1946), p. 70.

8. Introduction by Karl W. Deutsch to Karl Jaspers, *The Idea of the University,* (London, 1960), p. 15.

9. W. G. R. Hicks, 'German Education. A Retrospect and A Reassessment', *German Life and Letters,* 2, (1937-8), p. 51.

10. Adolph Loewe, *The Universities in Transformation,* (London, 1941), *passim*; especially p. 23.

11. Sir Fred Clarke, *Education and Social Change,* (London, 1940), pp. 8, 11; S. J. Curtis, M. E. A. Boultwood, *An Introductory History of English Education Since 1800,* (London, 1960), pp. 264-5; Sir Richard Livingstone, *Education for A World Adrift,* (Cambridge, 1943), pp. 39-42; Sir Walter Moberly, Chairman of University Grants Committee, *Universities Ancient and Modern,* (Manchester, 1950), pp. 11, 27; Moberly, *The Crisis in the University,* (London, 1949), p. 171; A. D. Lindsay, 'This Freedom', BBC Lecture, 25 March 1940, *The Listener,* 11 April 1940, pp. 742 ff; Lindsay, 'The Universities', *Journal of Education,* 74, (Jan.-Dec. 1942), pp. 437-38; H. C. Dent, *Universities in Transition,* (London, 1961), pp. 111-112; Lindsay, 'A Reprint for the Times', *Rewley House Papers* of the Oxford Delegacy of Extra-Mural Studies, 3, (1961-62), pp. 3-4.

12. Moberly, *Universities and Cultural Leadership,* p. 21.

13. y Gasset, *op. cit.,* p. 1.

14. J. J. Finlay, *Arnold of Rugby. His School Life and Contributions to Education,* (Cambridge, 1897), pp. 198-204.

15. Sir Richard Livingstone, *Education for A World Adrift,* (Cambridge, 1943), p. 2. Topic of rise of new classes also in: Karl Mannheim, *Ideology and Utopia,* (London, 1936), p. 251, in nearly all publications by Lord Lindsay, and Drusilla Scott, *A. D. Lindsay. A Biography,* (Oxford, 1971), p. 388; Lindsay, 'The Function of the Universities', *Nature,* 116, (July-Dec. 1950), pp. 1009-1010; *Toleration and Democracy,* (Oxford, 1941); *I Believe in Democracy.* BBC Address, 1940, (Oxford, 1940) in: *A. D. Lindsay, Selected Addresses,* (Keele, 1957).

16. A. Amy Buller, *Darkness Over Germany,* (London, 1943), p.v.

17. Sir Walter Moberly, *The Crisis in the University,* (London, 1949), p. 19. Similarly Sir Fred Clarke, *Education and Social Change,* (London, 1940), p. 3.

18. Kingsley Martin, 'The Re-Education of Germany', *Political Quarterly,* 15, (1944), p. 147.

19. Robert Birley, The German Problem and the Responsibility of Britain. Burge Memorial Lecture, 3 Dec. 1947, (London, 1947), p. 24.

20. *Ibid.* p. 25.   20a. *Ibid.* pp. 15-16.

21. Robert Birley, 'Education in the British Zone of Germany', *International Affairs,* 26, (Jan. 1950), p. 41.

22. AUT, *The German University System,* (London, 1931), p. 21.

23. Association of University Teachers, *The Universities in the British Zone of Germany,* (London, May 1947), pp. 7, 9.

24. *Norddeutsche Zeitung,* 19 Feb. 1949; *Times Higher Educational Supplement,* 21 Jan. and 26 May 1972.

25. Drusilla Scott, *A. D. Lindsay, A Biography,* (London, 1971).

26. A. D. Lindsay, 'Notes on the Way', *Time and Tide,* 5 and 12 Sept. 1942.

27. Among unpublished Lindsay Papers, Keele University, 'Der Soziologische Hintergrund des Modernen Universitätsproblems'. Undated minutes of a discussion. Internal evidence points to 1949.

28. Undated Memorandum (c. 1949) among Lindsay Papers, 'University Reform and Workers' Education'.

29. *University Reform in Germany.* Report by a German Commission, (London, HMSO, 1949), p. 6.

30. *Hansard,* Lords, v. 147, (1946-47), col. 701, 14 May 1947. Similar : W. B. Gallie, *A New University, A. D. Lindsay and the Keele Experiment,* (London, 1961), p. 112; Scott, *op. cit.,* p. 276.

31. *University Reform in Germany, op. cit.,* p. 11.

32. 'Die Rolle der Universität in der Gegenwart'. Undated MS (c. 1950) among the private papers of T. H. Marshall, Cambridge. *Gutachten zur Hochschulreform,* (no year [London, 1948]), pp. 77-78.

33. *University Reform in Germany, op. cit.,* p. 32.

34. Lindsay Papers : Letter to L., 23 Nov. 1948.

35. Lindsay Papers : Memorandum of eleven lines with marginal note 'From Wilton Park, 24 Oct. 1948'.

36. Lindsay Papers : Ständige Konferenz der Westdeutschen Kultusminister, 'Niederschrift über die Tagung der Kultusminister mit den Rektoren der Hochschulen in Hamburg am 13.1.1949'. Mimeographed MS of twenty-seven pages.

37. Lindsay Papers : R. Birley, 'Meeting of Ministers of Education and Rektors of Universities of the three Western Zones to consider the Report of the University Commission', Hamburg, 13 January 1949. Confidential Report. Mimeographed MS, seven pages; dated 19 January 1949.

9. Technical Education and the 'Zweiter Bildungsweg'

A. W. J. Edwards

The time-span covered in these notes includes the period from October 1946 to November 1948 during which I served in the British Control Commission for Germany as University Control Officer of Aachen Technical University and the period from December 1948 to November 1951 when I was Technical Education Specialist for North Rhine-Westphalia. Some of my subsequent work as Technical Education Specialist for Western Germany with the UK High Commission for Germany has been included as it was largely a continuation of what I was doing during the last stages of the Control Commission. The transition was not as abrupt in practice as in law. Having given advice when we could still have given orders, we were able to persuade when our advice had lost authority.

Writing about thirty years after the events and without access to any documents worth mentioning I cannot claim detailed accuracy for my recollections, but they may have some value as an impressionistic account of the educational climate of the time and of the interaction between the thoughts and attitudes of British officers on the ground and the German officials with whom they were dealing.

The development of vocational education in the British Zone of Germany which resulted in what has become known as *der zweite Bildungsweg* (the alternative educational route) will be used to illustrate these relationships.

The circumstances in which this dialogue took place looked at first anything other than propitious. Until June 1948, when the currency reform gave a foretaste of the German economic miracle yet to come, the material conditions under which our German opposite numbers lived were such that any activity not dictated by the need to survive was sheer self-immolation. I can think of only one exception. An ecclesiastical dignitary presented one of my colleagues with a piece of marzipan and, seeing his astonished face, remarked: 'The Church no longer requires martyrs', a jest which would have come better from a less

weighty source. In the main the description which Victor
Gollancz left us in his book *In Darkest Germany* is correct
although I think he generalises too much when he depicts the
life of members of the Control Commission. No doubt there were
some officers who found a way to enjoy gentle living, but my
own experience and that of most of my colleagues was that food
was far from plentiful and accommodation far from luxurious.

An unexpected outcome of the situation at that time was that
cordial co-operation between the two sides was readily established. That was not just the Englishman's proverbial love for
the underdog. One could not help but respect a man whose mind
was concerned with creating a better world for future genera-
tions while his body cried out for food and warmth. No doubt
we occasionally trusted people who ingratiated themselves with
us as they had with the Nazi hierarchy but such cases were rare.
There were more profitable things to do than to talk education
with the British. Here I feel I must mention the devoted service
of our secretaries and other German personnel whose faithfulness
was left unrewarded when they were no longer required.

If today we can find only few structural changes in the
German educational system which show a British influence, this
is not due to any aloofness on our side nor to a lack of concern.
At the time when we had real power we were more concerned
with giving such practical help as we could than with enforcing
changes other than the removal of obvious relics of the Nazi past.

When I arrived at Aachen the physical damage to the university was obvious and expected. There was little I could do about
it. I pleaded for the allocation of more building material payable
in Reichsmarks which no one wanted. I gave my word that
potential students who worked for one semester on repairing the
buildings would be accepted at the beginning of the next and
had an uneasy time, quite expecting that we might be unable to
keep the university open. Of the voluntary relief organisations
I found the Quakers the most helpful. On one occasion I asked
them whether they could fetch the papers and some furniture
of one of the professors who had fled from the Russian sector of
Berlin to Aachen. I got the cryptic answer : 'This is something
we would like to do'. A fortnight later the precious cargo arrived,
having travelled 800 miles over war-damaged roads and past
two Russian checkpoints without causing a diplomatic incident.

Of the gift parcels which began to arrive I could only obtain two for the university which was at the end of a long pipeline, but a substantial quantity of bacon, a gift which came from the Republic of Ireland, did find its way to the refectory and undoubtedly saved lives. The Senate, not being quite up-to-date in the history of the British Isles, decided to commemorate the event by establishing a permanent scholarship for one English student.

The situation in other universities was similar. I was told that when one of the renowned physicists of Göttingen University was awarded the Nobel prize he travelled in a British military train as far as the German frontier and, as is customary, appeared at the Stockholm function in full evening dress provided by one of my colleagues.

These things seemed very important to us at the time. In retrospect it would be difficult to claim that they come under the heading of German educational reconstruction, but they may have created an atmosphere within the universities which made it more difficult for extreme nationalism to re-emerge.

The damage to the intellectual life of the university and to its academic standards was more severe than I had expected. After a few weeks of studying the situation I came to the conclusion that if the Hitler régime had continued, Germany would have become a backward nation. We now know that it was our superiority in the physical sciences, particularly electronics, which enabled us to preserve our liberty. Immediately after the War, however, we overestimated German science and technology and I was genuinely surprised when I found textbooks for first and second year students which were below sixth form level. The explanation could usually be found in the preface where the author would explain that he had written a 'simplified' text because in the past the demands of scientific studies at *Gymnasium* and university regrettably had not left enough time for 'physical training' and 'education for citizenship'. To my regret overtly Nazi contributions to science, such as Aryan mathematics, had disappeared before I got to Aachen. It would have been interesting to see what heights of imbecility a well-trained human mind can reach. The cock had crowed; the *Walpurgisnacht* was over. When I tried to get a copy of *Mein Kampf* I could not find one anywhere. The ten million copies had vanished. What remained were the bones and ashes of 40 million human beings.

The question was what to put into the empty spaces in German university libraries. Books of a kind were already appearing in 1946 but most of them were little more than expurgated reprints of earlier titles. To help German university teachers to regain lost ground Education Branch obtained from a panel of British experts a list of texts in use in British universities and invited the universities in our Zone to place orders. At the same time a list of scientific instruments was sent out. Payment was to be made in Reichsmarks at an artificial rate of exchange which would have made the books and instruments a free gift. In due course the books arrived and were stored in the cellars of a Hamburg publisher, who had been entrusted with the distribution. He had underestimated the magnitude of the task. The books stayed in the cellars for months and became musty. Suddenly the currency reform was upon us and the books had to be paid for in Deutschmarks which at the time were in very short supply. We had no option but to sell the books at a considerable loss, to anyone who wanted them. Aachen University took some and also honoured its pledge to buy three theodolites although plenty of German instruments had suddenly appeared on the market.

The Aachen professors were well aware that their teaching standards had fallen, but they were unable to assess their position as far as research was concerned and this could not be ascertained by looking at textbooks written for undergraduates. In common with their colleagues in other German universities they had been virtually cut off from foreign universities for ten years and completely for seven. This alone would have been sufficient to cripple German research but there was also the Nazi purge of 1933-4 in the course of which fifteen per cent of the academic staff of the universities had been 'removed from office'. Amongst them had been some of the most brilliant scientists. By contrast the denazification of Aachen University, of which I had first-hand knowledge, removed no one but one or two opportunists whose contribution to science had in any case been negligible. The position may well have been different in universities with strong faculties of law, economics and the arts. Perhaps it should be mentioned that the purpose of denazification in theory and in

practice was not to punish but solely to remove Nazi activists
from positions of influence.

All this was common ground between us and the Germans
with whom we were dealing. What I, for one, did not realise
was the isolation German scientists had suffered in their own
country. The Weimar Republic had held them in high regard,
for which it received little thanks. Hitler's régime of 'marginal
men'—almost all of whom had been educational failures—was
not satisfied with the abject submission of the universities but
singled out the intellectuals as a group for a campaign of vilifi-
cation which intensified as the War progressed. The expression
die Intellektuellen became a term of abuse. Even Goebbels himself suffered under the odium of having a doctorate and it may
be significant that none of the leading Nazis accepted an
honorary degree. Being of a suspicious turn of mind it was some
time before I accepted that the Aachen professors were sincere
when they told me that what they suffered most from was a
feeling of isolation, but it is only now after reading up the
history of Nazism, that I fully understand their feelings.

In spite of a gap of at least ten years there were still professors
at German universities whose names were well known to British
workers in their fields. It was to be expected that in some way
they would play a part in the return of German scientists to the
international scientific community. The first form, however, in
which this took place was as unintentional as it was ludicrous
and had nothing to do with Education Branch. Amongst the
reparations to be extracted from Germany were the results of
German research in industry and the universities. For this purpose German research workers were taken to England for
'interrogation' in the hope of gaining valuable information from
them. As far as academic research was concerned it would, of
course, have been cheaper to give them facilities for publishing
their results in the English scientific press but that thought had
occurred only to the National Coal Board which later published
a translation of Professor Fritsche's book on horizon mining, a
fact which he reported to me with considerable pride. The news
of these 'interrogations' soon reached Aachen and caused some
hard feelings. No one had been whisked away from there and
some professors felt slighted and hard done by. To leave the
misery of a destroyed German city behind to be taken in a train

with real seats, and upholstered ones at that, to a destination where a warm room and three square meals a day were waiting but above all to have interesting talks with English colleagues about developments in one's own field during the previous ten years was as enjoyable as it was flattering. One of the Aachen professors felt particularly hurt and kept asking me when his turn would come. I had no idea of how to set about satisfying his wish but told him that I would do my best. A few days later a gentleman arrived at my office and told me in strictest secrecy that he would take the professor to England that night and did I think that he would offer resistance? I told him that I did not think so provided it was made clear to him that this was all my doing.

It had been the original intention that there should be reparation, denazification and re-education. It would be less than honest to pretend that re-education had always been completely alien to the policy of Education Branch, although we never had the self-confidence and the revivalist zeal of our American colleagues. However, our programme of visits by British lecturers to German universities and other educational institutions did have a bias towards such subjects as 'The Growth of Democracy in England'. In spite of their obvious moral these lectures were well received. I remember the first visit of an English lecturer, Aubrey Douglas-Smith, to Aachen in September or early October 1946 before I took up my post there. I had accompanied him as guide and interpreter on a tour of universities in our Zone which had been planned with a fine disregard for the state of the roads. By the time we got to Aachen we were over an hour late, but the large lecture room was still packed with academic staff and students. The Rector introduced the speaker in the most welcoming terms pointing out the historic significance of the occasion. The audience, consisting almost entirely of scientists and engineers, responded well although the subject was by no means of professional interest to them. What really counted was that a member of an English university had gone to the trouble to come to Germany so shortly after the War. This was taken as an offer of reconciliation and good will, which indeed it was.

As these visits became more frequent, the range of subjects was enlarged to include science and technology. We also began to arrange conferences and symposia using groups of lecturers including the occasional speaker from a 'neutral' country such as Switzerland, who had to be brought into Germany at our expense. The first international conference, at least as far as Aachen was concerned, took place towards the end of 1947. It may be useful to give the background of this, in itself unimportant, event because it shows that although the unity of European science had not been completely destroyed it was not always easy to restore the broken connections.

The initiative came from Professor Piwowarsky, who before the War had arrested the decline of the cast-iron foundry by developing a new material, spherulitic cast iron. As a result he was considered the grand old man of the industry throughout Europe and the annual symposium he used to organise became a popular event, particularly with English workers in this field. He told me that he would attempt to revive these meetings if we would bring over some English experts. I was not quite sure whether this would be possible. It was one thing to bring British lecturers over as part of an official scheme controlled by us and another to spend the British tax-payers' money and use the facilities of the British army of occupation to transport, accommodate and feed a number of visitors who wanted to discuss their specialism. To my pleasant surprise the project was authorised. Having got that far, Professor Piwowarsky asked whether he could confer an honorary doctorate on one of the visitors, Mr J. G. Pearce of the British Cast Iron Research Association. I consulted the Rector, Professor Paul Roentgen, whose absolute integrity and sound judgement I respected. He told me that shortly before the outbreak of the War, the British Cast Iron Research Institute had found a way of producing spherulitic cast iron which made Professor Piwowarsky's own process obsolete. The immediate reaction of Professor Piwowarsky had been to propose that an honorary doctorate should be conferred on Mr Pearce, but the Nazi authorities had vetoed the proposal. Rather nervously Professor Roentgen added that he felt that the time was not yet ripe to repair the damage. He for one felt so ashamed of the Nazi past that he was embarrassed by the proposal and afraid that the gesture might be misunderstood. As I could not be sure that Mr Pearce would not feel embarrassed himself I agreed and we decided to wait until the 1948 symposium. This was just as well because when the matter was put to our London office a year later, the motives behind the proposal were indeed misunderstood and it took some effort to get an entry permit and travel facilities for Mr Pearce who was the first Englishman after the War to receive an honorary degree from a German university.

I am not competent to judge how effective the symposia were in promoting scientific progress but socially they were a great success in spite of the austere conditions under which they took place. I think it should be said that from the very beginning of the Occupation the professional bond between our technical men and their German counterparts was very strong, particularly in such dangerous occupations as mining and metallurgy. The University of Aachen owed it to a visit of British mining experts that it received a regular supply of coal during the terrible winter of 1946-7 when there was not always enough fuel to bake such bread as there was and the ink froze at the tip of my fountain pen as I was writing.

The second international event at Aachen was the Summer School which took place in August 1948. The titles of the principal lectures convey the range of the subjects that were discussed :

Dr A. C. Crombie, University College, London : The Philosophy of Science (six lectures)

Professor H. Cremer, Aachen : The Development of Mathematics and its Relationship to Technology and General Culture (two lectures)

Mr G. L. Rogers, University College, Dundee : Relations of Science to Ethics (two lectures)

Professor B. Schachner, Aachen : Technology and the Soul of Man (two lectures)

Professor R. von Schoefer, Aachen : Technology, Culture and Style (two lectures)

Professor W. Fuchs : Is Technology to be blamed? (two lectures)

Mr Leo de Syllas, ARIBA : Foreign Influences in modern English Architecture (three lectures)

Professor O. Gruber, Aachen : Foreign Influences in German Architecture (two lectures)

Professor Mathieu, Aachen : Present Problems in Industrial Organisation (two lectures).

The course extended over two weeks and was well attended. There was a small contingent of British and Belgian students. The physical needs of all participants had still to be met mainly out of British resources. The summer school was repeated in the following year with a stronger international participation. It is now a permanent feature of the life of the university. Similar developments took place in other universities.

This work would have been quite impossible without the wholehearted support of the British universities whose attitude towards the German problem never departed from the concept of a common European civilisation. Before and during the War they had accepted German refugees as students and teachers, some of whom spoke hardly enough English to make themselves understood. During the immediate post-war years they interpreted their rules of admission most generously and did not enquire too closely into the academic standards of German applicants at a time when university places were not as plentiful as they are now. When early in 1948 Education Branch organised a scheme for placing German lecturers for one year in British universities they again responded well. Through the good offices of Professor G. R. Potter, who from the very beginning had been a frequent visitor to Aachen, Dr Geller, a lecturer in theoretical metallurgy was accepted by the University of Sheffield. He became so popular that he was made warden of one of the halls of residence and was able to bring his wife out. As he told me later he made academic history on his first evening as warden. Unable to read a word of Latin he replaced the long Latin grace put before him by an impromptu translation of a German child's prayer: 'Come Mr Jesus, be our guest and bless what you have given us'.

What has been described so far can hardly be called an attempt at the reconstruction of German education, unless one includes the creation of good will in the term. Reconstruction implies going back to a former state, the state before the Nazi régime. As the Weimar Republic had left the German universities unchanged this would have meant going back to the days of the Kaiser. We, therefore, made an attempt to remodel the government of German universities, which for all practical purposes was in the hands of oligarchies of senior professors, in the hope that we would thereby prevent the recurrence of what had happened in the past. I think most of us had by then freed ourselves from the misconception, quite common in England during the War, that the rise of Nazism had been largely the work of unemployed graduates, but the similarity of Professor von Treitschke's theory of history—'a country which cannot defend itself has no right to exist'—and Hitler's practice fifty years later was too close to be ignored, not to mention minor academic figures who had done all they could to prevent the Weimar Republic from gaining the confidence and respect of the German people. The problem was how to preserve the traditional right of German professors to teach what they liked, at the same time making it less likely for aberrations of the human mind to find shelter in the protective atmosphere of a university and—what is more—to reach citizens like Adolf Hitler in the form of penny pamphlets a generation later when the academic world had forgotten them. As it was our policy not to make any changes which would have disappeared after our departure, the problem was handed over to a German commission with the suggestion that government of the university by a council, consisting in the main of representatives of the community, might be a solution. The only contribution I was able to make to this work was to translate and annotate the Royal Charter of the University of Leeds and hand it to the Aachen member. The commission were given facilities to travel and British army rations. In due course they presented their report which was discussed but did not lead to any action. Nothing is more difficult than fighting the past.

As far as the present was concerned the state of society in Germany could not have looked more democratic. The need was to survive. The survival value of a peasant was higher than that of a craftsman and his was higher than that of a professor. Class distinction receded. But this is too simple a picture. The Nazi régime had established a hierarchy of its own which was classless in the conventional meaning of the word. By penetrating the existing social structure it had weakened its class basis. The manual worker, who had never been the docile robot our newspapers had made him out to be, had been the first to resist Nazism and the last to be won over. In the process of wooing him, the Nazi propaganda machine romanticised him and made him into a cult figure. Now he was watching the slow rise of democracy, rubbed his eyes and expected equality for himself and for his children. Had he demanded superiority, 5,000 tanks were ready to intervene on his behalf. For our part we had been sent into Germany with the mandate to secure equality of educational opportunity for all.

To any British educationist of the time this meant above all the introduction of something akin to our system of tripartite education. I realised that the main battle would be fought on the school front, but I also realised that it would take at least fifteen years before any changes at school level could produce a substantial number of graduates with a working-class background. The *Gymnasium* held the key not only to the universities but, together with a few *Mittelschulen,* also to all other forms of higher education. In theory the *Gymnasium*—like the Ritz—was open to all, but in practice it was extremely difficult for the children of wage earners to gain access to it and, what is more, to succeed in the course. The immediate cause of this was so obvious that few people saw it. The shorter the school day, the more scholastic success depends on the time that a mother has to look after her children and the quality of home she can provide. As all German schools closed their doors at 1 pm the children of wage earners who succeeded in reaching the *Gymnasium* were only very rarely able to go beyond what we would call the 'O' level stage, even if the parents were in a position to find the school fees and maintain their children beyond the age of sixteen. Of these some went to full-time colleges of technology as there was no part-time education at that level. In England a system of part-time technical education had developed in response to a similar, though not so extreme, situation. It consisted of a series of courses each one of which led to a certificate which was a qualification in its own right and a stepping-stone to the next higher course. Until 1961 this system was open to all, independent of any school qualifications. It began at crafts level and ended with the corporate membership of one of the professional institutions and/or an external degree of the University of London.

The only point at which I could influence developments while at Aachen was at the border between the colleges of technology, then called *Höhere Fachschulen,* and the technical university. If it were possible to establish a way of progressing from the one to the other the number of university students from working-class families, which at that time was negligible, could be increased. Traditionally there was no link between college and university, as it was widely held that only a nine-year course at a *Gymnasium* culminating in the *Abitur* could produce a mind capable of benefiting from a university course, apart from a few exceptions who were adequately catered for by the *Begabten-prüfung* (examination for the gifted), a term which made me wonder for whom the *Abitur* had been designed. This belief was strongly defended by men whose intellectual integrity I respected, but was it true? Was there not an element of self-deception, a subconscious defence of the monopoly of the *Gymnasium* as the instrument with which the middle classes had broken the privileged position of the aristocracy and which now served to defend their own? My own experience had been that quite a number of English workmen with far less general education than the students at *Höhere Fachschulen* possessed were able to reach a depth of understanding and a discipline of mind which would enable them to follow a university course with ease, as some of them actually did.

The most frequent explanation I was offered as to why the children of manual workers were under-represented at the universities may be called 'the two generation argument'. In Germany it took the form: 'The father by moving one step up the social ladder provides the environment which enables the son to reach university'. As a statement of existing facts this was undoubtedly true, but it was no justification. In Britain a genetic explanation had been introduced into the same argument which became educational orthodoxy. The idea is succinctly expressed in a comment written by an unknown hand into the margin of a report I submitted at the time: 'The universities want the cream of the brains and not a representative cross-section of society. Brains are normally found in the children of those who have bettered themselves and are no longer in the working class.' But the socio-political situation demanded that as many future parents of this kind as possible should be enabled to go right to the top. Where they got their talents from and whether they passed them on to their children was irrelevant.

As I set about my self-imposed task to persuade the professors of Aachen to accept a few finalists of the *Höhere Fachschulen* I was unaware of an order by the Nazi *Reichsminister* of education, dated 29 April 1939, which ordered all technical universities to accept all finalists of the *Höhere Fachschulen* who applied, provided they had passed their final examination with average and above average marks and that they were 'of German or kindred blood' and 'could be relied upon to defend the National Socialist State at all times'. In itself the existence of this order made little difference as, like all other Nazi regulations concerning education, it had been suspended pending a review by the *Land* Minister of Education, but I now realise that the professors were very kind to me, for during the conversations we had not one of them pointed out that it did not become a representative of the occupying powers to try to resurrect a piece of Nazi legislation. My argument was that any lack of general education was a misfortune for the individual because it deprived him of some of the enjoyable things in life, but that it was neither fair nor, in the existing economic and political state of Western Germany, expedient to deprive him of the possibility of developing his technical talents to the full. Some professors agreed, others were not quite so sure, but the opposition was not nearly so strong as I later experienced outside the university. There was one counter-argument with which I had to agree, namely the difficulty of judging from the marks obtained in technical education whether the student still had sufficient reserves left for a study at higher level or whether he had reached his ceiling in one last supreme effort. I mentioned that in England it was customary to interview such students. This was alien to German tradition.

It must have been at the beginning of the academic year 1947-8 when Dr Ing B. Schachner, Professor of Architecture, told me that his faculty had decided to accept one student from the local college of building. This was surprising, as of all professions the architects were the most insistent on a good general education. I never saw the young man, nor did I know his name. It would not have been politic to take an interest in him for fear of creating the impression that he was my protégé. I did find out, however, that he did exceedingly well. So there was hope, for no professor wants to miss a potential source of good students. Some years later I was told that he had come out first in his degree examination. In October 1948 the Minister made a regulation which legalised the acceptance of graduates of the *Höhere Fachschulen* without the *Abitur* by Aachen University. The regulation was only to be provisional but it remained unchanged for eleven years. It showed a remarkable skill in adapting German traditions to new requirements. The examining panel of the college was to include a representative of the university. This gave him the right to take part in the viva voce examinations of the candidates in question. If the panel so decided and he agreed the candidate's certificate was to be endorsed 'suitable for admission to university'. As North Rhine-Westphalia was economically the most important *Land* the others were bound to follow. In 1971-2, the last year for which statistics were available at the time of writing, five point two per cent of all students entering West German universities came from the *Höhere Fachschulen*. As most of them will have found their way into the technical universities the proportion is in the order of ten per cent. This figure is not likely to increase as the *Höhere Fachschulen* have been upgraded to become *Fachhochschulen* and the salaries of the engineers leaving them are now so close to those of university graduates that there is little inducement to study for another four years.

My next attempt at influencing educational developments was abortive and is only related in order to show the conflicts of opinions and interests which were soon to bedevil attempts at educational reforms. I had been given the free use for educational purposes of a building which would have made a good residential college. As it was too far away from the university to be used by it, I hoped that it might become a residential college preparing mature students for the *Abitur*. As someone had to finance the maintenance of the students my thoughts turned to the *Deutscher Gewerkschaftsbund*, the German equivalent of the TUC. The idea was to invite this body to sponsor students nominated by it and to take an active part in the running of the college. Ample time would be set aside for trade union studies which would be entirely in the hands of the DGB. The hope was that by careful selection and by making good use of the residential facilities the students would be able to pass the normal *Abitur* in two years. They would then proceed to the technical university to study any subject they liked. Although, of course, they would be under no obligation to serve the trade

union movement it was not unreasonable to assume that many
of them would do so.

At that time—in fact until quite recently—Germany industry
was for all practical purposes controlled by technical men and
I felt that it would be of advantage to the trade unions to have
a few technical experts of their own. To my pleasant surprise
the *Rektor* of the university supported the idea and in a very
short time we had found a number of lecturers and teachers at
the local *Gymnasium* who were anxious to take part in the
scheme. At this stage—it was shortly before the currency reform
of June 1948—I went to see Herr Hans Böckler, the grand old
man of the German trade union movement. He received me
most cordially but could not be moved to sponsor the scheme.
I had expected that he might find it difficult to raise the money
but his argument was that my proposal would mean that his
movement would lose a number of its most able men who, in
the natural course of events, would emerge as leaders. I replied
that there was many a bishop in the Church of Rome who had
studied at university at his co-religionists' expense without turning into a heathen. Not a very good argument, but neither was
his when in return he pointed out that Dr Joseph Goebbels'
studies had been financed by a Roman Catholic trade union.
Herr Böckler's attitude was understandable. The German universities unlike their English counterparts had never taken a
great interest in workers' education before. Although I am sure
he did not suspect my motives, he may well have been suspicious
of the gifts I was carrying. Not much later the DGB came out
strongly in favour of the *zweiter Bildungsweg*.

What one might call the alienation theory, advanced by
Herr Böckler, was an argument which I encountered in two
forms : one stressed the impoverishment of social groups through
educating their ablest members above the norm of their group,
the other emphasised the stress on family bonds and friendships. These arguments, as I now know, had a long history and
continued for some years afterwards. As late as 1958 an article
appeared in *Die offene Welt* in which the author argues that
the whole of democratic life depends on talented people remaining in their original position.[1] In 1956 Bruno Conradsen still
found it necessary to point out in *Die Neue Deutsche Schule*
that a boy who reached technical college by part-time education

was in no danger of being alienated from his parents.[2].

While still at Aachen I met Herr Conradsen, who was the head of the Vocational Schools and Technical Colleges Department at the Ministry of Education of North Rhine-Westphalia. I consider him the father of the *zweiter Bildungsweg* in Western Germany. Without realising it I gained his confidence as soon as he came to my flat. I showed him a few simple hand-tools I had brought with me from England, unaware that in Germany such treasures had been freely on sale throughout the War. We became good friends and later he told me that his thoughts had been : 'If these few tools give him so much pleasure, he must be a decent chap'. Almost immediately I told him about my disappointment over the residential college. He thought for a while and then said : 'I think I can get something like it established in Düsseldorf, but without the trade union connection'. At a loss for a short name for such an institution he asked me what we would call it in English. My reply was 'college'. He decided there and then to use the German *Kolleg* which at that time had only one meaning : a series of university lectures. When I mentioned this he said something which to me sounded like : 'I make a word mean exactly what I want it to mean'. A college was established and called the Düsseldorf Kolleg. Herr E. Kuhlmann, head of the Vocational Schools section at the Ministry told me later that its director, contrary to the philosophy of the foundation, had 'played safe' by giving preference to applicants who had failed in the *Abitur* before, thus giving them a second chance instead of giving a chance to those who had none before. The result, so he told me, had been a failure and the college was closed down. In Lower Saxony a similar college was established at about the same time, early in 1949, the Braunschweig Kolleg, which is still going strong and has no formal entrance conditions. I cannot recollect that there was any connection between the two foundations although the word *Kolleg* suggests it. There was no other such foundation until 1953 when the Oberhausen Kolleg was established in North Rhine-Westphalia. By that time the *zweiter Bildungsweg* had been sufficiently developed in this *Land* to provide the college with a regular intake of holders of the *Fachschulreife*, a term which will be explained later. Not counting denominational foundations there are now in North Rhine

-Westphalia eight such colleges of which the Wilhelm-Hein-
rich-Richter Institut is the most interesting. It was founded by
the Düsseldorf Chamber of Crafts, a statutory organisation of
what the French call the *artisanat*, small firms of master-crafts-
men employing only a few assistants each. The declared purpose
of the college is to prepare selected journeymen for university
admission in the hope that they will later become leaders of the
artisanat.

I do not think that any one thought that *Kollegs* would ever
make a numerically strong contribution to the education of what
are now called the educationally underprivileged. In 1964
eighteen *Kollegs* existed in Western Germany with about 100
students each. According to the 1971-2 statistics the *Kollegs*
together with the evening *Gymnasien* contributed three point
one per cent to the student intake of the universities.

A more substantial contribution amounting to a break-through,
the *Bildungsdurchstoss* of the reformers, could be expected from
giving the well-established *Berufsschulen* (compulsory vocational
day-release schools) an additional function. This type of school
owes its origin to Georg Kerschensteiner (1854-1932) who as
Chief Education Officer of Munich succeeded in overcoming,
at least in one field, the neo-humanist prejudice against com-
bining vocational studies with general education, which he
considered as two aspects of one and the same thing. Attendance
at the *Berufsschule* between leaving school and the age of eighteen became compulsory throughout Germany. It was the last
educational opportunity for the great majority of Germans. This
function it fulfilled very well. While the *Gymnasien* were turning from their original neo-humanism to an encyclopaedism
which was becoming more and more illusory, the *Berufsschulen*
helped their pupils to understand the work they were doing
and the world around them. While the *Gymnasien* could never
quite free themselves from nostalgia for the 'good old days
before 1914', the *Berufsschulen* were more concerned with turning their pupils into good citizens of the Weimar Republic. The
textbooks and readers which had survived from this period
showed that, although the teaching had sometimes been pedes-
trian and not always free from romanticism, Kerschensteiner's
original aims had been preserved. The *Berufsschulen* which I
visited had returned to this tradition and it would have been

churlish to criticise. I was also conscious of the fact that the percentage of *Berufsschule* teachers and administrators, particularly on the technical side, which we had to dismiss for Nazi activism was well below that in the full time sector of education. It was also becoming evident that when the interest in lecturers we brought over from England declined elsewhere Herr E. Kuhlmann and Frau Professor E. Wingerath, the official in charge of *Berufsschulen* for women, were always able and willing to provide an audience of *Berufsschule* teachers.

Clearly these schools had a tradition which singled them out to play a key role in opening the door to higher education to all those for whom the selective schools for a variety of reasons had been closed. The idea was not entirely novel. It had been discussed in *Berufsschule* circles, albeit in rather philosophical terms, during the decade before Nazism came to power and put an end to the formation of opinion from below. Now the debate was being resumed and Herr Conradsen, who had played a prominent part in the pre-Hitler discussions, was making practical plans for his own *Land*. He cut out all arguments by saying: 'Let us dig a second channel and see which way the water will flow'. He had decided on two principles which we discussed on numerous occasions: the scheme had to give young wage earners a sporting chance—*eine reale Chance*—to go to the top, and it had to be 'fail-safe', that is to say it had to be so designed that a student who decided to test himself by pursuing a more demanding course was not compelled to forego another educational opportunity well within his reach, such as a crafts-apprenticeship. The main question was: what is a sporting chance? I was often asked whether our system of part-time education provided it and my answer was 'Yes'. I had to add, however, that the percentage of failures was very high. There is no more contradiction in this than in the uncertainty principle of physics. If one accepts only those candidates whom one regards as certain to succeed one can keep the percentage of failures low, but then one automatically rejects many more who could have done equally well had they been given a chance.

Using English terminology the scheme at which Herr Conradsen arrived can be described as a craft course with optional provisions leading to a technician's qualification, which in turn gave access to a sub-degree course. The craft course was of the

normal day-release kind which in Germany automatically accom-
panies the traditional apprenticeship of three years. (Similar
arrangements exist in the commercial sector.) At the end of their
third year all students were to take their craftsman's examination.
This was in keeping with the 'fail-safe' principle. From the end
of the first year selected students were to be offered additional
tuition (twelve periods per week) in evening classes. The selection
was not to be strict. A pass in the work done so far and the basic
knowledge of a good pupil of the all-age school (*Volksschule*)
was deemed sufficient. Herr Conradsen was prepared to accept
high drop-out and failure rates. After the craftsman's examination these students were to spend an additional year in industry
in order to gain a wider experience than a man trained in
only one craft. During this year they were to attend evening
classes (ten periods a week) to be prepared for the technician's
examination.

From an English point of view there was, at least outwardly,
nothing very unusual in this scheme. At that time it would
have been possible to find similar arrangements in some of our
colleges, although separation of future craftsmen and technicians
after the diagnostic first year, with the possibility of transfer
from one group to the other, was the preferred pattern. There
was, however, one significant difference. Only about half of
the additional instruction to be received by the technician group
was to be technical and that included mathematics and science.
Whereas our Ordinary National Certificate is primarily a technical qualification in its own right and its function as a stepping-
stone to the next higher qualification is secondary, for Herr
Conradsen the break-through to higher education was the
primary objective. By introducing a substantial element of
what is traditionally called liberal education he forestalled, as
far as this was possible, the protests from the defenders of the
humanistisch-christliche Kultur des Westens who were pointing
to what was happening in East Germany, an argument which
could not be dismissed out of hand. To emphasise his point still
further he named the qualification awarded *Fachschulreife*
(certificate of maturity to attend colleges of technology) as a deliberate parallel to *Hochschulreife* (certificate of maturity to
attend universities) which is the official name of the *Abitur* of
the *Gymnasium*. In effect, this left German industry without

the full equivalent of our ONC—a most useful technical grade —but if there was to be a choice between placing the emphasis on improving the technical efficiency of German industry or on increasing the degree of social mobility of German wage earners, the circumstances of the time demanded the latter course. All I could do was to applaud and hope that the scheme would be approved by the Minister of Education.

Since the currency reform social differences had begun to re-establish themselves. As the West German life-boat was being towed into port its passengers, who had huddled together for warmth, were beginning to sit upright again—and further apart from each other. If anything, education as the basis of social status was more important than ever before because wealth, apart from a very few large fortunes, had disappeared. What would have been an easy matter before, had now become a political issue. At the time the party in power in North Rhine-Westphalia was the CDU (Christian Democratic Union) which was not given to innovations. Even so modest a reform as the abolition of school fees had been delayed. The chances were that it would not be possible to persuade the Minister of Education to sign an order which was bound to weaken the position of the *Gymnasium.* When the ministerial order came out on 31 March 1949 it went even further than I had hoped. The existing mode of entry to *höhere Fachschulen,* namely a satisfactory school report at the end of the sixth year of the *Gymnasium,* followed by two or three years of practical experience in industry without an examination at the end had been abolished. In fairness to all, the *Gymnasium* report was recognised as giving exemption from those papers of the *Fachschulreife* examination which tested general education. The order included not only all colleges of technology but also colleges preparing for the social services and colleges of business studies and economics.

The scheme took a very wide section of German youth to the doors of higher education but to this day there is no German equivalent to our Higher National Certificate. The German qualification at this level can still only be obtained by three years of full-time study. At the time this presented a serious obstacle to some of the students who had obtained the *Fachschulreife.* However, anything more would have been expecting too much. Ten to twelve periods of evening class attendance

G

up to the age of nineteen was already more than many people in Germany considered feasible. To expect anyone to give up practically all his spare time to evening classes and the home-work that goes with it right into the middle twenties or even longer was not acceptable in a country without a puritan tradi-tion. This became clear to me when I took parties of German educationists round English technical colleges. On one occasion —it must have been at Birmingham or Leeds—we left a college, which had been open since 8.30 am, at 9.30 pm and found a number of girls with their scarves over their heads sitting demurely in a sparsely furnished room. We were told that they were waiting for their boy-friends to come out so that they could have as much of their precious time together as remained of the cold winter's evening. This made a deeper impression on the visitors than anything else they had seen.

At the time we were developing in Great Britain the sand-wich system of higher technical education. In Germany some-thing similar came into being spontaneously. In the absence of an adequate grants system students intending to enter the colleges of technology would save up for the first year of the course. Having completed it they would find themselves a slightly better post and save up for the second year. In the third year they could reckon to obtain a full grant. This solution would have been quite impossible without the traditional generosity of German firms who do not enquire too deeply whether they get their money's worth out of students working for them. At one stage some German industrialists demanded the intro-duction of an officially supported sandwich system, but so far as I know nothing came of it.

Amongst the voices opposing the new scheme that of the colleges of technology themselves had to be taken most seriously. Their social status had been kept artificially low. At the time they were not allowed to award any diplomas. The only thing which singled them out as colleges of higher education was their conditions of entry. Now they were asked to accept students who had not been to a *Gymnasium,* nor even to the somewhat less exalted *Mittelschule.* The situation was serious. The first trickle of students from the *Berufsschulen* was expected at the beginning of the academic year 1952-3, to be followed by a sizeable output the year after that. In 1952 it became clear that the directors of the colleges were still hostile to the scheme. If the *Berufsschulen* did their work well there would be more students than ever before asking for admission. Selection would have to become more rigorous and it was not difficult to see who would be the losers. At that time I investigated 125 questionnaires which I had sent to former students of these colleges who had applied for some scholarships we were offering. I found a negative correlation between the number of years the applicants had spent at the *Gymnasium* and the results of their final examination at college. The few students who had risen from the ranks of craftsmen did best. The worst grades, on average, were obtained by the holders of the *Abitur*. While neither Herr Conradsen, to whom I showed the results, nor I interpreted them as indicating that the longer one stayed at a *Gymnasium* the more stupid one became, they did suggest that the colleges were overestimating the value of grammar school experience and were not very clever in assessing the intellectual ceiling of the applicants.

Shortly after taking up my post with the newly-created High Commission I wrote a report to the Head of Education Branch Mr (now Professor) G. C. Allen in which I said : 'Unfortunately the new system, sometimes described as a piece of *Kultur-bolschewismus*, is encountering so much opposition that it is doubtful whether it will ever become fully effective. Even the Directors of the *Fachschulen*, who occupy the key position in this struggle, are not paying more than lip service to an idea which cuts across their own ambitions. Here we could help by convincing the directors that it is possible for students to advance from the lowest level of education to university level and beyond'. Mr Allen had personal experience of teaching adult workmen and was also familiar with the high degree of social mobility the American system of technical education provided. In response to my plea I received an increased share in the budget for visits to England by German educationists and for visits of lecturers from England. In making this decision Mr Allen went not only against the orthodox genetic explanation for the scarcity of the children of wage earners in institutions of higher learning, but also against a certain technophobia which was then very common in England, probably as a reaction to the technology of war.

As far as I personally was concerned the support of lecturers from England was most welcome. I had only one lecture on this subject, not a very good one, which I had repeated with minor modifications between 1948 and 1951 whenever Herr Kuhlmann invited me to meetings of educationists. It had been published twice and new voices were badly needed. The first request for a lecturer on 'Technical Education and Social Mobility in Britain' came back from the Foreign Office with the question : 'What is social mobility?' After some explanations we had regular visits mainly from principals of colleges of technology whom I accompanied as guide and interpreter to other *Länder* of the Federal Republic where the *zweiter Bildungsweg* was still in the discussion stage.

Even in North Rhine-Westphalia the development was not rapid. From a note I have it would seem that the first real break-through came in the engineering college of Essen where in 1956 more than half of the students had come up from the *Berufsschule*. In this year the winds were beginning to blow strongly in favour of the good ship *zweiter Bildungsweg*. In North Rhine-Westphalia Professor Paul Luchtenberg, a Liberal, had become Minister of Education of a coalition government. While in opposition he had consulted Herr Conradsen and was strongly in favour of the idea from the very beginning. Now his government came out with a policy declaration promising to develop the *zweiter Bildungsweg* with all speed. The Social Democratic Party of Germany also made it part of their educational programme, and the Standing Conference of Ministers of Education of the *Länder*, the nearest thing to a Federal Ministry of Education existing in Germany at that time, began to co-ordinate the respective regulations in the different *Länder*.

By 1957 two-thirds of all students at the colleges of building and one third of all students at the colleges of engineering in North Rhine-Westphalia had come up through the *zweiter Bildungsweg*.[3] Such figures could not have been achieved without tolerating high drop-out and failure rates at the lower stages. According to research carried out for the academic year 1962-3[4] the proportion of pupils who discontinued their studies or failed in the examination for the *Fachschulreife* ranged from fifteen per cent in one *Land* to eighty per cent in some other. The norm seems to have been fifty per cent.

It was to be expected that the evening class element of the *zweiter Bildungsweg* would decline as Germany became more prosperous. It never fitted too well into the convivial pattern of German life. Soon there was also no more need for it. The 'economic miracle' has made a grant system possible which is so generous that no student from the age of fifteen upwards need have any financial anxieties whatever courses he attends. The evening classes have been replaced by full-time courses of the type known in Britain as 'bridging courses'. These are offered either by the *Berufsschulen* or in separate junior technical or commercial colleges which had already existed but played a minor part. This development had been anticipated in the original scheme, where it was included as an alternative to evening classes.

In 1972 some 25,000 young men and almost 23,000 girls obtained the *Fachschulreife*. This is approximately six per cent of the respective age group.[5] Although the majority of young people who take the hard road from the workbench or the typewriter to higher education no longer do so out of economic necessity, the *zweiter Bildungsweg* will remain to serve those who by virtue of their environment or their natural inclination develop their talents best if they can stay close to the world of work which, after all, is our portion.

NOTES

1. Quoted in Helmut Belser, *Zweiter Bildungsweg* (Weinheim, 1965) p. 143.
2. *Ibid.*, p. 146.
3. Belser, op. cit. p. 77.
4. *Ibid.*, p. 214.
5. Bundesminster für Bildung und Wissenschaft. *Strukturdaten* 1974 p. 33.

10. *Allied Policy in Berlin*
Marion Klewitz

This paper will be concerned primarily with the influence of the occupying forces on the general schools system in Berlin; it will not deal with other sectors of the educational system. Of the four occupying powers in Berlin the French will be left out of account, since they do not appear to have exercised any serious influence. Even in the French Sector, one can only perceive a few, not altogether successful initiatives, such as the introduction of a lycée and of French as the first foreign language in the fifth year of some of the Sector's primary schools.

I shall refrain from making any distinction between British and American educational policy in relation to the examination of the institutional change in the Berlin school system which is my chief interest here. The similarities in British and American attitudes may be explained above all by the particular political situation in Berlin. In discussions with the representatives of the Soviet authorities and of the influential school reform movement in Berlin, British and American officials adopted similar positions. They minimised disagreements about educational aims and measures, or at least do not appear to have expressed them publicly.[1]

The analysis of policy is based substantially on those documents that were accessible in the archives of the City Council, the political parties, the Churches, the trade unions and the press, and on the published resolutions of the Allied Kommandatura, especially of its Committee for Education and Religious Affairs (1945-48).[2]

When considering the Allied influence on the Berlin school system, and particularly with reference to British policy, the informal nature of the advisory work should be taken into account. But here sources are meagre. They do not permit authoritative statements either about the form of such contacts or the actual influences on teachers and administrators. For this reason the wide field of informal contacts and advisory activities will be omitted. This seems justified since in any case the British representatives in the Allied Kommandatura had to share in the joint responsibility for the administration of Berlin schools.

My chief interests are the binding decisions of the Allied Kommandatura and their effect on the Berlin school system. For reasons of time I shall not be able to examine in detail the different concepts in the policies of the occupying powers and I must likewise largely exclude any description of the school system as it existed then.[3]

Confrontation over Schools Policy, 1945-6

From the beginning, British and American education officers in Berlin had to follow procedures that were different from those adopted in their own Zones because the Soviets had, in the two months before the arrival of the Western Allies, already exerted an influence on the school system as part of their general policy for social change. It should be remembered that they had since 1943 included the reorganisation of the school system in their detailed plans for an 'anti-fascist' restructuring of the German economy and of German political life. Whilst according to British and American thinking, denazification was to be the chief task during the first phase of the Occupation, Soviet planning saw the process directly linked to reforms.

As early as May 1945 the most important positions in the educational administration of Berlin were filled; in June the school superintendents in most of the city's twenty district education offices were appointed. Denazification was pursued rapidly and resolutely. On 11 June 1945 the Commander-in-Chief of the Red Army had the schools reopened through a decree of the *Magistrat* (City Administration); this had been reconstituted especially for the purpose by the 'Ulbricht group'. It was explicitly a question of 'emergency measures for the immediate future' since 'in view of the deep spiritual and moral decay of the German school system' and the material damage, 'there can be no question of regular school activity in Berlin'.[4] Clearing up operations, surveys of teaching materials and the vetting of teachers, who had to report to the district offices, were rapidly carried out, in view of the imminent arrival of the

Western Allies. By this means the Soviets succeeded in stealing a march on the Western Allies who arrived later. They did so partly through the appointments they made and partly through directives for institutional reforms.

A bare two months after the arrival of the British and American forces in Berlin, at the beginning of September 1945, it was established in the Allied Kommandatura that all fundamental changes in the work and administration of the Berlin schools had to have the unanimous agreement of the Education Committee and the approval of the Kommandatura itself.[5] So in their own sectors the occupying powers only had the right to deal with minor internal school matters and the informal advising of teachers, not their training.

The 'Order' of 3 September 1945 did impede what had been close co-operation between the Soviet Military Authority and the Central Education Authority in Berlin. However, most of the district KPD and SPD members in leading positions appear to have preferred working with the Soviets, so that even in their own districts the Western Occupying Powers could only gradually achieve influence through individuals sympathetic to their views. Moreover, denazification, which the British and American authorities saw as the first decisive sphere of activity, had largely been carried out in the Berlin teaching force already.

Taken together, the decisions of the Allied Kommandatura on questions regarding the Berlin school system in the second half of 1945 and the first half of 1946 show a tendency to reverse or render ineffective the reforms and measures initiated by the Soviets. These were concerned with (i) the planned unification of the school system; (ii) the abolition of the private schools; (iii) the isolation of religious instruction and (iv) the furtherance of the 'anti-fascist reorganisation'.

The Planned Unification of the School System

The *Magistrat's* decree of 11 June 1945 on the resumption of school activity spoke exclusively of the *Volksschulen;* other schools were not mentioned. The *Volksschule*, the only school for the vast majority of the rising generation, was to be the core of the publicly proclaimed educational reforms. The minutes of the *Magistrat* meeting of 11 June 1945 stated:

'The new German school system shall be one in which every child, irrespective of social class and political or religious persuasion, can work his way through all types of school from the primary to the university stage. Ability shall be the only decisive factor'. The plans were directed against the intermediate school and the various types of eight-year secondary schools. Through local initiatives, however, most of these opened their doors again like the *Volksschulen*.

Not only the Soviet Occupation Forces and the *Magistrat* but also many other advocates of school reform in Berlin wanted to prevent the re-establishment of the various secondary schools. At the beginning of the 1945-6 school year the *Magistrat*, with the broad support of the school reform lobby, asked the Allied Kommandatura for authorisation to abolish the intermediate schools and to set up an *Aufbauschule* for the school years seven to thirteen. The *Aufbauschule* was to be the first institution to make provision for late transfers from a primary school or a *Volksschule* to a secondary school and so to the *Abitur*. The Allied Education Committee rejected the Assembly's proposal. It also turned down a subsequent proposal along similar lines to the 'Law for the Democratisation of the German School System' which was brought into effect in the Soviet Zone before the beginning of the 1946-7 school year.[6]

We may infer from the statements of British and American officials in the press, at school inspectors' conferences and in conversations with teachers and headmasters that both sides rejected the proposals for the same reason : the fact that the Berlin *Magistrat* had not been legitimised by election but installed by the Soviets, and the thoroughly inadequate provision for public discussion contravened their basic requirements for a democratic process of decision-making; changes in the structure of the school system should be decided on the basis of the broadest possible agreement of a democratically elected self-governing body for Berlin.

This attitude is particularly interesting with regard to the American side since many of their representatives had from the beginning regarded educational reform as imperative. The Soviet Zone's 1946 law which introduced an eight-year common school, was emphatically welcomed : 'The political significance then of the *Einheitsschule* system lies in the fact that it contributes

G*

directly to breaking down the caste system of German society'.[7]

The German proponents of the *Einheitsschule* in Berlin knew that they could not count on the basic support of the Americans even when a democratically elected assembly had been elected, and had to accept the temporary postponement of the reform. Meanwhile they saw the established types of intermediate and secondary school being consolidated while the *Volksschule* retained its lowly place in the traditional tripartite hierarchy.

The Abolition of the Private Schools

From the beginning, the Soviet authorities and the *Magistrat* had rejected the private schools even more emphatically than the state intermediate and secondary schools. However, they had not prevented five Catholic *Oberschulen* from opening at the beginning of the 1945-6 school year. Three years later, nine per cent of secondary school pupils were being educated privately (eleven per cent of the population of Berlin was Catholic).

Soviet officials, representatives of the Central Education Authority and school reformers with socialist views condemned the private schools as privileged institutions for minorities and children of the upper classes. They stood in the way of a standardised school education and an all-embracing state school system. On the other hand, the British and American authorities supported the private schools and defended them against the disapproving Soviets. In so doing they supported the claims of the CDU, the LDP, the Protestant and Catholic churches and of specific minorities such as the proponents of anthroposophical education in the schools named after their founder Rudolf Steiner. The British and American authorities also welcomed the different individual initiatives on the German side as reactions against the Nazi régime.

At the insistence of the British and Americans, the Allied Kommandatura recognised the legality of the newly-opened private schools. It also maintained the right to recognise the foundation of further private schools 'in exceptional cases'.[8] The decree in question strengthened the hand of all those who were against a standardised state school system. These critics were also the ones who did not want to see traditional forms of secondary education, state and private, affected by any improvement in the *Volksschule* sector, even granted this was necessary. So British and American delegates in the Allied Kommandatura had provided for a liberalisation of the Berlin school system but had postponed provision of greater equality of opportunity.

Isolation of Religious Instruction

Liberalisation also benefited from the attitude of the British and Americans in the controversy over the isolation of religious instruction. Here it was a question of gaining recognition for the traditional norms of large sections of the population in the face of demands for a secular monopoly in the school system.

The *Magistrat's* decree on the resumption of school activity on 11 June 1945 stated: 'All parents are free to let their children take part in religious instruction. It should be given as an extra lesson at the beginning or end of the school day by ministers or teachers so authorised by the Churches.' This regulation harked back to the secular schools and to the *Simultanschulen* which had been predominant in Berlin before 1933.

The British and Americans took an opposing line; they pursued an education policy favourable to Christian interests, speaking out against the total separation of school and church. The Allied Kommandatura Orders of January and April 1946 stipulated that the *Magistrat* should guarantee to provide in every school religious instruction for those children whose parents wanted them to have it. It was further laid down that for those pupils who were enrolled for it religious instruction should be a compulsory subject.[9]

The Furtherance of the 'Anti-fascist Reorganisation'

With the reopening of the first schools, the Soviet Occupation representatives began the political instruction of the teachers. Those of them who had emerged with a positive rating from the denazification procedure and the newly appointed ones with very short or no training were to begin 'anti-fascist' teaching. That is to say, they were to support the political, economic and social reforms which had been introduced or were being planned by the Soviet Military Government for its Zone. The chief school supervisor in Berlin declared: 'At the present time,

semi-trained teachers of proven anti-fascist persuasion are more
important than fully trained teachers who have no intention
of supporting the aims of the new State'.[10]

Nonetheless in the first months of the period of Occupation,
the Soviets followed their Block policy to the extent of tolerating
a wide range of 'anti-fascist' activities and expressions of opinion.
They even encouraged teachers who had reservations about the
Soviet Occupation to put their views forward. This explains
the fact that when the Western Allies arrived, a broad school
reform movement was discernible, one which looked beyond
mere denazification to various forms of reorganisation.[11] This
spontaneous reform movement began to wither when the Soviets
proclaimed increasingly rigid 'anti-fascist' aims for day-to-day
school work and for reorganisation of the school system. As a
result, from the autumn of 1945 the British and American representatives felt impelled to formulate an official policy even on
matters of curriculum, particularly the 'anti-fascist' items. Basic
differences of opinion became evident when at the beginning of
the 1945-6 school year, the Soviet army began to promote
current affairs instruction which pronounced the new economic
situation (land and property reform had been in progress in the
Soviet-occupied Zone since September 1945), the new political
conditions, the new parties, organisations and organs of self-
government as part of 'progressive development'.[12] Soviet education officers supervised history teaching vigilantly to ensure that
'anti-fascist' work was being done. It was made clear to teachers
and students that they were expected now more than ever not
only to reject National Socialism but to conceive of the 'anti-
fascist' reorganisation as the only way of overcoming it.

From the end of 1945 current affairs instruction initiated by
the Soviets met with increasing misgivings from the British and
American representatives in the Allied Education Committee.
As in the case of religious instruction and the private schools they
made an example by rejecting the history programme which had
been prepared in accordance with guidelines issued by the central
authority in the Soviet Zone and had previously been approved
for the school year 1946-7.[13] It is likely that the Western Allies'
protest in Berlin was in part a way of objecting to the collaboration between the Soviet occupying power, the administrative
authorities of the Soviet Zone and the Berlin Assembly. They

saw this as a breach of the Four Power status of Berlin. But it was also probably a reaction against historical materialism and the Stalinist conception of history.

The ideological opposition becomes clear when one considers an American military regulation on 'Democratic Trends in Textbooks' where it is stated that :

It is not enough to eradicate from school texts Nazism or Prussianism. . . . German authors or events of definitely democratic trend should be included. The following are examples of subjects which might be included : the liberals in the days of Bismarck; the idealist proposals of Kant and Herder for permanent peace; the moral courage of the Göttinger Seven; Mommsen's attack on Treitschke's anti-Semitism; the broad liberalism of the Weimar Constitution; and Stresemann's work for international understanding.[14]

It is noteworthy that this list gives no indication of reasons for defeat or extremely limited success, nor does it take any account of socialist movements and their conception of democracy. Unquestionably the American trend represented by this quotation could not be reconciled with what the Soviets would recognise as a progressive view of history.

It is symptomatic of the stalemate in the Four Power Government of Berlin, that for lack of unanimous resolutions in the Allied Kommandatura, the teaching of history was forbidden until the city was split in November 1948. Thus both the Soviet and the Western representatives deprived themselves of an important formal and informal means of influencing the teaching in schools.

Confrontation over Schools Policy: A Summary

Almost inevitably one is led to the conclusion that the education policy of the Western Allies, particularly in school matters, restored and stabilised the pre-1933 status quo. But as a complement to this frequently made statement it should be pointed out that in contrast to the Western Zones the restoration of the Berlin school system was achieved despite the Soviet and German reform initiatives in three respects. Firstly, the British and Americans did not support either the expansion of the *Volks-*

schule or a reduction in the range of the schools. They allowed the re-establishment of types of schools which had been discriminated against under National Socialism and during the months of Soviet Occupation in Berlin—*Mittelschulen,* various types of *Gymnasium* and private schools. Secondly, running counter to the movement favouring a State monopoly of schools, the solution adopted for religious instruction restored a closer link between education and the Churches. Thirdly, the three-year ban on the teaching of history also had a conservative effect: although doubtless none of the Allies approved, the Berlin teachers were largely able to avoid discussion of historical questions. So in 1948-9 (in West Berlin) they reverted all the more readily to their previous opinions, since the conflicting viewpoints of the Allies had strengthened their scepticism about new or unusual ways of thinking.

British and American Attitudes to the 'Einheitsschule'

Whilst the traditional institutions of the school system were restored, the school reform movement which had been active since 1945 sought legal sanction for the *Einheitsschule.* The proponents of reform were mostly Social Democrats and members of the teachers' union; some of them were members of the LDP and the KPD/SED. The grouping was yet more complex and ambiguous as far as attitudes to teaching were concerned. It was above all a matter of the aims and experiments of the pre-1933 *Reform* movement being revised and applied to the present situation in Berlin.

After intensive discussion in 1947, the *Einheitsschule* law was passed in November of that year by eighty-six votes to thirty. The CDU delegates and a minority of the Liberal party voted against it. The SPD (which had polled about fifty per cent of the votes in 1946), the SED and the majority of the Liberals voted in favour.[15] The SPD set great store by the support of the Liberals and in this way they also met the requirements of the British representatives who had insisted on widespread assent as a prerequisite for the reform.

The Berlin *Einheitsschule* law was the first complete school reform law passed in Germany since the one for the Soviet Zone. The law prescribed eight years' education in the *Grundschule* for all children. From the fifth class they would learn a modern language and from the seventh class they would all be taught mathematics and science. Supplementary courses were to be provided in the seventh and eighth classes to cater for special abilities and inclinations. After the eighth year the *Einheitsschule* would divide into a practical branch with a ninth year of full-time instruction and three years' part-time vocational education, and a four-year *Oberschule* leading to the *Abitur*. The principle of equality of opportunity was stressed by the provision of free instruction and school materials.

Despite the tenacious opposition of Liberals, of the CDU representatives and the Churches, the supporters of the reform had achieved total State control; according to the law, the private schools were to be run down and closed. (The provision of religious instruction was to be the responsibility of the Churches, in accordance with the compromise of 1946.)

The British and American Occupation representatives had an ambivalent attitude to the Berlin School Law. There was complete agreement with the German side only on the fact that it was a German responsibility and a matter for parliamentary decision. On the nature of the reform, opinions were divided.

The British, though less inclined to commit themselves than the other allies in Berlin, obviously preferred more cautious measures. The introduction of the eight-year *Grundschule* was seen as a difficult educational problem which could scarcely be mastered under the given circumstances. The planned abolition of the private schools was unacceptable. It was also suggested that the cost of the reorganisation of educational institutions, plus free instruction and school materials could not be met. In view of the wide scope of the reform it was argued that reorganisation in individual German *Länder* and in Berlin should not jeopardise a future standardised reform in Germany. In general the signs are that the British had fundamental doubts about the Berlin reform law.

The American side greeted the prospective *Einheitsschule* as a guarantee of democratic equality of opportunity. However, if it was perceived, the socialist basis of the *Einheitsschule* was not endorsed. In official statements accepting the law all one finds are continuous references to the ideology of self-advancement and success. This attitude implied a far greater economic

determinism than appeared in public discussion.[16] In this connection a semi-official declaration on American educational
policy in Germany written in October 1948 may perhaps legiti-
mately be quoted with reference to the events of 1947 :

> Those who would strive here for the un-accomplished ideal
> in the United States have no place in an environment which
> generates realism . . . The democratic ideal and practice will
> not be secured by courses of study, lectures or discussions on
> the subject. The Berlin air lift is a daily reminder of the
> strength of the democratic countries. Let action, practice and
> precept supplant the term. We shall develop an intellectual
> and cultural air lift.

The priorities of American educational policy demonstrate its
distance from the dominating beliefs of the Berlin reformers. The
ideological gap also explains why the American representatives
did not range themselves solidly behind the champions of the
Einheitsschule reform in Berlin.

The educational policy makers in the SPD and the teachers'
union had long been aware of the reservations on the British
and American side. For this reason, despite their own criticism
of the Soviets, they had been at pains to secure their support and
to co-operate with the SED in matters of school reform. Conversely, the coalition between the SPD and the SED seems to
have disappointed those on the British and American side who
had hoped for a massive vote against the Soviet line.

It was the principle of total state control in the Berlin School
Law which the British and American representatives in the
Education Committee of the Allied Kommandatura were not
prepared to accept. In a compromise worked out with the
Soviets, the Education Committee confirmed its resolution of
February 1946 : a passage in the law was amended to the effect
that the private schools which had been licensed should remain
open and that 'there was a possibility of authorisation of a small
number of additional schools to be set up in accordance with
agreed procedures.'

There was another objection to the law. It was declared, at
American instigation, that classes nine to twelve of the two
branches of the *Einheitsschule* (the ninth school year plus the
vocational school, and the academic *Oberschule*) were as a

matter of principle to be housed in the same building and as far as possible taught by the same staff. The socialist educational policy makers in Berlin had deferred the merging of the upper school tracks because it did not seem a practical proposition for the time being. At that time in the USA, commissions were trying to merge the high school and the various vocational institutions. One is tempted to think that the American representatives in the Allied Kommandatura welcomed the opportunity of taking a progressive position vis-à-vis the Soviets. The British members, who as a matter of principle always weighed up the feasibility of any new project, apparently could not or would not in this instance prevail against their stronger political partners.

That the American amendment was casually planned is suggested by an official report on the School Law and its passage through the Allied Kommandatura; this states that: 'the elimination of the traditional two-track German educational system was the result of a proposal by the US representative of the Committee, who suggested that academic and vocational students no longer be separated after the first six grades'.[18]

British and American Policy: A Summary

The ambivalent attitude of the British and American representatives to the Berlin reform movement reflected their educational policy in the Allied Kommandatura. In the name of liberalisation and especially of the protection of minorities and parents holding traditional opinions, the interests of the Churches and of other groups were supported. The renewed sanctioning of private schools ran counter to the beliefs of the social-democratic reformers. This strengthened the opponents of the reform law and all those who did not want to see any of the traditional educational institutions disturbed.

After Berlin had been integrated into the West, the CDU, the Liberals and the churches were able, barely three years later, to carry out a revision of the *Einheitsschule* law, abolishing the institutional innovations which had scarcely got under way. They were replaced by a tripartite school system following a *Grundschule* which was now six years, and including the possibility of private schools, as supported by the British and

Americans against the wishes of the Soviets and the Berlin Social Democrats since 1945.

This brief account deserves further elaboration. It is brought in here simply to support the thesis of this paper, that official British and American educational policy, taken as a whole, strengthened the conservative or 'restorative' tendencies in the Berlin school system. The influence of the informal discussions and of the exchange programmes would however also have to be taken into account.

NOTES

1. Major sources (i) British : The British Zone of Occupation, in : *The Yearbook of Education*, 17, 1948, pp. 513-524; H. Liddell et al., *Education in Occupied Germany*, (Paris, 1949); R. H. Samuel and R. Hinton Thomas, *Education and Society in Modern Germany*, (London, 1949); R. Birley, 'Education in the British Zone of Germany', in : *International Affairs* 26, 1950, pp. 32-43.

   (ii) American : US Department of State, Publ. No. 2793, (Washington, 1947); M. Knappen, *And Call It Peace*, (Chicago 1947); H. Zink, *American Military Government in Germany*, (New York 1947); H. Zink, *The United States in Germany*, 1944-1945, (Princeton, 1957); K.-E. Bungenstab, *Umerziehung zur Demokratie?* (Düsseldorf 1970).

2. Decisions published since 1947 : AKB, *Official Bulletin of the Allied Kommandatura Berlin*, 1947ff. The papers of this Committee, selected by OMGUS and filed in US National Archives have recently become accessible. An analysis of allied education policy based on these documents, by the present author, is to be published in a special edition of *Zeitschrift für Pädagogik* 1977.

3. For such a description see M. Klewitz, *Berliner Einheitsschule 1945-51*, (Berlin 1971).

4. Unpublished proceedings of the 'Magistrat', 11 June 1945.

5. Order of 3 September 1945, in : Senate of Berlin, *Kampf um Freiheit und Selbstverwaltung 1945-1946*, 2nd ed., (Berlin 1961) 4.9.45/8 b.

6. H. Schützler : Die Unterstützung und Hilfe der Sowjetunion

für die anti-faschistisch-demokratischen Kräfte Berlins (Thesis Humboldt-Universität Berlin, 1963), p. 232; *Kampf, op. cit.,* 21.8.46/50 d, 2.9.46/6.

7. Information Control. Intelligence Summary, No. 61, 23 September 1946.

8. BK/O (46) 77, 1 February 1946, in : Senate of Berlin, *Berlin, Quellen und Dokumente 1945-51,* (Berlin, 1964), No. 323. Cf. Control Commission for Germany (British Element), *Education: Brief for Official Visitors to Germany,* 1948, p. 9; *Monthly Report of the Control Commission for Germany (British Element),* Vol. 3, 1948, p. 19 ff.

9. BK/O (46) 63, 24 January 1946 and BK/O (46) 159, 4 April 1946, in : Berlin, *Quellen und Dokumente* . . . op. cit. No. 320 and 324.

10. Proceedings of the 'Magistrat', 11 June 1945.

11. Proceedings of the Conferences of District School Supervisors, Pädagogisches Zentrum Berlin. Unpublished.

12. Schützler op. cit. p. 75 ff.; G. Uhlig, *Der Beginn der anti-faschistisch-demokratischen Schulreform 1945-1946,* (Berlin, 1965), p. 87 f.

13. Berlin. *Kampf,* op. cit., 31.1.46/95; 8.8.46/17; 1.9.46/1; 20.9.46/56.

14. Military Government Regulations. Office of Military Government, US Zone, 8-421.2.

15. *Stenographische Berichte der Stadtverordnetenversammlung von Berlin, 1.Wahlperiode, 47.* (13 November 1947). The law was published with the amendments by the Kommandatura— referred to below— : *Verordnungsblatt für Gross-Berlin,* 1948, p. 358 f.

16. Cf J. Gimbel, *The American Occupation of Germany,* (Stanford, 1968), p. 249.

17. US Department of State, *Germany 1947-1949. The Story in Documents,* Publ. No. 3556, Washington 1950, p. 543.

18. OMGUS, *Monthly Report,* No. 36, June 1948.

11. *A British View of Education in Berlin*

Trevor Davies

Berlin was different from the rest of Germany in several ways :
it was the capital, it had been a centre of educational reform in
Weimar days, and it was the meeting place of the victors from
East and West. These factors made the Berlin atmosphere something special, which was sensed by all visitors. Not a few of these,
after a day or two in Berlin, would ask : 'Do you always live at
this pace?' They had been whirled from an *Abitur* examination
beginning at 8 a.m. (with a view of the snow-covered Russian
Zone through the window) to a session of the Schools Parliament,
then they had visited a Youth House, and finished up at a school
performance of *Midsummer Night's Dream* in English, with
animated discussions all day.

A year after the end of the War, Berlin presented the same
sights as other German towns : acres of ruins, roads littered with
rubble, people crossing to Tiergarten by ferry (the bridges had
been destroyed), bare-footed men pushing belongings on home-
made carts, women piling up masonry, wearing layers of clothes
to keep out the cold. The single sheets of the newspapers gave
lists of those who had died of cold and hunger, infant mortality
(much of it a delayed result of Russian occupation) rocketed.
Children took it in turns to wear the family shoes to go to school,
yet English visitors expressed astonishment at their neat and
clean appearance. Women took on heavy work so as to get out
of the lowest category of food rationing—the Russians, who
arrived a month before the British and Americans, had devised
five categories, the highest being 'creative' (pro-Communist)
intelligentsia. The juvenile prisons were full to overflowing with
young blackmarketeers, made criminal by need.

It was in these conditions that the schools resumed their work.
Former teachers who had been removed by the Nazis flowed
back enthusiastically and were often given responsible jobs.
Among them was a high percentage of those who had been
active 'school reformers'. There was naturally a wish among
them to forget the differences (mainly between SPD and KPD)

that had weakened resistance to Hitler, and this explains why some of them, when the division of Berlin came, hesitated about which side to take. Many, however, made up their minds early —they realised that despite ideological differences the methods of the Communists were close to those of the Nazis and that both organisations attracted the same sort of *apparachiki*. Some teachers spent years in Nazi camps and then vanished into Communist prisons or camps for years more.

These bitter experiences help to explain the crowds who packed school halls to hear lectures on nursery schools or adult education. An English lecturer might arrive in a room with one candle on the table in front of him and start addressing the darkness on the workings of Parliament. It was not until the lights suddenly came on—the blackout for that area having come to an end—that he realised the room was full. On one such occasion the chairman was not aware of the change: he was blind, having spent years in prison without medical attention for his opposition to Hitler.

There was a real longing to hear what had been going on outside Germany during the twelve years of isolation, to hear questions discussed from more than one angle, to be able to put questions and even to voice disagreement. Lectures delivered by us in the Eastern Sector became political demonstrations against the new totalitarianism. Audiences who asked questions of Russian speakers received bland answers, such as that no one in the Soviet Union wanted to form a youth group that was not Communist.

Until the split, the City Assembly met in the Russian Sector, and the Ministry of Education was situated there, as were the University of Berlin (renamed the Humboldt University) and the Pädagogische Hochschule (Teachers' Training College). To get to a debate was like entering a Heath Robinson world or a building devised by Monsieur Hulot: one went upstairs to get to the next room and walked along planks suspended in mid-air, but this building had been chosen because it was less damaged than the surrounding ones. It was here that Frau Dr Gertrud Panzer stood up to the Russian Commandant, as recounted elsewhere in this book, just after the former Director of Education for Manchester had left the room.

This visit of Mr Lester Smith is worth mentioning because it shows how the policy of sending a steady stream of educationists to Berlin ensured both that the Berliners felt that they were not isolated and that thinking circles in Britain were informed of what was going on.

Although the Berliners continued to take a lively interest in education abroad—whether it was Britain or Borneo—they needed contact on the purely human level most of all. This is an appropriate point to recall the contribution made by thousands of people in this country. On several occasions young Germans told one that their time as POWs had been the happiest in their lives till then, and one never sensed resentment—quite the contrary. The same is true of the visits to Britain organised by the Education Adviser. They often led to lasting friendships, just as some of the young English and German exchange teachers found husbands and wives in Germany and Britain.

It became clear after a time that it was even more important to inform visitors about the Berlin scene than to enlighten Berliners about Britain. This was partly a matter of language and the educational systems—English was learnt by every Berlin child from the fifth class (roughly age ten onwards), and many teachers had a good knowledge of our history, literature and institutions on which they could build—but also because our development had been more or less consistent, whereas it was difficult even for Germans to keep track of their fragmented history and geography. After a time one found that quotations from *1066 and All That* or *Alice in Wonderland* provoked immediate response from a German audience, indicating a wide range of knowledge on their part. There were even one or two who understood the Irish question as well as the average informed Englishman. It was not unusual for a candidate in the oral of the school-leaving examination to be asked about Frank Cousins or Kwame Nkrumah.

As for comprehensive schooling, it was we who asked to have it explained by the Germans. Dr Klesse, of the Pädagogische Hochschule, gave Education Branch an exhaustive lecture on the German conception of the *Einheitsschule* in 1948. The School Law which was passed in that year converted the whole system of education in Berlin into a highly organised comprehensive system from the age of six to nineteen. It was based upon ideas which Berlin educationists traced back to the Gotha programme of the Social Democratic Party in 1875. In a centralised system such as the Germans have, experiments are obviously much easier to carry out and assess. After three years, there was a partial setback: at the age of twelve (although in fact age is not the decisive factor in Germany, since passing up is not automatic after the first two years), pupils were once more split up into three types of school. The reason for this modification of the original law is in dispute. Some people said it was the result of three years' experience, others that it was a political compromise. Certainly the name *Einheitsschule* did not help— anything associated with 'unity' suggested a link with the 'unity' forced on Social Democrats and Communists in Communist-occupied Germany.

Something of the original reform remained: the universal mixing of boys and girls, the introduction of compulsory English, the raising of the age of selection from about ten to about twelve, and the attempt to make the range of subjects offered in the three types of school similar in the interest of late developers. It must be mentioned, however, that transfer from *Mittelschule* to *Oberschule* had been fairly common before, and special classes and schools to facilitate this movement *(Aufbauklassen* and *Aufbauschulen)* existed in Berlin as in other parts of Germany. The *Einheitsschule* in Neukölln survived the change in 1951. It was spared because it had existed before 1933 and had strong local support. Not everyone agreed with the principles of the *Einheitsschule* that remained: one headmistress insisted on keeping classes for girls who wanted them, subject specialists complained that bright children had been held back; interestingly enough, in the light of our own experience, this was particularly the case in English.

The German system of grammar school education helped in the creation of these reforms. Everyone takes all subjects to the age of nineteen or twenty, so that virtually every teacher can teach the elementary stages of any subject. In practice, some teachers opted out of English and traded maths or games for it with a colleague. The Pädagogische Hochschule was planned to provide teachers who could teach the early stages of all subjects and the middle stages of one or two. Possession of the *Abitur* was a condition of entry. Some young men had been English interpreters in POW camps, some girls had become interpreters and

secretaries in Military Government, so they made up in command
of the spoken language what they had missed in not attending
university. Our officers were able to help by taking classes with
these teachers or giving occasional lectures. The library provided
by the British Centre was as useful as visiting speakers were
stimulating. Many of the lecturers who visited Berlin were of the
top flight and included Bertrand Russell, T. S. Eliot, Herbert
Read, Harold Nicolson, Stephen Spender, John Summerson,
Father Copplestone, Vera Brittain, Elizabeth Bowen, Noel
Annan. Humbler mortals were just as well received—in schools
they were often more effective because they were closer to their
hearers, although Anthony Wedgwood Benn produced a great
effect in the school that he visited. Berlin felt that it was being
treated as a capital, at least by the British. These were the days
when it was thought that some elements in Western Germany
were not as interested in the former capital as they should have
been.

The publishing house of Cornelsen was early in the field of
textbooks for learning English. They took great pains to get the
language and background correct, and here our advice was
sought on points of detail. They also worked in close collaboration with the teachers in the schools, who pointed out which
chapters were too difficult or not interesting. Each new edition
brought improvements.

In the first few years there was real hardship among teachers
and taught through want of food, clothing and heating, not to
mention shortage of paper and books. When the Free University
was founded, at the time of the split in the city, the Educational
Adviser, Mr Birley, was able to make a gift from the west of
thousands of books, some duplicate copies of which were actually
diverted to the Prussian State Library, Unter den Linden. In
this way, for example, Isaac Deutscher's *Stalin*, which had just
appeared, found its way to the East.

At the same time as dissident students and professors came
over to the West to found a university free from ideological
control, the same thing happened with the Pädagogische Hochschule. The catalyst appeared to be the visit of an English
professor from London University (Professor Robson-Scott).
Until that moment the Western Allies had had little to do with
this important institution, and the Russians regarded it as their

property in the same way as they claimed the university was theirs. (It was because of this that the British concentrated on developing the range of the Technische Hochshule, Charlottenburg, now the Technische Universität). The Russians were annoyed that students of the Pädagogische Hochschule had attended the professor's lecture and sent a representative shortly after to make good the damage. He delivered a ranting harangue, in which he treated his audience as a crowd of unrepentant fascist beasts. After that the students took what each could carry, came over to the West and were given a building in the American Sector to found a new Pädagogische Hochschule—hence the phoenix that has since appeared on its publications.

The aim of the Pädagogische Hochschule was to provide teachers for the *Einheitsschule,* but on how this was to be done there were divergent opinions. Some felt that it should be part of the university (this view was adopted by the powerful *Lehrergewerkschaft*), others felt that the university outlook was not appropriate and that the primacy of educating children would suffer unless a new type of autonomous institution were founded. It was to train teachers for the first nine classes of the comprehensive school (six to fifteen) and for the (compulsory) dayrelease schools *(Berufsschulen)* and the various types of special schools. The possession of the *Abitur* was a prerequisite, although this was relaxed for the *Berufsschule* teachers. The course lasted three and a half years. Its heads of departments were professors and students were able to attend lectures at the university in addition to their own.

Our relations with the Pädagogische Hochschule were always close and one of our number became a full-time lecturer there.

We looked upon the young men and women who came out from Britain to teach in German schools as very much our concern. Several married Berlin wives or husbands and they were almost all very reluctant to leave the city. They helped in the production of English plays and entered into the life of the schools. One came out of a play rehearsal to find that his pupils had wrapped up his diminutive car in brown paper and tied it up with string like a parcel. One was imprisoned by the East German police for going to sleep in a train and being carried on into the Russian Zone; another pursued and helped to arrest an

offender against the law in the West. Another became Professor
of German at a British university.

The Berlin Cultural Relations Group worked from the British
Centre and felt a part of the life of Berlin. There was probably
not a school in West Berlin, and hardly any kind of educational
institution, with which we did not have dealings of some sort.
One got to know where the art or music was particularly good,
who gave splendid lessons to ESN children, who was interested
in the sonnets of Michelangelo. Each new visitor from Britain
provided an opportunity to get to know a new school or play
group or other facet of education. A number of visitors sat
through the oral part of the *Abitur*—a fascinating experience,
especially as oral exams were hardly known in England at that
time. Professor Lauwerys of London University Institute of
Education, did some quick marking of written papers in physics
during one of these orals and awarded the same grades as the
German examiners. On another occasion, a prominent Jewish
member of the LCC, Mrs Helen Bentwich, was amused to hear
history candidates at the Pädagogische Hochschule answering
questions on the social forces represented by Isaiah, a compulsory part of their studies. A member of our group was regularly
invited to keep the minutes of oral exams in English and French
at the Free University.

Both sides took this co-operation for granted. British people
who had come out to purge the German education service of
National Socialist influence began by rubber-stamping permits
to publish books, scrutinising questionnaires on the political
activities of would-be teachers and actually ordering the removal
of toy soldiers from shop windows. Before they had realised it
they were a kind of Anglo-German civil service working in
German education. We seemed to have unconsciously become
District Officers on the model of the old Colonial Service, provided with the most hazy terms of reference but seeking to cope
with what turned up. Is it over-optimistic to believe that the
result was more lasting—and certainly more beneficial to both
sides—than the execution of clear orders to indoctrinate, such as
Wolfgang Leonhardt describes in his experiences as a servant of
Soviet Communism?

Denazification could only mete out very rough justice. A girl
who had had some position of trust in the BDM and was ex-

cluded from teaching in 1947 revealed casually about ten years later that she had been prevented from studying medicine under Hitler because of her Jewish grandmother. One question in the questionnaire asked how the person filling it in had voted at the last free election before Hitler was firmly in the saddle. All the Jesuit fathers of the Canisius School wrote : 'electoral secret'. They were the only ones to do so. Many people with something to hide fled to the West, and almost all those who filled leading positions knew each other from Weimar days, and they had left teaching under Hitler, so that the atmosphere in Berlin was very healthy.

This was particularly fortunate because the memory of the Third Reich was soon driven into the back of people's minds by the need to cope with Communism. Stories of midnight arrest and gruelling interrogation in the Soviet Sector and Zone, of kidnap and attempted blackmail or bribery were heard every day. Teachers were under greater pressure, probably, than they had been under Hitler : the Nazis to some extent used the Hitler Youth as a rival organisation to the schools, whereas the Communists inculcated their ideology through intellectual education; history was a particularly important subject in their eyes. The teaching of the mother tongue involved writing essays on : What our teacher has told us about Stalin, or What Mother and Father talk about at home. Issue after issue of the Communist *Lehrerzeitung* devoted its main article to discipline, e.g. 'The leading role of the teacher'. Teachers were criticised for showing 'a lack of partiality' or of 'ideological clarity'. Stories for the little ones told how a quiet, clever boy in a Russian school was always ready to help his classmates but never let them copy. Josef Vissarionovich was to be their model.

One could never forget that Berlin was surrounded by a Communist state, in which hardline Stalinists ruled. One young man came into the office one day to talk. He had just arrived from Leipzig, where he had been at the university. Having criticised the 'elections' he had been interviewed at midnight and had taken the first train to Berlin on his release. He went back to Leipzig, was caught distributing leaflets, and reappeared in the office just two years later after an amnesty, with a few teeth missing and in a bad physical state. Another student of medicine, who lived in the basement of a Control Commission house, had

failed his *Abitur* in the East the first time for giving the
wrong answer to the question : Was the American War of
Independence an Imperialist one? The answer at that time was
yes.

One of our borough directors of education had been thrown
out of his school in the Eastern Sector because a *Life of Scharnhorst* had been found in the school library. The real reason was
no doubt that he had refused to leave the SPD for the Socialist
Unity Party. A few years later Scharnhorst was proclaimed one
of the heroic sons of the German people, together with Karl
Marx and Walter Ulbricht.

One of the earliest readers for learning English in the DDR
was called *The Gordons*. It purported to tell the life story of a
typical English working-class family and was written by a lady
who had spent the Hitler years in England. One of the children
asks his mother for an orange and is told he will get one when
she can afford one, at Christmas. One of the girls goes for a
typing job and meets her predecessor, who is being dismissed
because she will not accept a reduction in salary. Another book
entitled *English School Life* had extracts from Dickens and *Tom
Brown's Schooldays,* but only the bullying scenes. No ray of light
entered the darkness of this gloomy, brutal world. The compiler
of this collection was an intelligent, widely-read scholar. A member of his family had been recently arrested, and perhaps that
is the explanation.

In spite of all this, there was widespread approval in Berlin
educational circles for some aspects of the educational changes
in the DDR, and as late as the early 1960s a few educationists
from East Berlin came over and addressed a large audience in
the Pädagogische Hochschule on polytechnic education. In
private they admitted that it was far from working as it was
supposed to. As under Hitler, teachers still find a way to educate,
but it must be at great cost in nervous energy and ingenuity.
One suspects that some of the articles in the educational press
were written tongue in cheek : suggesting for example an im-
proved wording for 'two men plough a field in x days'—'two
members of the collective form "Harmony" plough a field
together with a tractor from the Machine Pool . . .'.

In the field of adult education, British members of the group
and young assistants gave isolated talks or session-long courses in

English, but there were also annual courses and meetings in which British lecturers from home participated; one of the first was a recent graduate called Anthony Crosland. As time went on, the emphasis changed here too : it became more necessary for the visitors to be informed, for Germans were now making great use of their opportunities to visit Britain, first at our expense, then by private arrangement. One such course was addressed by a visitor from the East who spoke in favour of the régime. As the talk progressed, the temperature seemed to fall. One of the British participants, who had taken a rosy view of the DDR, looked more depressed than anyone else.

The Germans were particularly interested in our university department of adult education. Some university teachers did involve themselves in adult education, but on a purely private basis. There was a society called *Humanitas* in which professors addressed sixth formers on aspects of their subjects. The *Abend-gymnasium* was also revived; this was an evening institute preparing working people for the *Abitur,* the key to university entrance. This was probably a more formidable hurdle than evening study which led to London University's external degrees. In the last two decades a lot of attention has been devoted to the *zweiter Bildungsweg* and the Open University has been greeted with enthusiasm. In short, the yeast is still very active.

The British centre was to some extent neutral territory. We were able to invite guests at that time that German bodies could not invite without arousing opposition. Father Copplestone's lecture in the dark days of the Blockade was chaired by a woman member of the Philosophical Faculty of the Humboldt University, East Berlin. (Interestingly enough she later transferred to the Theological Faculty). We had made her acquaintance at the house of another professor of the university, a member of the SED, who lived in the West. Those were the days when all food was in short supply, even with us, and the preliminary interview was a battle between rapid consumption of buns and her irrepressible eloquence. She had been beaten up by the SA in 1933 and her fiancé murdered, but possessed that resilience that one so admired in the Berliners, particularly the women. On another occasion Ludwig Renn came to a reception and expressed his dissatisfaction with the tendency of the younger generation in the East to conform. Members of the Brecht theatre, the Berliner

Ensemble, including Brecht's wife Helene Weigel, were occasionally seen at lectures of theatrical interest.

Co-operation with other nationalities, particularly the Americans, was cordial and lasting. One of our members was on the
Committee of Mittelhof, run by American Friends, and of the
Società Dante Alighieri. Bertrand Russell met Westermann, the
authority on African languages, in an unlikely place—a tea
queue in the American Harnack-Haus. Sometimes ex-German
Jews took the decision, a very hard one, to return to the scene of
their childhood or youth as some kind of exorcism, but they had
little idea of what they would find or what memories would be
awakened. One remembers accompanying a lady and her
daughter through the Jewish cemetery in East Berlin on
Christmas morning. We passed the massive mausoleums of
Wilhelminian Jews who had died wealthy and distinguished, but
every so often a name appeared 'deported to the East' or 'died
while being deported'. Nevertheless, it was a pilgrimage they
had to make, and they bore it with traditional Jewish cheerful-
ness. One also remembers accompanying a German teacher
through the three controls on her escape from the East to the
West, breathing a sigh of relief every time the People's Police
failed to detect that her passport, provided by a Jewish friend of
her schooldays, was forged.

After a time, we acquired a certain reputation as all-purpose
guides to Berlin, particularly its educational and cultural life.
And so one was never surprised when someone turned up on
somebody else's recommendation and asked to be taken to the
places or people that interested them: Swiss educationists who
simply wanted to see their Consul and were disgusted to find he
spoke only *Hochdeutsch*; an Australian psychologist who felt
that his journey had been really worth while when he was taken
to the fascinating, self-built house of a White Russian doctor to
hear a concert given by disabled people; the charming young
lady mathematician from Santiago de Chile, speaking perfect
Württemberg German, inherited from her grandfather, who had
a UNESCO scholarship to travel around Europe enquiring into
the validity of educational statistics; a Pakistani missionary from
the Ahmadiyyah movement who was horrified by the frivolity
of Berlin children (they were always singing or producing plays
instead of learning that life is serious) and produced an em-

barrassed hush in a session of teachers-in-training by his courteous reference to their great leader Adolf Hitler (his turn came in the next school, when an equally polite headmistress paid a sincere tribute to the achievements of Mahatma Gandhi).

Our contacts with the Russians were of a different order, especially after the split in the city. A Russian attaché did come to the Deutsch-Britische Gesellschaft, but it became clear after a short time that his object was to recruit one of us as an agent (we did not know that Blake had just been arrested and there may have been some connexion). After waving hundred mark notes in the face of the person whose home he visited once a week on the pretext of exchanging English and Russian conversation, he progressed step by step from sweets and toys for the children to Russian classics and finally a bottle of vodka, which he seemed to think would do the trick. At the end of a pleasant evening (he and his wife were likeable people), he had to be more or less carried to the car and put on the U-Bahn. Shortly after he called to say he had been recalled to Moscow, much to our regret.

None of this episode was reported to higher authority on the British side. It was enjoyed as one of the pleasures of living in Berlin. Berlin was different. Everyone, however, finds the Berlin he is looking for. It may centre like Mr Norris's around the Wittenbergplatz or it may linger in the memory as a bright schoolroom on a frosty morning at eight o'clock just before Christmas. The occasion is the practical examination of a young teacher, a girl born just before the outbreak of War. Through the window one can see the snow-covered fields of the Russian Zone, and the table is laid with an Adventskranz with candles lit. Before discussing the English lesson that she has just given, the examiner says: 'Well, Fräulein Schmidt, let's sing a carol. What do you suggest?' They sing, and then get down to discuss the lesson with Prussian gravity and scepticism.

My own contact with Germany began at Oxford where I first came upon the work of Rudolph Steiner. His ideas were so trenchant that I continued to pursue them in Germany. During the Second World War I was a schoolmaster in Bristol and then engaged in intelligence duties at Bletchley Park, which kept me in close touch with what was happening in Germany. Subsequently I received an invitation to attend an interview with the prospect of doing educational work in Germany after the War. My name had been put to Control Commission by the Vice-Chancellor of the University, Sir Richard Livingstone, on the recommendation of Dr W. T. S. Stallybrass, the Principal of my college, Brasenose.

Towards the end of the next month I arrived in Münster. Before leaving Britain, there had been a training course but little time for preparation or reflection; we were pitched into an unprecedented situation. Within a few days I found myself driving around Westphalia with the Monuments and Fine Arts Officer assessing which of the old churches—the Patroklikirche in Soest, the cathedral in Paderborn and others—needed to have their roofs temporarily repaired, wondering whether anything ought to be spared for monuments when the housing need was so overwhelming. The head of Education Section in Westphalia was Lt-Colonel George Savage, a Canadian with little knowledge of German or Germany but with much energy and goodwill. He asked me to go with him to see Pastor Friedrich von Bodelschwingh of Bethel near Bielefeld, a home for physically and mentally handicapped young people; en route I was able to tell him how courageously von Bodelschwingh had withstood the Nazis and saved his charges from euthanasia.

After a few weeks on general educational duties at Münster, I was posted to Arnsberg, the administrative centre of *Regierungsbezirk* Arnsberg, the southern half of Westphalia, with a population of 3.5 million. The local head of the Education

Section was Squadron-Leader John Ozanne, a Channel Islander
with a good knowledge of German. He asked me if I knew anything about youth work and, when I replied that I did not, he
said the other educational posts were already filled and this was
of some urgency. He explained he had to know immediately
because Field-Marshal Montgomery was coming the following
week, was very interested in youth work and would have many
questions. 'Oh, and who is going to answer the questions?' I
enquired. 'You,' he replied. In no time I was immersed in the
problems of German youth!

Having known Germany before the War through work and
study within the Steiner movement and the Christian Community, I was in a better position than most of my colleagues to
know what had been going on and what needed to be done. And,
by a stroke of good fortune, there came together a group of
people who soon developed into a harmonious and effective
team. There was the *Regierungsbezirk* Commander, Colonel
D. A. Stirling, who had been captured by Rommel in the desert
and had been among those who had escaped from the British
Generals' Camp, Campo 12, near Florence. There was John
Ozanne's successor, Lt-Colonel Rudolph Elwes, a devout Roman
Catholic. On the German side there was *Regierungsdirektor*
(Chief Education Officer) Ernst Müller, socialist and pacifist, who
had suffered greatly under the Nazis; and *Bezirksjugendpfleger*
(Area Youth Officer) Clemens Busch, whom Müller appointed
at my suggestion. There was my secretary, Helene Koenig, and
my driver, Helmut Koch. The aim was clear: to encourage
co-operation between the various youth groups which quickly
occupied the vacuum left by the Hitler Youth, between organised
and unorganised youth and between German and European
Youth.

Catholic and Evangelical youth were quickly off the mark,
having been kept going in some sort of way, however covertly,
under the wing of the Churches throughout the Nazi period.
the *Falken* (Social-Democrat) and *Freie Deutsche Jugend* (by
and large Communist), which had been sustained abroad, were
soon re-established. There followed sports and trade union
groups, and, more problematical, the *Bündische Jugend,* which
certainly harboured vestiges of the Hitler Youth (I remember an
exchange of correspondence with Adolf von Thadden, later to

H

lead the National Democratic Party, who wanted to have uniforms and flags and tests of courage). Groups belonging to all these organisations and others such as the *Sauerländischer Gebirgsverein* (Sauerland Mountain Club) on a more local basis were recognised and registered by Military Government, the politically oriented groups not without some hesitation and reluctance (but it was pointed out that the Churches in Germany exercised political influence and yet were allowed to have their own youth organisations). Our effort went into fostering goodwill and co-operation between the various organisations and served to lessen recrimination and friction. In Arnsberg we were particularly fortunate in having a team of people who, though holding widely divergent religious and political views, yet had trust in each other's integrity; if there was reluctance to co-operate on the Catholic side, Rudolph Elwes would mediate, twice taking me to see the Archbishop of Paderborn; if on the Protestant side, I would seek out the leader of Evangelical Youth, Pastor Johannes Busch in Witten; Ernst Müller would pacify the Social Democrats.

The best way of avoiding a unitary state movement like the Hitler Youth was not for each group to go its own way but to co-operate willingly in the interests of all young people. These were not easy arguments to advance in a foreign language, often to those who had been victims of totalitarian concepts and practices, but we had some success and there was no relapse into the conflict between Catholic, Protestant and Socialist groups which had led the way for the Hitler Youth. The Zonal Youth Leadership Training Centre at Vlotho provided a successful forum for discussion. Great care was taken when scouting was introduced into Germany as the Hitler Youth had borrowed some of its features. Every effort was made to bring together all interests in one organisation and, although this proved impossible, a federal association was set up comprising Catholic, Evangelical and Free Scouts, working closely together.

One movement which merited unreserved support was the German Youth Hostel Association. It was an indigenous growth, and had spread from Germany throughout the world. It had been from the beginning a meeting ground for all young people, irrespective of religious or political differences, and had remained so at a time when the Hitler Youth was making headway by exploiting the division of German youth into mutually hostile factions. Its founders, Richard Schirrmann and Wilhelm Münker, deposed by the Nazis, resumed their activities.

The Secretary of the International Youth Hostels Association, St John Catchpool, was a frequent visitor to Germany and Arnsberg. During the War and immediately afterwards, Youth Hostels had been taken over for welfare purposes such as old people's homes and refugee centres but as soon as alternative accommodation could be provided, we tried to make some of them available. The British officer in charge of forestry in the area reported to Colonel Stirling that he had come across a large house being built using a great deal of timber without permission. To protect the forests, it was forbidden to use timber without a permit and those breaking this regulation were liable to imprisonment. The builder had sworn that he was building the house not for himself but as a hostel for young people. The forestry officer found this difficult to believe, since most Germans had enough to do looking after themselves in those days without bothering about others. Colonel Stirling asked me to investigate. Jupp Schöttler was building, almost with his bare hands, the youth hostel of Finnentrop-Bamenohl, the first to be built after the Second World War. Military Government turned a blind eye and in due course I was happy to attend the opening ceremony in the presence of Richard Schirrmann. Another youth hostel, the picturesque Burg Bilstein in the heart of the Sauerland mountains, became a centre for our youth activities: young people came from all parts of *Regierungsbezirk* Arnsberg, including much of the Ruhr; there was a free exchange of opinion, no youngster was ever rebuked or reported for any view he or she expressed, however confused or reactionary.

Field-Marshal Montgomery took a close interest in German youth and, at an early stage, he had given instructions that in each district 'a good German' was to be appointed whose task would be to promote the interests of young people within the community. It was this instruction that had led to the nomination of Clemens Busch as *Bezirksjugendpfleger* (Area Youth Officer) and which led to the appointment of a *Kreisjugendpfleger* (District Youth Officer) in each of the twenty-five *Kreise* of the *Bezirk*. Clemens Busch and I kept a careful eye on the appointments and held regular meetings with the

twenty-five *Kreisjugendpfleger,* giving them all the support
we could. In co-operation with them a policy of reconciliation between the various youth organisations, between
organised and unorganised youth and, later, between German and European youth was pursued which had an effect
throughout the whole area. A *Kreisjugendring* (District Youth
Council) was set up within each *Kreis,* bringing together the
various youth groups in joint consultation. In each *Kreis* there
was also a *Jugendamtsauschuss* (Youth Office Committee) comprising councillors, officials and youth representatives, to foster
the youth welfare and activities services within the local community. I tried to visit each *Kreis* at least once a month and to
attend a meeting of the *Jugendamtsausschuss* so that I had some
idea of the problems of youth welfare and activities throughout
the area.

I was assisted in this work by Joan Dunning, Andrew Finlay
and my colleagues in Education Branch, notably Rudolph Elwes
and Fred Brand all of whom gave support to our work. Another
great source of strength were the relief teams which were concentrated within the Ruhr but operated throughout the area and
included the British, Swiss and Swedish, in the Guides International Service, the Salvation Army, and the Quakers.

One day early in 1949 Ernst Müller came to see me. He said
that, for the sake of democracy in Germany, the co-operation
which had grown up between British and German educationists
in the British Zone of Germany must be continued into the
future. He asked what he could do to ensure that we stayed in
Germany for many years to come. I replied that there was little
he could do along those lines, that various pressures, economic
and political, would necessitate our withdrawal in the not too
distant future. What could be done, however, was to form and
foster direct links between similar British and German local
education authorities which would continue to grow from
strength to strength long after we had departed. He immediately
offered his full support for this idea, backed by the educational
resources of *Regierungsbezirk* Arnsberg.

It remained to find an area in England corresponding to
Arnsberg, which had a similar contrast between densely indus-
trialised conurbations and rural districts, with a population of
about 3 million. Lancashire and Yorkshire were the obvious

possibilities; the West Riding seemed to be the closest match. That summer I spent a fortnight in the West Riding studying new developments in education and at the end of my stay put the idea of a link with Arnsberg to the Chief Education Officer, Mr Alec Clegg, who also promised his full support.

First there was a year of unceasing negotiation with education and youth committees, Mayors and Lord Mayors, Clerks of Councils, Chief Education Officers and their Chairmen, universities, youth organisations, His Majesty's Inspectors, the *York-shire Post*, the Bishop of Sheffield, and the Lord Lieutenant of the County. I was attempting to engage the machinery of local government in the cause of international understanding, bringing local authorities and communities into fruitful collaboration and so to perpetuate the bond of friendship which had grown up between British and German educationists.

In the summer of 1950 I went to the Hook of Holland to meet the first boat bringing young people from the West Riding. Although there had already been twinnings between individual towns of Britain and Germany, notably between Bristol and Hanover, this was the first Regional Exchange Link to be established. Not only were the West Riding and *Regierungsbezirk* Arnsberg connected in this way but links were also formed between cities and towns within the two regions including Leeds and Dortmund, Sheffield and Bochum, Wakefield and Herne. With the support of Des McGlynn, who was responsible for youth work at *Land* level, this campaign spread throughout North Rhine-Westphalia and, after our return to England led to a series of successful congresses of Linked Local Authorities; the most recent was in October 1974 in York, the sister-city of Münster. Starting from this first regional exchange Link, all parts of Britain and Germany have now been linked, for example Scotland with Bavaria, Wales with Baden-Württemberg, the South-West with Lower Saxony.

This has been part of the story, told without access to sources, of what happened in one *Regierungsbezirk*. But what has scarcely been mentioned is the welfare side: the distribution of food and equipment in the early days, the running of camps, relief teams, the treatment of delinquent youth, the approved schools, the introduction of probation, the setting up of child guidance clinics. There was a vast field to be covered and each British

youth officer was able to contribute according to his own interests. It was a dedicated group of colleagues—we had an
establishment at one time of 200 youth officers though I do not
think we ever had a full complement—working at Zonal, *Land*
and *Bezirk* level, pursuing very different paths within wide
limits of policy. We were grateful to Donald Riddy, Sir Robert
Birley and to T. H. Marshall not only for all they did to further
the cause of educational and youth work but also for providing
us with a field in which we could develop our own initiatives. A
similar tribute should also be paid to Alan Andrews who led the
group of youth officers.

13. *The British Influence on German Adult Education*

Fritz Borinski

The education policy of the Control Commission in the British Zone was not based on a rigid model but gave the Germans a wide measure of freedom. This was also true of the reconstruction of adult education in Germany after 1945. The British administration limited its involvement to general supervision and support. The supervision included the crucial and very difficult area of personnel policy—especially denazification. The support given lay not only in the realm of materials and ideas but also of administration and spiritual regeneration.

It should be remembered that the reconstruction of the adult education system in Germany immediately after the collapse was first and foremost a practical emergency activity. To refer to that period in terms of an ideological restoration of the adult education principles of the Weimar period is to misunderstand completely the situation at that time. There was no time in those days for ideological discussions, it was simply a case of getting down to practical, pragmatic action. In this we found the British occupation forces, and especially the education officers of the Control Commission, understanding and helpful. Together we had to care for the desperate bands of refugees and of prisoners of war who were returning from captivity and trying to find their homes in a world that had been ravaged and transformed; for the great numbers of homeless young people roving around the country, for German personnel employed by the British armed forces (the German Service Organisation) who had found temporary lodging in this way. The latter lived in camps under military discipline, had not adjusted fully to everyday civilian life and often were still strongly National-Socialist at heart. They constituted a serious social-psychological problem for the British occupation force. Education officers urged that the *Volkshochschulen* should help to solve this problem. In the residential *Volkshochschule* in Göhrde we ran about thirty GSO (German Service Organisation) courses. This was an exciting, intensive and very personal activity. There was also a central GSO school in Hamburg, directed by Ernst Hessenauer.

The pragmatic and urgent character of the work is reflected in the first Conference for Directors of *Volkshochschulen* in the British Zone. This took place in Hanover in April 1946 as a result of a British initiative, amidst all the difficulties of communication, provisioning and accommodation in a city badly damaged by bombs. In his opening remarks Adolf Grimme reminded the participants that only a year earlier the battle had been raging to defend the Weser bridges but that now, despite hunger, cold and destruction, 'the life force of our people is stirring once again'. 'The mere fact that this conference is possible,' he said, 'is a source of encouragement.' The conference programme did not consist of papers and discussions about educational aims and principles but was concerned with immediate, practical questions : 'How can we communicate with young people between the ages of eighteen and twenty-five?' 'Suggestions for teaching materials . . . bearing in mind the paper shortage', 'Where are the teachers going to come from and how are we going to train them?' 'Can *Volkshochschulen* educate people to political responsibility and if so, how?' 'What can *Volkshochschulen* do to help evacuees and refugees?' In a resolution on publications, we read : 'The Conference participants therefore request the central office of the Control Commission to issue a binding decree along these lines to all the units under its control'. This binding decree was to provide for the release of paper for timetables, recruitment posters and for duplicating purposes.

In this practical and pragmatic reconstruction the education officers responsible for adult education in Germany gave valuable material, organisational and pedagogic help. When I say material help I am not simply thinking of the provision of rations for school meals or the allocation of paper. I mean also the concern and active involvement of education officers which helped to create the atmosphere of trust which was an essential prerequisite for the work of reconstruction. May I refer, as an example, to the end of a three-month course at the residential *Volkshochschule* in Göhrde? This course, for men, was threatened with closure in May 1947 because of the food supply situation. It was saved by the timely intervention of the Swedish Red Cross who allocated to us food from their school meals stock. Then in June, when the course was due to shut down, the participants, who as former soldiers had often wandered through the forests, wanted to have a dinner of wild boar. In the large Göhrde forest there was only one forester who was allowed to shoot wild boar and he had to obtain the permission of the British administration before he could do so. So we took our request to the education officer in Lüneburg. He then approached a colleague at military headquarters who duly gave permission. The men thus got their way and the course ended with a convivial dinner to which the British Major, the chief forester of Göhrde and the forester who actually shot the boar were of course invited. In this way the education officer helped to provide us with an unforgettable 'educational experience'.

The shortage of suitable adult educationists was just as significant as the shortage of food. In the shadow of total Nazism and of denazification it was often very difficult to find the right kind of people for the work. The education officers helped in this respect too. A colleague and friend of Adolf Grimme, Otto Haase, reports how in the summer of 1945 soon after his release from a Nazi prison camp Adolf Grimme turned up unrecognised at the offices of the district authorities in Hanover looking for his friends. When he could not find them he went away again without telling anyone where he was going. And so it seemed that the chance for getting the right man to head the new education authority had slipped by and been lost for ever. But two English officers—Major Beattie and Captain Aitken Davis—whose spirited and prompt, if somewhat unusual initiative saved the day. They recognised the need for immediate action and sent out a search party in a military vehicle with orders to follow Grimme's trail and bring him back to Hanover. They eventually found the fugitive somewhere near Hamburg, brought him back again and the work began.

The British administration also helped to organise the rebuilding of *Volkshochschulen,* their amalgamation into regional groups, the formation of *Landesverbände* and regular contact between the *Länder* and the Zones, in which the Soviet Zone also took part during the first few years. In addition there was the intellectual help, given in the form of advice and recommendations as well as of active participation in lectures, courses

H*

and conferences. As an example I would mention the papers given by education officers at the first Conference for Directors of *Volkshochschulen* in Hanover and the lecture given by Mr Birley on the occasion of the founding of the Association of *Volkshochschulen* in Lower Saxony in Celle on 21 September 1947. His text was Goethe's statement: 'No amount of learning guarantees the power of judgement'. The delegations of British adult educationists who travelled through the Zone were also a great help. They would meet together at the beginning of their journey at a *Volkshochschule* for informative discussions with education officers and German colleagues. Then they would spread out over the whole Zone and come together again after a fortnight to exchange impressions and hold discussions. Professor Ross Waller of Manchester wrote about one such visit in July 1947 in the *Manchester Guardian*. Waller was critical of the excess of aesthetic lectures and at the same time he drew attention to the great need for 'reconstruction' and above all to the shortage of people suited to the work. He recorded that according to a reliable source of information there were only twenty adult educationists left in the British Zone who had been employed in adult education at the time of the Weimar Republic.

The education policy of the Control Commission gave the Germans a fair amount of freedom in the development of a new democratic adult education system. But it was important that this freedom should not lead to arbitrary disorganised activity and the growth of the new system was not allowed to go unchecked. Both the Germans and the English were agreed on this point. In a documentary report of the Conference of Directors of *Volkshochschulen* in Hanover published by Heiner Lotze in his series *The Practice of Adult Education* (1946) we read 'For the first time since the collapse of National Socialism there has been a demonstration of the desire for and achievement of a *genuine* adult education, shaped by our new Germany'. In the concept of 'genuine adult education' the German adult educationists were at one with the English, who wanted to help with advice and suggestions in the development of a free, democratic adult education system in post-fascist Germany. The British recommendation was characterised by four demands: (i) liberal education (ii) education for democracy (iii) education for a social purpose (iv) close co-operation between those responsible for adult education and the universities.

These are the four essentials of the British recommendation and they are also woven unobtrusively into the lecture given by Robert Birley in Celle.

According to British theory and practice, *liberal education* stands in contrast to *vocational training*. It is in this sense a disinterested and general education which concerns itself with the whole personality. It affects the totality of human existence. It teaches a person to make the most of life. Thus it is more comprehensive and goes deeper than mere preparation for a trade or profession. But if we are to get the most from life we cannot be purely concerned with the individual. Liberal education puts the individual alongside other human beings, alongside his fellow citizens in society and State. Liberal education is at the same time *education for democracy*. After the collapse of Germany, education for democracy was imperative in a situation where the anti-democratic, authoritarian régime had been destroyed and people, especially young people, had to learn how to live together in freedom and responsibility, criticism and tolerance.

But in our society education for democracy means *education for a social purpose*. The education movement is linked with the social movement. Thus in England the Workers' Educational Association is the principal vehicle of modern democratic adult education. It is impossible to have education for democracy without involving the work force. It is not possible to leave the workers out of this movement; they must be drawn into it, their aims and associations must coincide with those of adult education. This had already been tried in Germany in the Weimar period, notably by the Leipzig school of the adult education movement, and fostered through contacts with England. Then after 1945 there grew up in Lower Saxony a strong and permanent partnership between the trade union movement and the *Volkshochschulen*; this was called *Arbeit und Leben*. It was founded in the autumn of 1948 and after only a few months it had spread throughout the three Western Zones. The founding itself arose out of a purely German initiative but the Workers' Educational Association was quick to show interest and to give advice.

The link with the university is just as indispensable as the link with the trade unions for the development of democratic adult education, but also just as beset with tensions and difficulties. Reference has already been made at this conference to the fact that a University Commission had been set up by the Military Governor of the British Zone in the spring of 1948 to look into the state of the universities in Germany and to make recommendations for the reform of higher education. The Chairman of the Commission, Henry Everling of Hamburg, was a leading figure of the co-operative movement. Among its members were Lord Lindsay of Birker, Bruno Snell, Karl Friedrich von Weizsäcker, Katharina Petersen and the trade unionist Franz Theunert. The Commission's report was published late in 1948 in Germany and an English version was published officially in London in the spring of 1949. The ninth chapter of this report deals with adult education. It links 'specialist training' with 'liberal social education', or 'political and social education'. The report says: 'If this type of adult education is pursued properly, it is concerned with activating a sense of social and political responsibility. Thus it is not teaching in the ordinary sense of the word . . . in this case men and women come together to talk about their common problems . . . and to do this they need education and understanding of academic thinking.' This form of adult education is carried on in small groups, in which there is active co-operation between teachers and those being taught. The students should participate 'not only in the course, but also in the organisation running the course'. Thus close co-operation between the social organisations and the universities is a prerequisite for this kind of educational activity.

This 'liberal social education' was developed in Scandinavia, Great Britain and the British dominions. In Germany the relevant findings and experiences had been discussed theoretically and tested practically. Hohenrodt and Dreissigacker could be quoted in this context. But, in the words of the report, 'It is a pity that the universities in Germany have, as yet, taken little part in the development of this adult education.'

The Commission does not take the matter any further. It does not make a concrete recommendation for the development of a system of university adult education in Germany. It does, however, refer with approval and confidence to the new development of 'social academies' (*Sozialakademien*) in the British and American Zones (Frankfurt, Dortmund, Hamburg, Wilhelmshaven-Rüstersiel) which, attached to the university, retain their academic freedom. 'They must not become institutes for the vocational instruction demanded by outside organisations'.

At the time of the publication of the report produced by the Everling Commission a newly formed committee, made up of professors from the University of Göttingen and representatives of adult education in Lower Saxony, met in Göttingen. The purpose of the meeting was to try to develop a suitable form of co-operation between the universities and adult education in Lower Saxony. The initiative was again taken by the Germans. But they followed the example and advice of the British. After many difficulties and changes, the plan to base adult education in the universities by means of internal and extramural courses, led eventually in the winter term of 1955-6 to permanent co-operation between the University of Göttingen and the *Volkshochschulen* in Lower Saxony and to the founding of seminar courses at Göttingen by Helmuth Plessner, Erich Weniger and Willy Strzelewicz.

The four essentials of the British recommendation—liberal education, education for democracy, education for a social purpose and permanent co-operation with the university—have shaped the development of adult education in West Germany up to the present day. Even after twenty-five years, in a completely different world, they characterise and determine to a considerable extent the theoretical foundations of adult education.

It may often seem as though 'continued education', that is to say education specifically directed towards professional needs, has taken the place of liberal education. This is only a superficial and one-sided view. Professional training and education can and should supplement and make a practical reality of liberal education which is concerned with the totality of human existence. Even the pragmatic *Strukturplan* of the German Education Council (*Deutscher Bildungsrat*) of 1970, cannot avoid making an attempt to link professional training with personal, social and political education. Educationists and politicians, who want to keep democracy alive, must be especially vigilant in a highly technical and specialised society in order to ensure that powerful

interest groups are not allowed to dominate everything and
to undermine and devalue the essential nature and rights of
the individual. The precept of liberal education becomes increasingly important at a time when personal freedom and
humane liberalism are for the most part misunderstood and
suppressed. Learning for living is the unavoidable prerequisite
for every demand for a better quality of life.

The content and method, importance and aims of an 'education for democracy' are now being questioned once again
in the Federal Republic. Is political education one subject
amongst many others or is it a comprehensive principle underlying all education? Does it aim to bring people to terms with
the existing order or to promote radical or revolutionary change?
Should it provide unbiased, factual information or should it try
to encourage ideological commitment? Should it set store by
objectivity or aim at educationally effective participation?
Should it try to build a unified whole or should it show up and
explore areas of conflict?

After the policy of the Occupation period, the German *Volkshochschule* was concerned to develop democratic adult education in the form of humanitarian, social and political education.
Perhaps the work of political education was made too easy in
many places—too positivistic, too uncritical, too harmonious,
encouraging the unqualified acceptance of the status quo, of
established values and structures. Recent years have seen a reaction in the form of an intense concern with politics. The
German adult education system must face this. And in discussions and confrontations it must seek to defend and demonstrate the foundations of humane and realistic democracy, the
principles of 'liberal and social education'. It must refute and
overcome the dangerous alternatives—political totalitarianism
or escapism from political reality.

This also applies to workers' education (*Arbeiterbildung*).
For many years social and political problems have been treated
too lightly, too pragmatically and too optimistically in many
parts of the adult education system as well as in the trade unions
and the *Arbeit und Leben* movement. Workers' education lost
its existential, elemental character and became more functional
a kind of employee training specially programmed to meet the
needs of contemporary society. Since 1967 the demand for a

more existential, emancipatory workers' education has been taken up again with renewed enthusiasm. There have been attempts to draw up a new, neo-Marxist theory for workers' education. Left-wing trade unionists and students want to continue the revolutionary struggle against present-day society for the emancipation of the workers' movement, young extremists want to try to establish a lively contact with workers through the medium of workers' education. I cannot go into the background of these efforts here. At all events it is apparent that the affluent society has done nothing towards solving the problems of class differences, class-bound education in general and working-class education in particular. It has not met the hopes of the working class and a solution of these problems remains a task for democratic society and thus for democratic education in the changed social conditions of today.

Finally, university adult education. As I mentioned earlier the first secretariat for adult education at a German university was established in the winter term of 1955-6. Several meetings had preceded its formulation. I will mention only the conference at the residential *Volkshochschule* of Göhrde in the summer of 1950 in which Ludwig Raiser and Wolfgang Abendroth, Rectors of Göttingen University and the Social Academy of Wilhelmshaven respectively took part as well as Professor Evans of Cardiff and Wilhelm Flitner, both of whom gave papers. In December 1952 another conference, called by the Universities Council for Adult Education, took place in Oxford. Among the German participants were Bruno Snell, *Rektor* of Hamburg University, Walter Merck, Director of the UNESCO Institute in Hamburg, Helmuth Plessner, a sociologist from Göttingen, and Werner Stein, a university lecturer from Berlin. It was in Oxford that Plessner was won over to support for the new project at Göttingen; Werner Stein, who is at present Senator for Higher Education and the Arts in West Berlin, was the first German Education Minister to make adult education a legally prescribed duty of the university.

Since the beginning of the 1960s Secretariats, Institutes or Departments of Adult Education have been operating at a number of German universities and other institutions of higher education, among others Berlin, Frankfurt, Hanover, Bochum and Cologne. Nevertheless the problem of university adult education and of the integration of adult education into the university has by no means been solved in the Federal Republic. People have failed to understand that this integration must be an important part of the controversial democratic higher education reform that is currently taking place in the Federal Republic. Indeed, the present ambiguity about the situation of the universities in the Federal Republic, their vacillation between total politicisation and exaggerated academic specialisation diverts attention from the real demands of adult education and hinders the understanding of its true nature, of both its academic and its political role. The real purpose of university adult education cannot be appreciated and fulfilled either in a situation of total politicisation of knowledge or in one-sided professionalism, for example in the total concentration on academic refresher courses.

The education policy of the British Occupation forces helped to give impetus to a fresh beginning for democratic adult education in Germany in 1945. We are deeply indebted to those who worked in this field at that time for the human understanding that they so often showed and for their material and intellectual support. Adult educationists in Germany have sought to learn from democracies and to develop their own forms of democratic educational activity without unthinking imitation. In the very different world of today we face new problems and new tasks. These problems and tasks are, however, not restricted to the Federal Republic alone. They also apply in large part to our colleagues in England. Let us then strive to overcome these problems together through the mutual exchange of ideas and practical co-operation.

14

Adult Education for a New Society

Werner Burmeister

The Nazi régime had cut off the Germans from contacts with the outside world. People were prevented from forming or expressing their own views. Instead Nazi propaganda presented them with a world picture designed to produce predetermined reactions. Overwhelmed and corrupted by this propaganda, they were mostly unable to form their own opinions. To a larger extent than is often realised all of us depend on truthful information, on the ability to exchange views without fear and to obtain occasional confirmations of our views from others.

Not all of those who later claimed never to have been Nazis were dishonest—many had simply acted and thought in accordance with the orders they received. As they emerged from the holocaust and surveyed the scenes of devastation and defeat, many began to ask questions about the past as well as the future, often with feelings of shame and guilt. Others wanted to restore their links with Western culture and there was therefore a great and spontaneous response to the revival of adult education.

The most common form of provision for adult education in Germany had been the *Volkshochschulen*, to which the nearest British equivalent is the adult evening institute, and the residential colleges often maintained by voluntary associations or political bodies. Residential colleges in particular often catered specially for people interested in political ideas or wishing to promote a reform of society involving a new style of life. Some of these had their roots in the German Youth Movement. Generally those who joined their courses were in fact rather younger than their counterparts in Britain.

Although the Nazis exploited the ideas of the Youth Movement, especially the desire for a simple open air life, they closed all residential colleges which were not prepared to transform themselves into Nazi institutions. The non-residential *Volkshochschulen* either withered on the stem—since they were no longer permitted to deal with controversial subjects—or were replaced by ideological training institutions controlled by the Nazi Party. In the course of the War most of them closed their doors.

Even under the appalling conditions of the immediate post-war period, the demand for adult education showed itself in the large attendances at lectures and courses, often held in badly lit and unheated halls in half-destroyed buildings, reached along precarious 'rabbit tracks' between ruins and heaps of rubble. After languages, chiefly English, the main interest was in art, literature, philosophy and related subjects. Only a small proportion of programmes were devoted to the study of politics, history and the social sciences, a weakness frequently attributed to the lack of suitable tutors. A large and growing part of the work was directed towards vocational needs.

As the local authorities were reconstituted in the British Zone, they began to support the organisation of these courses and there was a gradual review of the *Volkshochschulen* which gathered speed as the local authorities were reconstituted under the Allied Military Administration. Soon the British Military Government and later the Cultural Relations Division of the UK High Commissioner in Germany started to organise educational visits by British adult teachers and from 1947 onwards consider-able numbers of German adult educationists visited Britain to see what university extra-mural departments, local authorities and the WEA were doing in this field and to take part in summer schools and conferences. Heads of ministerial depart-ments in Germany, leading representatives of local education authorities there and of the newly constituted trade unions came to Britain to study our methods and institutions while British delegations went to study the development of adult education in Germany. All this was done in equal partnership with those Germans who wished to see their country's future based on honourable co-operation with other free nations.

The *Länder* which came to constitute the German Federal Republic are autonomous in the field of education. Inevitably there were variations not only in their educational systems but in the financial provision made for adult education by the Governments of the *Länder*. Within the *Länder* the *Volkshoch-schulen* formed their own *Land* Associations. Early in 1953 these in turn formed the German Volkshochschule Association which held a memorable national conference in Berlin on 17 June 1953, the day when the workers of East Germany and East Berlin rose against the Communist government imposed on them by Russia. Thanks to the energy and skill of Walter Ebbighausen, its national secretary, the new organisation quickly gained considerable influence in the Federal Republic and has contributed powerfully to the advance of adult education.

By 1953 when the German Federal Republic had attained sovereignty, well over 1000 *Volkshochschulen* had been established within its territory, differing of course widely in size, character and the quality of their activities. In the larger cities they had full-time directors (but as yet scarcely any other full-time academic staff) whereas in the smaller places the heads of the *Volkshochschulen* often acted in a part-time capacity. For their financial support they relied, apart from student fees, upon grants from the Ministry of Education of their *Land* and from their local authorities. The volume and significance of their work was already considerably greater by then than it had ever been during the days of the Weimar Republic.

In addition to their British contacts, German adult educationists also established close relations with interested people in Denmark, Sweden and Switzerland. In the American Zone large numbers took part in visits to the United States facilitated by the American Occupation authorities in Germany.

Residential adult education also rapidly revived after the War and within a few years a network of residential colleges (*Heimvolkshochschulen*) were established. They were either private foundations aided by public grants or supported by organisations like the trade unions, the farmers' union (*Bauernverband*) or the churches. The trade unions in particular felt the need to develop a programme of systematic training and education for their shop stewards, branch officials and representatives of public bodies, in well equipped residential colleges up and down the country, financed out of union funds. It could well be argued that the effectiveness of the German trade unions owes much to this high degree of priority which they have given to the continued education of their members.

On the other hand, their teaching methods were often rather unsatisfactory. There was too much lecturing, too much pressure to cover a given amount of ground, without sufficient regard to the interests and reactions of the students, not much discussion and not enough effort to elicit the views of the students or to stimulate them into formulating their own thoughts.

Adults studying the history, political development or economic organisation of their society required tutors who, by deepening the student's understanding of the processes of social change, increase his ability to influence those changes and thereby strengthen that sense of participation which is indispensable to a free society. Classes dealing with the study of the subjects therefore depend to an exceptional degree on the qualities of the tutor. This is particularly true in a society which has been deeply unsettled and therefore stands in special need of the contribution which adult education can make to the steadiness and tolerance of public opinion and the successful functioning of free institutions.

Perhaps we might quote here the shrewd comments made in a report by a British Delegation whose members visited both the northern and southern parts of Western Germany in November 1954.[1] They said that they soon realised that the character of German adult education was in many ways different from their own :

> Its inspiration is different and it serves different social pur-
> poses. In Britain much of our adult education began as a
> radical movement. There was in it a strong element of protest
> against established institutions, ideas and policies. The study
> of economics and the other social sciences was not unconnected
> with the aspirations of the 'under-privileged' to social and
> economic 'emancipation', and the approach to such matters
> as philosophy and religion was essentially a critical one. . . .
> It is hardly too much to say that the aim of adult education
> was to achieve a new social order, a new understanding of
> philosophy and theology, rather than to condition people to
> be useful citizens of the existing society. . . .
>   In Germany we felt that the whole spirit of adult education
> was a more constructive one vis à vis the existing society and
> the traditional culture. The aim, particularly in the *Heim-
> volkshochschulen,* was to enable young people to live a fuller
> and more useful life in the society and vocation to which they
> were born. . . . Similarly, a course on Industrial Organisation

in an industrial town was explained to us as a means of equipping workers for the positions now allocated to them in the management of particular industries.

Much has changed since that report was written and there are now rather more critical attitudes to be observed among those who teach or participate in German adult education. But it is perhaps worth quoting from a later paragraph in that report :

It is dangerous to try to explain the difference between the German and British approaches without deeper study. At first we were inclined to attribute it to the relative inexperience of the Germans in democratic methods and to their more clearly defined class structure. But while these are undoubtedly factors in the situation, it must not be forgotten that the *Volkshochschulen*, especially the residential ones, are modelled to a very considerable extent on the Danish pattern, and the chief characteristic of Danish adult education is that it is a constructive education for young people, the emphasis being on appreciation rather than criticism, on synthesis rather than analysis. . . . And Denmark is a fully-fledged democracy !

We must also remember that at that time most Germans probably had had their fill of social and political change and were longing for some stability.

Before long and prompted by the effects of rapidly rising prosperity, many Germans began to talk critically of 'restoration', the re-emergence, as they saw it, of a materialist society now directed towards the acquisition of wealth rather than territory. There was of course truth in that. The Chancellorship of Dr Adenauer in many ways symbolised this development. As an outstanding representative of the old German middle class he became the father figure of the new Federal Republic. Yet the society which was now emerging had in fact many new features. The War and its aftermath, the destruction of cities, the ruin of the economy, the amputation of the eastern provinces, the avalanche of refugees—all these had some of the effects of a social revolution.

Some of the most important features of the old society had disappeared together with the Nazi organisation—the old army and its Officers' Corps, the Junker families whose names could

be found among those executed after the attempt on Hitler's life
in July 1944. Prussia itself had disappeared from the map,
Prussia which, contrary to general belief abroad, had proved
more resistant to the Nazis than other parts of the Weimar
Republic.

The old class structure had been broken. The political parties
which came to dominate the scene were for the most part
pragmatic rather than ideological, and in addition to the Social
Democrats and the Liberals there was now for the first time in
German history a Conservative Party, the CDU, which accepted
the rules of parliamentary government and whose members did
not reach for their guns when democracy was mentioned.

The middle class that emerged with the rapid economic
recovery after the currency reform had many new members and
it soon became clear that millions of industrial workers were
poised to adopt its standards and perhaps even its outlook.

Reference has already been made to the shortage of suitable
tutors for adult classes studying modern history, politics and the
social sciences. One obvious reason for this was of course Germany's recent history, another was the negative attitude of
German university teachers to adult education. Many of them
considered it beneath their dignity to go 'into the market place'.
To this must be added the distrust felt by many adult educationists towards the universities, partly because of the reactionary
political tendencies of German universities before and under
Hitler, but also because the *Volkshochschulen* fear an academic
tradition which tends to cloud live issues with a fog of abstrac-
tions.

The German universities therefore did not make any significant
contribution to adult education. Only two or three universities
showed an interest in this work or felt that they had any
responsibility outside the sphere of academic teaching and research. Göttingen, encouraged by a sympathetic high official in
the Ministry of Education in Hanover, Hans Alfken, went so far
as to establish something like a department of extra-mural studies
which has continued to flourish. (It may be recalled that the
students of Göttingen University in 1953 forced a Nazi sym-
pathiser to resign from the post of Minister of Education in their
Land of Lower Saxony.) That Göttingen felt able to do so was
also in large measure due to the efforts of the *Land* Association

of *Volkshochschulen* in Lower Saxony where Professor Borinski was very active at that time, and to the enterprise of Dr Strzelewicz, the first head of the university's extra-mural department. The 'seminar courses' which they organised in co-operation with the *Volkshochschulen* of the region resemble our tutorial classes with their insistence on continuous study, systematic reading and students' contribution to the work of the class. But few other universities followed this example.

Most university teachers tended to keep aloof and did not believe that their knowledge and learning could or should be made available to ordinary people. Indeed many German adult educationists at that time doubted whether the universities, in that frame of mind, could make a worthwhile contribution or would in fact be able to appreciate their problems. Nevertheless experiments in co-operation between *Volkshochschulen* and universities were started in some places, notably in West Berlin, where Professor Borinski, who had retained many contacts in this country, now occupied the chair of education.

The educational efforts made by the German trade unions very soon after they had reformed deserve closer consideration because they were on a scale never attempted in this country. There were good reasons why the need for a special educational effort was so readily recognised by the German unions. Before Hitler's rise to power, German workers had organised themselves into socialist, catholic and liberal unions, allied to the respective political parties. The socialist unions, connected with the Social Democratic party, had been by far the strongest, although at some crucial periods towards the end of the Weimar Republic they had suffered crippling internal divisions because of the communists within their ranks. Support for the Christian trade unions was centred on industrial areas with a predominantly Roman Catholic population like the Ruhr and Silesia. Clerical workers formed the backbone of the much smaller liberal unions.

Although all the unions usually adopted an agreed policy on the more important economic and industrial issues, their resistance to the rising Nazi party was greatly weakened by their political divisions. After their dissolution on May Day 1933, Hitler's 'Day of German Labour', and the confiscation of their funds by the Nazi's 'German Labour Front', many of their leaders were united—but inside the concentration camps. It was

this agonising experience which helped to bring about the resolve
to establish a united trade union movement, a resolve supported
by the mass of the members, who had suffered the disastrous
results of former divisions.

British trade union experience was also of considerable influence upon German developments. Britain had given shelter to
a considerable number of leading German trade unionists in
exile. Moreover, the most important industrial area in Western
Germany, the Ruhr, was under British control. Ernest Bevin as
a former trade union leader and now Foreign Secretary in the
Labour Government naturally wanted to see the trade unions
re-established. In the early stage, therefore, the British authorities encouraged the organisation of trade unions and British trade
union experts were seconded to Military Government to give
help and advice.

The unions themselves were conscious of the fact that their
functions and responsibilities were bound to be much wider than
they had been earlier, particularly as they began to formulate
their plans for the promotion of industrial democracy and for
co-determination in the basic industries of coal and steel whose
former masters had given such powerful support to Hitler. A new
streamlined structure of powerful industrial unions emerged and
both the German TUC, the *Deutscher Gewerkschaftsbund*
(DGB), and individual unions quickly established short-term
residential colleges in some of the most attractive parts of West
Germany.

By 1953 the DGB alone maintained seven of these colleges
(Bundesschulen) and a similar number was established by the
affiliated unions. Their task was to educate trade unionists for
their various functions in society, especially for their activities as
members of works councils or of committees dealing with the
administration of health and unemployment insurance and joint
management in the basic industries. Unfortunately the educational work often lacked some of the qualities essential for its
success. Syllabuses tended to be too narrowly confined to trade
union subjects and there was again too much emphasis on lecturing and not enough time for discussion and individual study.
But the volume of the work done remained impressive and so
did the energies and resources devoted to it so soon after what
seemed to be a total collapse of society.

The provision of degree courses for mature students from the trade unions proved rather more difficult. In view of the attitudes still prevailing at that time in most German universities, the unions felt that special provisions had to be made by arrangement with individual universities considered suitable and sympathetic. This led the DGB to support the Social Academies in Dortmund, Frankfurt and Hamburg by granting scholarships to promising students who had been active trade unionists and had successfully passed through the courses in the *Bundesschulen*. The function of the Social Academies was similar to that of Ruskin College, Oxford.[2]

Purely cultural activities are taken much more seriously in Germany than in England and from an early date the DGB did much to interest its members in the arts. The outstanding example of activities in this field has been the Ruhr Festival, held since 1948 in the town of Recklinghausen and organised in co-operation with the town council and the *Land* of North Rhine-Westphalia. During the freezing winter of 1947 some Ruhr miners had worked extra shifts to provide coal for heating the concert hall of a symphony orchestra, and the orchestra came and played for the miners. Thus the idea of the festival was born and subsequently the organisers brought to Recklinghausen every summer some of the best productions of the German stage and concert hall as well as exhibitions of art and design. Another feature was a programme of public discussion by people prominent in the intellectual life of Europe. Trade unionists from all over the Ruhr, including thousands of young people, came to Recklinghausen in fleets of buses and the spirit of the enterprise triumphed over the sometimes ill-suited premises where meetings and performances took place, until in later years the splendidly equipped new Festival Hall arose.

Arbeit und Leben, a co-operative venture established jointly by the *Land* organisations of the DGB and the *Land* associations of the *Volkshochschulen* owed a great deal to the advice and example of the WEA in Britain where it is the practice of students in adult education to determine their own educational activities and even the syllabus of the course they join. *Arbeit und Leben* was conceived as an additional means of providing working people with educational opportunities for social and political responsibilities and presented a most serious effort on

the part of both organisations to provide a continuous and progressive form of part-time study. These courses, particularly the
way in which they sought to equip the individual member with
a technique of study, constituted another German approach to
the three-year tutorial class developed in Britain in co-operation
between the universities and the WEA. The subjects covered in
each course include—in addition to basic skills such as the use
of language, the writing of papers and methods of study—
history, politics, economics, industrial relations and management.
It was a form of study which made considerable demands upon
the stamina of students with two weekly meetings over a period
of thirty-six weeks a year.

The success of these courses, and to some extent their methods
and standards, differed in the various *Länder*. They were
probably most successful in Lower Saxony where the movement
began and where it had some of its most distinguished leaders.
The average age of students was much lower than in comparable
classes in Britain and to some extent this may have accounted for
the fact that German tutors argued that it was not possible to
expect an informal discussion, especially since young people at
that time found it impossible to supplement class attendance
with home study because of their cramped housing conditions
and the shortage of suitable literature in public libraries which
were only just being rebuilt.

As a rule students in adult classes in Germany were given little
opportunity to exercise an effective and continuous influence
upon the shaping of programmes and activities or to practise the
art of self-government. Certainly there was not much demand
for such influence—people were after all just emerging from a
strictly authoritarian period—and those who organised the work
had enough problems to face and not much energy to spare for
stimulating such demands. There was no movement comparable
to the WEA and in the absence of a student movement initiative
and responsibility tended to remain in the hands of officials. The
provision of adult studies was considered to be the responsibility
of the authorities rather than a co-operative enterprise. Perhaps
this was inevitable in a society still deeply unsettled, in the most
literal meaning of that word. Millions of people had been expelled from their homes in the eastern territories and were still
drifting about seeking new opportunities for work and settlement.

At that stage they were bound therefore to leave the initiative to others more familiar with local conditions.

However, some German adult educationists did recognise that the participants of adult education should be involved in planning and organisation and that the adult class, whatever the subject studied, can provide education and citizenship, giving its members the chance to train themselves in self-government by practising it. They saw that if men and women are to have an incentive to democratic behaviour they must be given an opportunity to exercise responsibility and to make effective decisions. In many *Volkshochschulen* this led to the establishment of students' councils whose job it was to help in programme planning.

Contacts with their British colleagues probably helped to encourage German educators in these developments. British visitors, on the other hand, had much to learn from the energy with which the Germans in many places set about the provision of purpose-built accommodation for adult education, ultimately leaving Britain far behind. The position has been well described by a keen observer in Germany throughout those decisive years:

> The second real achievement (after the reorganisation and rehabilitation of youth groups) of Education Branch . . . was the re-establishment of adult education centres in the towns and the opening of many new resident centres in the country. Here again the main initiative came from a few German enthusiasts. But the enthusiasts had to be found, the premises had to be secured, and all kinds of facilities had to be provided by us at first. The keenness and thirst for knowledge of the participants in these first rough courses were remarkable. . . . The WEA in particular took a deep interest in this work in Germany and probably had a decisive influence on developments in the same field there. Our Education Branch officials acted as organisers, planners and helpers with all these contacts.[3]

The emphasis at that time, on both sides, was on providing opportunities for what in this country is called a general or liberal education, designed to develop intellectual independence and the spirit of critical enquiry. The German educational system in the past had made very adequate provision for vocational train-

ing and had perhaps been rather too much directed towards
those needs. The priority now was to promote knowledge and
understanding of those values and achievements which would
enable people to build a free society and to defend their freedom.

Many of the contacts and personal friendships established
during those early days have stood the test of time and have
resulted in lasting co-operation. The problems of German society
—not only today but for at least half a century—run closely
parallel to similar problems of Germany's neighbours. All of them
have had to solve them in their own way. None of them can
offer ready-made answers for export. But they can share experiences and perhaps learn something from each others' mistakes or
successes. It is curious to reflect how, after an initial and fortunately rather brief period in which many people talked about
're-education' for Germany, almost as many now look keenly at
the efficiency of her economy and her industrial relations, at the
way in which devolution has been made to work and even at the
electoral system and wonder whether these may hold lessons for
us here.

NOTES

1. *The Tutors' Bulletin,* Numbers 97-99, December 1954-June 1955.
2. Lionel Elvin, then Principal of Ruskin College, together with
   Otto Kahn-Freund, John Wray, then TUC Education Secretary
   and the present writer took part in some of the preparatory
   discussions with the University of Münster which led to the
   establishment of the Sozialakademie in Dortmund.
3. Raymond Ebsworth, *Restoring Democracy in Germany. The
   British Contribution,* (London, 1960), pp. 171-2.

15

'GER': A Voluntary Anglo-German Contribution

Jane Anderson

This paper is a description and to some extent an evaluation of the organisation best known by its initials, GER. These originally stood for 'German Educational Reconstruction'. They were retained in the 1950s because they were familiar, but were reinterpreted as meaning 'A Society for Promoting Anglo-German Educational Relations'. The study is a preliminary one, based on a first reading of the papers which were deposited with the University of London Institute of Education when the society was dissolved in 1958. Though a few related texts have been consulted, and indeed quoted, the paper is essentially based on the archives. The questions they raise have been left open. No attempt has been made at this point to provide answers through supplementary research.

In 1941 a group of English people led by S. H. Wood of the Ministry of Education tried to persuade the Government to help German refugee educationists prepare for their eventual return to their own country. They were unsuccessful, and decided to pursue this work themselves within the framework of a voluntary organisation. Their enquiries revealed that a nucleus of German refugee teachers and social workers was meeting in London to study the collapse of the Weimar Republic and the rise of National Socialism, and to examine new ideas in their field. The groups joined forces in 1942 and began to extend their circle amongst English people and German emigrés; in 1943 GER was officially founded, under the presidency of Eleanor Rathbone. The members of the Board were English with the exception of Karl Mannheim; the Germans formed the Standing Committee. The joint secretaries of the society were Fritz Borinski and Werner Milch, and S. H. Wood was Chairman of the Board.

Since the non-theoretical bias of GER work will be the subject of another section of this paper, where it will be linked with the relative pragmatism of English educational policy in occupied Germany, it is worth noting at the outset the determination of

German as well as English members to work on a practical basis. Describing the earliest stages in the formation of GER, Fritz Borinski wrote (of himself, Werner Milch, Minna Specht and S. H. Wood):

> We agreed there should be no large, expensive organisation, no great publicity, no theoretical discussions or elaborations but a small group of reliable people, working quietly; people prepared to accept the practical implications of their activities, in a word, people who seriously intended to return to Germany when the time came.[1]

It is perhaps also worth noting here that GER, unlike certain other German emigré groups in wartime London, contained people of widely differing political and religious convictions.

Fritz Borinski has defined GER's wartime tasks as *Klärung, Vorbereitung, Sammlung, Kontakte.*[2] The society sent representatives to conferences organised by other voluntary bodies, held lectures, study groups and short conferences of its own, and arranged training courses for German refugees. Subjects included aspects of youth and welfare work, adult education and vocational training, reflecting from the beginning the characteristically broad interpretation GER gave to education. The emphasis within the organisation was never to be primarily on a restructuring of the German school system.

Various members produced pamphlets describing aspects of pre-war German education and lectured on these subjects in London and the provinces. Others chose the first of the so-called *Lesebogen* for young people, intended for distribution in Germany as textbooks and leisure reading. The society drew up memoranda on practical steps towards educational reconstruction and these were distributed to interested bodies, for contacts of all kinds were being established both in England and Germany. GER was in touch with individuals in government circles from autumn 1944 and in the Allied Control Commission for Germany from the summer of 1945. Through these official contacts, it claims to have taken an active part in assisting the return of German refugee educationists, some of them to positions of considerable importance.[3] How great GER's part was and whether the standing of the former emigrés was impaired or enhanced by this connection is open to question.

GER also helped other Germans in Britain in the immediate post-war period. From the summer of 1945, the society, working with the War Prisoners' Aid of the YMCA and other bodies, undertook educational activities of various kinds amongst prisoners of war awaiting repatriation.

With the gradual return of these and most of GER's German members to their own country, the first aims of the organisation were largely accomplished. Activity had now to shift from planning for the future to helping with work already begun. To discover the real educational needs of Germany and determine the shape of its new activities, GER held a conference in June 1946 to which it invited delegates from educational and official circles and two important German guests—Heinrich Landahl, Senator in charge of Education for Hamburg, and Adolf Grimme, who occupied a similar position in the Province of Hanover and was a member of the British Zone Advisory Committee on Education. They were the first German educationists to visit England after the War and GER claimed their visit had a wide-reaching effect in Germany.[4]

The new aims of the society were described in its *Bulletin* for December that year: it would act 'as a Bureau of Information, qualified to supply individuals and societies with reliable facts about the development of educational and social work in Germany; as a channel for establishing and maintaining personal contact between British and German workers in the educational field; as a medium for bringing about the exchange of university lecturers and students, school teachers and social workers'.[5]

Two specific activities mentioned in a draft by S. H. Wood and pursued with vigour, though not spelled out in the public version were giving practical help to German educationists by supplying books, periodicals, etc. and bringing pressure on the Control Commission to remedy ills which could be remedied.[6]

The guiding principle of all GER activities was the constantly reiterated desire to break the isolation of German educationists and to help those who were trying to rebuild the nation's education on democratic principles. There is, though, no record of any systematic debate on the issues raised by that most elastic of concepts, democracy in education. Ideas were to be transmitted person to person, mind to mind,[7] through 'a personal relationship within the field of education, based on free inter-

change of intellectual ideas and spiritual ideals; based in fact on
friendship.[8] This extreme faith in the value of the individual and
the rather English belief that sound policy would emerge from
exchange of ideas between men of good will were fundamental to
GER policy. Here, of course, it resembled British policy in
general. This contained a minimum of specific goals and, as an
American observer has commented :

> Even when fairly clear objectives existed, the implementation
> procedure was vague. The British relied mostly on the con-
> tinuous personal influence of British education officers, on
> information centres, exchange visits, jointly sponsored courses,
> co-operation with other agencies of international co-operation
> and on encouragement of co-operative progressive activity
> among German authorities. The method was informal per-
> suasion. The program was not specific, but the participants
> understood the general aims and functioned quite effectively
> with this understanding.[9]

From late 1946, then, GER embarked on the most fruitful
and intensive phase of its work. It had been strengthened, as it
was to be at intervals during the late 1940s, by donations from
charitable trusts. The Standing Committee now became an
Advisory Committee of Germans and English people. 'Corresponding Members' were sought from the voluntary societies with
which it was increasingly to collaborate. I shall not examine here
the working relationship between GER, these voluntary bodies
and the central and local government departments, training
colleges, schools and universities whose co-operation made so many
of the society's schemes possible, but it is an interesting one and
would repay further study.

GER entered its second phase under a new president and a
new secretary. Eleanor Rathbone died in January 1946 and
Professor Sir Ernest Barker was asked to become its second
president. In the autumn of that year, Erich Hirsch became its
secretary, a post he occupied until 1958. The archives suggest
that the particular character of GER as a mediating body, a
role it fulfilled as and when it could, was due in large part to the
appointment of this German educationist to the key post in the
English organisation. His correspondence with former members
of the wartime GER circle and with other German educationists,

and his smaller exchanges of letters with former guests of GER
show a man whose working knowledge of the problems of post-
war German education as seen from the German side undoubtedly helped him, and thus his organisation in its tasks.
Arguably, this rapport, and the society's independence from the
Control Commission eased its relations with German educationists and dissipated their resentment. But not always perhaps,
since the archives also contain a remark recorded by Charlotte
Lütkens that GER was seen as *Frucht oder Nachfrucht der
Re-Education.*[10] (To some members of the Control Commission,
on the other hand, GER, especially Hirsch, was an irritant).
Curious, too, in view of the wide range of political opinions held
by members of the wartime circle, is a German criticism, also
retailed by Charlotte Lütkens, to the effect that GER was
politically rigid.[11] Could such a remark about the later organisation be traced to a fixity of policy on the part of Erich
Hirsch?

The answers to these questions and their bearing on a final
assessment of GER must await further research as must an
appraisal of Erich Hirsch's personal role in post-war German
education. This would consider his part in the setting up of the
Psychologisches Institut at the University of Hamburg, his work
for the Victor Gollancz-Stiftung, and other matters not directly
related to his post with GER.

Suffice it to say that the archives would seem to reveal the
society as an educational and social nerve centre receiving
information about initiatives by Germans, Allies and neutral
nations. German-based members of the GER circle expressed
their frustrated criticism of obstructive attitudes among their
compatriots, mistaken Allied policies, practical difficulties, friction between the *Länder* or between Zonal military authorities.
They and British workers with the voluntary societies or Education Branch called on GER for help of all kinds. Its Chairman
and Secretary, both of whom visited Germany in 1947, saw
their organisation's help as very important. Erich Hirsch wrote:

Whether British or German authorities or individual personalities were concerned, everyone seemed to know of GER and to
expect the impossible. Everywhere it was necessary for me to
point out that GER is a very small organisation without

I

financial security and that, in consequence, GER is unable to do all that really is required. I realised, however, that the very fact means much already, that there are people in Great Britain ready to help in building a bridge to those in Germany who are willing to take part in constructive work. Should we, in the future, be able to intensify our personal relations with these people, thus by practical measures breaking their isolation, I firmly believe no greater encouragement could be given to educational reconstruction in Germany.[12]

S. H. Wood rather more grandiloquently stated:

I am immensely impressed with the responsibilities of GER. We are known to Germans throughout the British Zone, our work is genuinely appreciated by Education Branch and we still have much work to do. There is hope for German education if organisations like GER, in full co-operation with Education Branch, plan their work on the basis of conciliation, encouragement and friendship.[13]

How far can these fairly substantial claims be justified? Did GER, working with Education Branch and German educationists really contribute to the emergence of wise policy and enlightened practice? Or was it simply viewed by them as one of the many voluntary organisations which could help out in a chaotic situation by providing information, contacts and materials, arranging visits and so on? If GER proves ultimately to have provided only material and professional help, it need not, of course, invalidate the society's claim to have made a contribution to the re-establishment of German education. We are dealing, it should be remembered, with a time when a pencil or a pair of shoes could radically improve a child's way of life and when German correspondents could report that prospective guests or helpers of GER had in the meantime died of malnutrition.[14] It might also be argued that disinterested and unpatronising assistance to German educationists exerted a modest influence of its own. The question would then be, how widely did GER work and attitudes make themselves felt amongst German educationists at the time? At all events, these questions cannot be answered by the material in the archives and would entail further research.

We might now consider the activities on which these GER claims were based, always remembering that a short account will be distorting in that it will not record GER's help to innumerable individuals over a wide range of smaller matters.

Clearly, conditions in Germany just after the War were such that material help to German educators was vital. GER therefore collaborated with other voluntary organisations in sending relief parcels and concerned itself in particular with collecting and shipping school supplies and books of all kinds. (Forty-five tons of books were sent out between 1947 and 1949). It also administered a highly successful scheme initiated by T. A. Leonard whereby English people sent periodicals of general or specialised interest to individuals, colleges, universities and public libraries. Over 5000 British donors came forward during the first year of the scheme. Publication of the *Lesebogen* prepared by GER was undertaken by a German publishing house under the supervision of Martha Friedländer.

The *GER Bulletin,* published about six times a year until the early 1950s, not only kept English sympathisers informed about conditions in Germany and the efforts of educationists and social workers there, it also served to keep those workers in touch with movements in other parts of Germany. One British officer with Education Branch asked for it to be sent fifty English and forty German copies. The *Bulletin* provided a platform for constructive criticism of certain Allied educational, social and cultural measures, but on the whole, systematic discussion of education in the abstract was not one of its features. Specific abuses were exposed—the muddles over denazification for instance, or the banning by the textbooks branch in Bünde of certain German classics, though the correspondence between leading German members of the GER circle makes it clear that their privately held view of Allied shortcomings was in fact much more general. Similarly, the *Bulletin* reported isolated evidence of disagreements between conservative and progressive elements within German education—the reaction to the reintroduction of caning in Bavaria, for example, or disagreement over the position of Latin in the curriculum—but it made no attempt to give English readers a clear picture of the main trends and debates. The society would have been in an excellent position to do this, as the correspondence in the archives and the list of its German guests makes clear. Why did it not do so? Was it considered unnecessary or inadvisable or both?

Closer contact between educationists from the two countries was brought about during conferences which aimed at 'creating a common atmosphere and of opening avenues of mutual understanding, or at least, of realisation and explanation of divergent points of view'.[15] These were held at least once a year until the early 1950s, sometimes twice. The early ones were in England but the 1948 conference was convened at Fritz Borinski's *Volkshochschulheim* in Schloss Göhrde with the help of Education Branch and the newly formed German 'friends of GER'. The 1949 conference met in the Odenwaldschule at the invitation of Minna Specht.

Specialist conferences were a feature of GER activity in the 1950s, the first being one for economists at Oxford in 1949. Subsequent conferences were on history, political science, industrial relations, social security, safety and hygiene and old age welfare. Three were held for lawyers and two for teachers of English and German. It will be noted that only these last two were concerned with education in schools. I think future research may well prove that the strong emphasis on welfare and the social sector can be traced to the influence of Erich Hirsch. All the conferences seem to have been carefully planned and well run with some distinguished speakers and must surely be accounted one of GER's most solid achievements.

Between conferences GER entertained a stream of German visitors. Some of them were in England for courses or visits arranged by official bodies, notably the Foreign Office, the British Council and the Ministry of Education, but many were invited, either singly or in groups, by GER itself. The society, working through its German contacts, might select a certain individual and then request a permit from the authorities in the British or American Zone. (Collaboration with the French Zone was far less extensive.) But GER also invited the education officers in the three Zones to put forward suitable candidates themselves. The Americans recognised that it was practical to send certain visitors across the North Sea rather than across the Atlantic. And Great Britain, they felt, was politically if not educationally a good substitute for the United States, suitable terrain in which they might carry out their avowedly anti-communist policy for Germany.[16] They thus provided generous funding for certain visitors. This, however, was dependent on 'political clearance' which GER's own candidates from that Zone did not always pass. S. H. Wood actually feared that these political restrictions and the lavish hospitality bought by American money for certain GER guests in London constituted a threat to the society's independence. It is impossible to say at this stage whether GER simply facilitated the task of the education officers in the British and American Zones or whether, through them, it was able to make a contribution which in any way modified or complemented official policy.

GER guests included workers from all parts of the education sector from student teachers to Ministers Voigt of Lower Saxony, Hundhammer of Bavaria and Teusch of North Rhine-Westphalia. But there was also a large number of visitors from other branches of public life including journalists, policewomen, trades unionists, child guidance specialists, youth leaders, and marriage guidance councillors.

Undoubtedly the most deeply appreciated were the study visits of three to four weeks arranged and financed by GER for German educationists in the late 1940s when their material need and professional isolation were profound. The pattern evolved for such visits seems to have been highly successful: the guests were received in a residential centre where the first week or so was devoted to an orientation course on English education; then they dispersed, usually in pairs, to visit educational institutions in England and Wales, meeting again in London for reports and discussions on all they had seen. Letters from such visitors leave little doubt that they gained enormous benefit from these weeks of relative comfort and stability and the wholesome distancing effect of viewing German life and education in the context of another culture.

The question of influence, here as elsewhere, is problematic. Though the reports from these visitors dealt at length with the newly inaugurated tripartite system, their praise was reserved for the 'living democracy' of English education and public life; however, most of them were quick to point out that the qualities they admired were the fruit of a particular historical tradition and could not instantly be grafted onto the rather different German one.

During the later years of GER's existence, visits multiplied and diversified enormously. They also became to some extent reciprocal as did the youth work. This began early after the war with the linking of individuals and schools under the Penfriend Scheme. Later came school exchanges, contacts between training colleges, participation (arranged through GER) in all manner of camps, summer schools and university courses in England and Germany, tours by choirs and drama groups, and other similar undertakings. Most ambitious numerically were the Youth Groups Exchange Scheme which involved hundreds of young people annually during the 1950s, and the Student Harvest Scheme. GER took part in this for ten years and was the sole organiser after 1955 when the Ministry of Education withdrew. The society enabled over 5000 German students to work, earn and travel cheaply in Britain, an opportunity which was of particular value in the early post-war years before the currency reform and the lifting of travel restrictions.

Arranging individual exchanges was, with some exceptions, not part of GER work. It posed a problem to all the voluntary bodies which undertook to organise youth travel at that time, as the demand on the German side was disproportionately great. It was, however, Erich Hirsch who formed an ad hoc committee of members from these societies in an attempt to improve this particular side of the youth service.

The organisation of visits, particularly those of English groups to Germany, was greatly simplified by collaboration with GER's German Office. This had finally been established in Bonn in 1950 to co-ordinate the activities of the GER Friends in the various Länder. Its responsible officers were Charlotte Lütkens, Wilhelm Platz and Walter Weizel. Despite declarations of parity and the dogged insistence of the Bonn office on the expression 'sister organisation', the London office seems to have remained the senior partner, probably because of the years of expertise accumulated by Erich Hirsch.

It must have been difficult for the hard-worked staff in either office to believe that GER had fulfilled its essential purpose. Yet some committee members were suggesting that it had.[17] West Germany was now a fairly wealthy and independent nation with diplomatic representation in London. And with UNESCO as well as organisations like the *Bund für internationale Kulturar-*

beit, the Carl Duisberg-Gesellschaft für Nachwuchsförderung, Das Experiment, the *Deutsch-Englische Gesellschaft,* the *Deutsche Auslandsgesellschaft,* the *Europäischer Austauschdienst* the Anglo-German Association, the Educational Interchange Council, the British Council and the Central Bureau of Educational Visits and Exchanges, the long-term need for GER's services was becoming debatable. The constant demarcation disputes between the Bonn office and Frau Lilo Milchsack's *Deutsch-Englische Gesellschaft* suggested that the field was becoming overcrowded. However, other London committee members, and they were a majority, felt that as long as there was a need for the sort of services GER offered, that society should fulfil it.[18] Erich Hirsch argued that GER was the most experienced organisation devoted to Anglo-German visits and exchanges and had an important role to play as more and more *Jugendplan* and *Kultusministerium* funds were spent, sometimes on rather shakily organised ventures. His argument was not unjustified: his office was sometimes called in to rescue victims of other societies' inadequate organisation. Suggestions for major changes in the function of the society were considered at this time but apparently rejected.[19] The organisation, it was concluded, should continue as it was for the time being. This decision was endorsed by those GER Friends and former guests who replied to the questionnaire sent out in January 1952.[20] Isolation seems still to have been a real issue for these German educationists and many letters contained a plea for an increase in GER activities, albeit now on an equal and reciprocal basis.

In the event, the decision was forced on GER by financial considerations. More and more English societies of a similar type were competing for funds. And then, appeals for money to help Germany obviously did not now make the impact they had after the War. The GER report for 1955-6 stated that the last large grant it had received (in 1949) would ensure only two, or perhaps three further years' work. The report for the following year could record no fresh source of funds and the society was wound up in 1958.

I do not intend to repeat at this point all the questions which I have raised during this account. They can really be reduced to a discussion about the words 'help' and 'influence'; when does the first of these become the second? When should it?

Are we right, anyway, in inferring that GER intended to exercise influence when it insisted, in its policy statements, on the word 'help'? I feel sure we are. GER did not, of course, reflect official British attitudes to Germany. Its officers were often deeply out of sympathy with the policies of the Allies and with the ethos of Wilton Park. And the remarks about broadening the horizons of Dr Hundhammer are unique in the archives for their patronising tone.[21] Nevertheless, there was I think, in the early post-war years, always the assumption that England should try to influence Germany over the question of democracy in education, an aim it is hard to fault in the context. 'Democracy in education' we may interpret here as meaning chiefly a preparation in all sectors of education for life in a democratic society. The interpretation pursued with such missionary zeal by the Americans in Germany—that of providing equalised opportunity for an equalised, one might say standardised, education—was not so heavily stressed in England, either in government circles or by GER.

We may surely state unequivocally that GER, for a voluntary society of its size, offered substantial help to German educationists in the early post-war period. Could it have done more? Could a society of a different kind have done more? Does this help constitute an influence? Or conversely, if, as seems likely, no influence can be proved, does this discredit GER? The society did show large numbers of Germans in responsible positions alternative models for redevelopment at a time when they needed to rethink their own policies. Is this not achievement enough?

During its third phase, GER obviously intended to exert an influence, though now of a completely different kind. As we have already noted, the society had a fundamental belief in the benefit of international contacts, exchanges of opinion, shared activities. No one, surely, questions the great value of such encounters to the people concerned. But GER, with its extreme liberal faith in the power of the individual, went further and maintained that such personal benefit had a positive effect on international relations as a whole. Has that belief been vindicated, or is it one which events and a more sophisticated study of complex factors is forcing us to relinquish?

This paper was written at a point when only a cursory first reading of the archives (which contain well over 30,000 documents) had been possible. Two further years' work have thrown new light on some of the subjects it dealt with. For example, GER's role in helping its members to return early after the War to responsible posts in Germany, was more substantial than the paper implied. Or again, the *Lesebogen* scheme seems to have been really extensive, though tantalizingly few of the published texts remain in the archives. The society may also prove to have had a discernable influence on the development in Germany of child guidance, a topic the paper did not even mention.

However, discussions at the conference, both public and private, confirmed what looked a rather cowardly assertion at the time the paper was written : that the answer to the most interesting questions about GER would be found by research outside the archives. The reasons for the apparently small role played by Karl Mannheim—perhaps the most distinguished name associated with GER—were disclosed at Oxford by Fritz Borinski. The most important question for English scholars is surely whether GER succeeded in modifying the policy of the Foreign Office or the Control Commission for Germany. After the conference, it seems safe to say that the attitude of these bodies towards GER cannot always be inferred from the letters in the archives. The other important question—whether English ideas influenced the German educationists and social workers who came over on GER study visits, remains open; (the nature of foreign influences on post-war German education is difficult to establish). It seems likely that GER's influence, if any, would most easily be traced by a researcher taking as his starting point the post-war work of the *Gilde Soziale Arbeit*. Many emigré members had belonged to it before the War; after 1945 Erich Hirsch re-established contacts with the *Gildenleute* who had remained in Germany or taken refuge in other countries. They were amongst GER's first visitors; their letters form possibly the most interesting part of the archives' correspondence section. In retrospect it seems one might almost describe GER as an English off-shoot of the *Gilde*.

I*

NOTES

Document numbers refer to the archives of GER in the library of London University Institute of Education.

1. F. Borinski in *Erziehung und Politik—Minna Specht zu ihrem 80. Geburtstag,* Editors Becker, Eichler, Heckmann, (Frankfurt am Main, 1960), p. 80 : 'Wir kamen überein : keine grosse, teuere Organisation, keine laute Publizität, keine theoretischen Diskussionen und Konstruktionen am grünen Tisch, sondern ein kleiner Arbeitskreis vertrauenswürdiger Menschen, die in der Stille arbeiten und zur praktischen Konsequenz bereit, dass heisst, des ernsten Willens sein solten, zur gegebenen Zeit nach Deutschand zurückzugehen.'

2. Borinski, op. cit., p. 81.

3. James L. Henderson, *A Contribution to Anglo-German Understanding 1942-58* (the GER valedictory lecture given in 1958) p. 15 (doc. 1078).

4. *GER Bulletin,* July/August 1946, p. 2 (doc. 884).

5. *GER Bulletin,* December 1946, p. 1 (doc. 886).

6. doc. 828.

7. PPB (presumably Paul Bondy, the Editor), in *GER Bulletin* 1950, number 3, p. 14 (doc. 910).

8. GER publicity leaflet circa 1950, p. 2 (doc. 840).

9. Robert F. Lawson, *Reform of the West German School System 1945-62,* (Ann Arbor, 1965), p. 56.

10. Letter from Charlotte Lütkens to Schlange-Schöningen at the German Embassy, London, 20.2.53 (doc. 22245).

11. Letter from Charlotte Lütkens to Erich Hirsch 21.7.50 (doc. 9943).

12. *GER Bulletin,* June/July 1947, p. 9 (doc. 892).

13. *GER Bulletin,* December 1947, p. 9 (doc. 895).

14. See letters M. Pirani to Hirsch 11.4.48 (doc. 28995) and H. Polchau to Hirsch 19.3.46 (doc. 29004).

15. PPB (presumably Paul Bondy) in *GER Bulletin,* 1950, No. 3, p. 16 (doc. 910).

16. See, for instance, the American High Commission's preamble to their project on Higher Education in Political Science and Public Administration, under which two German specialists

were to be brought over to England by GER in 1951 (doc. 17664).

17. See for instance letters Barker to Hirsch 14.9.1950 (doc. 18484) and Wood to Burmeister 24.11.52 (doc. 19322), memorandum August 1951 'The Future of GER' by Wood (doc. 841).

18. See minutes of Board meeting 4 October 1951 (doc. 396).

19. See second of two memoranda by Wood with title 'The Future of GER', some time after August 1951 (doc. 842).

20. See correspondence section of Dassel Conference (docs.3356-98).

21. Unsigned carbon copy of a letter possibly by Hirsch but more probably by Wood to John Hynd MP 11.7.50 (doc. 17753).

16. *Retrospective View from the German side*

Hellmut Becker

The period of National Socialism has long been the subject of extensive historical research in Germany. Lately, however, greater attention is being paid to the beginnings of the Federal Republic of Germany. There exists a voluminous stock of memoirs dealing with the Third Reich. Reminiscences of the Adenauer Era are appearing with increasing frequency. What is remarkable is the fact that the Occupation period is barely touched upon. The years between the collapse of National Socialism and the emergence of a functioning federal republic remain shrouded in a strange semi-darkness. Because of this, it is most important that material dealing with this time be recorded; and for the same reason it is most difficult to classify it.

Looking at the Germans today, one could say jokingly that they want to eat and make love like the French and to make money like the Americans. In this connection it would not be untrue to say that, through the German occupation of the whole of France and the French Occupation of a part of Germany, the French and the Germans have learned more about each other than at any previous time in history. This experience of mutual occupation with all its horrors—perpetrated mainly by the Germans in France—formed the basis of communication between the two countries after the war. Of some significance also was probably the fact that the French from the very beginning adhered less to the non-fraternisation rule than any of the other Occupation forces. The differences between the Allies with regard to manifestations of their Military Government become clear when one bears in mind that in 1946 there were for every 10,000 of the German population eighteen French nationals in the Military Government, in the British Zone ten Britons and in the American Zone three Americans.

Today the Federal Republic of Germany is considered to be the most Americanised country in Europe. In France—and here the Gaullists and the Left are in agreement—there is more anti-

American feeling than in any other European country. German tourists mainly travel to the Romance countries—to France, Italy, Spain and Portugal.

There are as well more French and Italian restaurants in Germany than there ever were before. Whereas the Russians, with the help of German émigrés returned from Moscow, assumed very direct political control of government right from the beginning in Germany and set up their own particular type of political system, and whereas the Americans succeeded, in spite of all the errors of their Occupation policy, in propagating the 'American way of life', French policy underwent considerable changes at various times. After the failure of their attempt to split off the southern parts of Germany from the newly formed Federal Republic (the idea of an alpine union extending from the Palatinate to Austria had many supporters), they confined themselves to getting certain of their fundamental conceptions adopted, in particular in the field of education. Most important was the centralised *Abitur*, which still exists today in the *Länder* of the French Zone and which contradicts the spirit of the school reform of the 1920s. The establishment of new institutions of teacher training could be mentioned. Of considerable importance was the broad impact of French literature from Anouilh to Sartre, from Gide to Camus. This influence was quite characteristic of the early post-war years and German readers had the opportunity of becoming familiar with these writers through a variety of means and media.

And what was the attitude of the British at this time? This book shows clearly that the British were too experienced to want to set up any programme of their own in Germany. Rather than that, they confined their activities to giving assistance and encouragement to German-initiated projects and developments, to bringing people together, to providing practical aid—in other words, carrying on a very cautious educational and cultural policy. In this policy there is nothing of the conscious intention to direct the course of events characteristic of the French (which also brought about a counter-reaction), or the naïve belief in the beneficial effects of their actions, which was both a weakness and a virtue of the American Occupation. And of course there was nothing in the policy of the British resembling the unmistakeable ideological intentions of the Russians. British soldiers in Germany maintained the aloofness toward foreigners characteristic of their nation; the British education officers came with the also typically British idea of simply doing what was necessary.

Looked at today and from the German point of view, the policy of the British Occupation presents problems which should be clarified, particularly since so much good will was manifest from the British side. Was it right to allow the Germans their period of restoration? It is not without reason that one of the best known accounts of the period refers to the first two decades of German post-war education policy as the 'Two Decades of Non-Reform'.[1] Was it not possible to start from the unfulfilled reform programmes of the 1920s and make use of the shock of 1945 to make a really substantial advance? The British education officers saw quite early the clash between the reformists and the conservatives. Arthur Hearnden writes: 'It was British policy to keep out of this controversy'. But was this right? Can one exercise complete control as the Military Government did at the time, and still not take some clear stance on the real educational and social controversies? Was it not so, that the decision for de-centralisation constituted a clear decision against any radical change?

In the accounts given in this book we are told many times how in the years 1945-7 men of impressive and dynamic personality appeared on the scene with the urgent desire to influence developments in Germany in a progressive way. These groups included such people as the Minister of Education in Lower Saxony, Adolf Grimme, and the Berlin educational reformer Fritz Karsen. Both of them had their roots in the reform movement of the Weimar period. It would have required a conscious political effort to give adequate support to such groups, rather than to be satisfied with a cautious resumption of a discussion based on the views of the 1920s.

Was it right to set up again the centralism of the *Land* Governments, or even to develop it at all, by the policy of de-centralisation at a national level? Was it right to allow the State-supported expansion of the confessional school and thereby present the Federal Republic of Germany with a twenty-year long controversy over this question, which was not fully resolved until the 1960s? Was it right to begin again establishing the con-fessional primary school (*Konfessionelle Volksschule*) and the traditional German grammar school (*Gymnasium*), basing these on the values of the pre-National-Socialist era, without considering what part these values might have had in the nation's downslide into National Socialism? Was respect for individuals' resistance against the Nazis the right principle on which to select the people who were to be responsible for change in the German education system? At the moment of collapse of the Third Reich it was naturally very difficult to check whether even the low level of resistance offered by the Germans to the Third Reich was borne by the strength of tradition or vision for the future. Was it right simply to purge the school books of all formal and direct traces of National Socialism, without critically analysing the conception of society these books presented? Was it not necessary at this time to put certain types of capitalism, and colonialism in all its forms, openly to question? But again: could this be the proper task of the education officers of a British government? The question must remain whether the British did not carry their policy of cautiousness and restraint too far in these early post-war years, and from the German point of view it is regrettable that the British authorities abstained so strictly from taking sides, however much we respect the reasons for this neutrality.

When we hear today for instance that the OECD Report on German education policy criticises the Germans for overvaluing career-mindedness, when critics point to the bureaucratisation of the education system, when complaints are heard about the centralisation of decision-making procedures in the eleven *Land* capitals, when the lack of freedom and scope for experiment, innovation and modification is censured—there can be no doubt at all that the roots of these problems lie in developments which took place in the very first post-war years. The OECD investigation into the education policies of the *Länder* in 1971 represents perhaps the strongest criticism ever made of the policies of the Occupying forces in the years after the war, even though the word 'occupation' itself does not appear in the Report and not one single measure or action of this period is subject to criticism. But the centralism of the *Länder,* the re-institutionalising of careerism and the absence of concrete, specific reform measures in the institutions of education—all of these problems can be traced back directly to the first years after the War.

One fundamental problem in this connection is the question of the confessionalisation of the school system. This book makes it plain that the British Occupation forces did not take the decision to allow the reintroduction of the confessional school lightly. But were the British fully aware that confessionalism at this time was no true counter-movement to National Socialism, but rather that the Germans, faced with the collapse of one creed, wanted simply to find another as quickly as possible that would afford them security and some form of release? The brief duration of this pseudo-Christian fervour became evident very soon in the 1950s, and by the 1960s was quite obvious. Perhaps it would have been of value in those early years to realise that National Socialism was not brought about by the suppression of a Christian Church and community generously financed by Church taxes, but rather was made possible by the fact that in Germany the Enlightenment never became a decisive force capable of influencing the whole cultural and political life of the people. It would have been perhaps more important at the time not to seek to replace false values by past values, but to place enlightenment and critical consciousness at the centre of the education system, so that gradually a consciousness for new values could arise. By way of criticism, one could say that the British did give the Germans every possible pragmatic and practical assistance in the reconstruction of the education system, and with the fundamental policy decision for decentralisation they did allow the free development of variety and diversity in education. But in doing this the British indirectly encouraged the restoration of the old order. They helped the Germans in many ways, but they were unable to give support to those groups and persons in Germany who were perhaps capable of making real use of the opportunity given by the 'year zero'.

There is a ready answer to this criticism of the British Military Government's education policy, namely that the problem in the field of education merely reflected a fundamental problem present through all the early stages of the developments leading towards the founding of the Federal Republic of Germany. The re-establishment of German sovereignty on the basis of a free market economy with a full professional civil service structure and with a State whose main direction of purpose was not the encouragement of citizen initiative but rather the re-establishment of the traditional German State order, did provide the conditions for the economic miracle, and set in motion the moves towards a united Europe; yet it did not immediately provide for the development of a free society, of a society of citizens capable of free and independent action, or of a socially just education system. It would be true to say this was the Germans' own choice; the Allies did no more than clear the way for free elections in a very short space of time, and the decision that was then taken was not their concern.

No one can free the Germans from the responsibility for their own mistakes. An assessment of British policy during this time cannot, however, overlook the fact that although the education policy of the British Military Government was practical, helpful, tactful, not hasty or overbearing in taking decisions, it was apparently not able to help the Germans overcome their own basic failings and errors and open up new intellectual and social horizons for them. We know today that the rise of National Socialism was closely bound up with the developments and conditions in the pre-Hitler era, and that it would therefore be quite wrong simply to attempt to fall back on the values of the past. The State-run denominational schools and the *Humanistisches Gymnasium*, careermindedness in the public service, élitist universities, idealist philosophy and a permanent professional civil service—none of these could mark the path that would lead to a new Germany. But they did belong to a Germany that had once influenced England's own education system too, and the occupying power was therefore unable to object to the restoration of the old order if the Germans themselves seemed to want this. It was not the intention of British policy at this time to present any concept for change of their own. It would quite likely have been very difficult for the representatives of this country to do this, since they themselves must have had no clear idea of the direction education would take in their own country, in spite of the Education Act of 1944. For in contrast to the modern tenor of this Act there still stood the unbroken tradition of the prep. schools, the public schools and the predominance of the Oxbridge universities, in short a firmly established system of educational institutions which serve mainly the benefit of the upper class. It is understandable that in this situation the British did not feel called upon to decide on a

question for the Germans which had not yet been resolved for
their own nation.

On the other hand, it is quite intriguing to note in detail how
every single decision of any importance in education in the
Federal Republic of Germany has a history dating back to the
early years of the Military Government. An especially important issue in this connection is the comprehensive school. The
problem of the comprehensive school (at the time it was still
called the *Einheitsschule*) was much discussed in the period
immediately following the First World War. It was on the
agenda of the Imperial Schools Conference (*Reichsschulkonferenz*)
in 1919. It was part of the programme of the *Bund Entschiedener Schulreformer* in the Weimar period. As the accounts given
in this book show, it was in the main the Social Democrats who
again called for the establishment of comprehensive schools in
Germany in the period immediately after the Second World
War.

While the Americans made vigorous attempts to set up a
comprehensive schools system in their Sector, but failed because
of resistance from the Germans, the English were rather more
cautious and left the Germans to resolve the question among
themselves. And so the discussion within the German Education
Council and in the *Kultusministerkonferenz* (Standing Committee of the Ministers of Cultural Affairs), which eventually led
to the recommendation entitled *Einrichtung von Schulversuchen
mit Gesamtschulen* (1969) and a corresponding experimental
programme in all of the *Länder,* actually goes back to the
controversy of the early post-war years. For one who is familiar
with the extent of the problems involved in getting the comprehensive school established over the last few years alongside a
full-developed tri-partite school system, it is a matter for regret
that such schools were not set up at least experimentally as a new
beginning after the *tabula rasa* of the year 1945. The tri-partite
school system, with its class-based selection system, was re-
established for the time being at the expense of the comprehensive school, and the re-establishment was to all intents and
purposes absolute and unconditional.[2] Considerable time had
to pass before it became clear that granting free tuition alone
without effecting changes in the structure of the school system
itself could not bring about any diminution of the inequality of

opportunity characteristic of the traditional school system in Germany.

Faced with the physical destruction and the sudden collapse of political order around them, the Germans obviously sought immediate refuge in the familiar. The attempt to introduce six years of primary schooling as preparation for a comprehensive school system—a question given much attention particularly in the British Zone—also failed because of the resistance of German voters. This experiment was rejected at the polls both in Hamburg and in Schleswig-Holstein. The accounts given in this volume show clearly how the Germans themselves were responsible for dampening the general willingness for educational reforms in the years between 1945 and 1948 with the restoration of the pre-National-Socialist order. Only very much later were the reform proposals of the early post-war years to be taken up again and at least in part implemented by the Federal and *Land* governments, in the first instance within the framework of the *Deutscher Ausschuß für das Erziehungswesen* (1953-1965) and then in the German Education Council (*Deutscher Bildungsrat*) (1965-1975).

One gains the impression that particularly the pragmatic, practical measures taken during these early years proved to be of benefit in the long term. Here I do not mean just the physical reconstruction, or assistance in the provision of school meals and the like, but more the way the British Education Advisor invited the Education Ministers to his house for discussions, or how he was able to arrange a visit to the theatre. One finds here the beginnings of the Standing Committee of the Ministers of Education (*Ständige Konferenz der Kultusminister*), which represents to this day the vehicle which prevents the federal structure of the system from producing a total atomisation in German education. One realises, on the other hand, that the British accepted the federal principle as a political necessity without fully considering the dangers which later arose from this; today the demand for more power for the central administration in educational affairs has become a political demand particularly of German liberal politicians. It is so patently impossible today to separate educational affairs and policy from social policy, or foreign affairs, or economic policy, that at least the planning aspects of education are seen increasingly to be the concern of the national administration. Perhaps it was the British colonial experience which deterred them from encouraging centralism, so that in educational affairs they were prepared to accept the regional differences of the German *Länder* rather more readily than was in fact desirable.

The main problem the British faced in the question of centralism was that school education was not unified when the German *Reich* was established in 1871, but remained within the power of the individual *Länder*. Again, during the Weimar Republic, the *Reichsschulgesetz* (Imperial School Education Act) provided for in the Weimar Constitution foundered on the refusal of the *Länder* to agree among themselves. The only central educational administration that ever existed in Germany was set up by the National Socialists in the form of the Imperial Ministry of Education (*Reichskultusministerium*). Centralised educational policy was therefore felt to be typical of National Socialism and was abolished. Yet the question of federalism in Bismarck's Empire and in the Weimar State was a much simpler one, as Prussia constituted two-thirds of Germany and therefore educational policy matters were almost solely decided by Prussia. The *Länder* bordering directly on Prussia like Saxony or Hamburg usually followed Prussian educational policy on all questions of importance. The effects of this historical development in educational policy can be seen today in the continuing existence of clear dividing lines in educational affairs. In the 1920s, the great Prussian reform of the *Gymnasium*, the so-called Richert Reform, was introduced; the marked difference in the style of teaching and learning today in the *Gymnasium* in the Prussian successor states, on the one hand, and in Southern Germany, on the other, are due to the continuing influence of this reform. Federalism in education without Prussia naturally produced a whole new set of problems that went unrecognised in the early post-war years. Today, educational affairs must be seen as the responsibility of the nation as a whole. Vocational training, the school system and the universities must be considered in relation to each other within the framework of an integrated education policy. If it is to be effective, the responsibility for all educational planning must be organised on a supra-regional basis.

That efforts to restore the old order dominated the post-war period becomes particularly apparent in the case of the universities. In this area especially the work of the British Occupation Forces must be recognised. By this I do not just mean the sympathetic help in reconstruction itself, but rather the pushing for fundamental reforms. After 1945 the Allies, including the British, were understandably hesitant to interfere with the structure of the German universities.[3] After all, the British laid the foundation for basic structural reforms. They even went so far as to set up a German commission that was to produce a report on the reform of the German universities. This Report[4] became part of the history of German universities, and became known as 'The Blue Report' (*Das blaue Gutachten*). As long ago as 1948-49 the Report presented a clear statement on the responsibilities of the universities towards society, the importance of teaching in academic work, the need for a *Mittelbau* in the universities' staffing structure, and on many other matters. The Report's proposals were not instituted because of the resistance of the German professors and the *Rektorenkonferenz* (University Vice-Chancellors' Committee). If the reform proposals made at that time had been given proper and rapid attention, then the crises of 1968 and after would probably have taken a different course. In 1968 the German universities had to pay the price for reforms not carried out in the period from 1945-1950, just as the French were faced with the French Revolution because reforms had not been instituted at the right time. As in the French Revolution, sometimes the 'wrong aristocrats were beheaded'. A lowering of the prestige of the universities as an institution was an inevitable result not so much of the reforms of the period 1965-75, but of the delay in introducing them.

The way universities have developed to the present is seen to be even more disturbing when one considers that the Reform Commission of 1948-49 included such outstanding academics as the classical scholar Bruno Snell, the physicist and philosopher Carl Friedrich von Weizsäcker, and the Swiss historian and political scientist Jean Rudolf von Salis, alongside well-known educationists and a representative of the Trades Unions and the Co-operatives. Together, within the framework of an initiative of the British Occupation Forces, they presented a series of analyses and suggestions, the implementation of which was possible and realistic even then. When German professors today complain about too much power-sharing within the university

(*Mitbestimmung*) and about the lowering of the public standing of their scientific pursuits, then they should not forget that
the German universities did not make use at the proper time of
the insights offered by a German commission acting on the
initiative of Lord Lindsay and Robert Birley. Not only did they
not make use of these insights, they consciously rejected them.
The absolute masters of this university system, the German professors, must bear the blame for this development. It was to the
credit of the British Occupation Forces that they at least enabled
these questions to be asked, and some possible answers put forward. It would have gone against the character of British policy
to enforce the implementation of what they saw to be right
against the will of the Germans.

The Education Adviser in the British Zone drew attention to
four specific points which of all the well-known educational aims
of the *Kontrollratsdirektive No. 54* were to remain of especial
importance.

1. Free tuition and free school materials for pupils. This is
accepted today as a fundamental right in the whole of the
Federal Republic. Here we see how an idea promoted by the
Allies in the first years after the War could be established, and
affect the whole of the education system up to the present
day.
2. Teacher training should be carried out in the universities
or at institutions working within the framework of the universities. The realisation of this idea too is in sight after many
long battles.
3. No legislation in educational questions should preclude any
development towards six years of primary schooling. This
desideratum fell victim in the meantime to the political trend
towards restoration of the old order in the post-war years.
However, the *Bund* (Federal Administration) and all eleven
Länder agreed in the 1973 *Bildungsgesamtplan* on the overall
policy to combine the fifth and sixth classes into an orientation
class. The CDU- and SPD-governed *Länder* have not yet
been able to agree whether this orientation class should be
organised within the context of the existing school forms, or
whether some new organisational form should be found. In
any case the proposal has remained on the table and is now

likely to be developed along lines very similar to what the British Education Adviser at that time had wanted.

4. The rights of private schools to continue in existence should be respected. The reason given for this by the British was in particular that the private school system in Germany had traditionally provided a healthy climate for experimental education. Since then the guaranteed right of existence for private schools has been written into the Constitution in Article 7, paragraph 5; in practice this right is supported still more by the fact that all recognised private schools receive high subsidies from the State. In some *Länder* in what used to be the British Zone, like North Rhine-Westphalia and Hamburg, these subsidies are so high they cover almost all the whole costs of staff to a level equivalent to comparable public schools.

In Germany school means in the main an institutionalised, State-run arrangement. It is therefore regrettable that although under English influence pupil representation was instituted very early on, the German tradition was too strong to allow any significant degree of autonomy for the school, or a degree of self-government for individual schools, to occur; for the same reason the school inspectorate and supervising officers could not take on a more advisory role. Respect for German traditions also prevented the British from initiating institutional reforms at the university level.

Developments in youth work and adult education took a different course from what happened in the schools and universities. Here, personal contact was more important, and the lively way many young English people set about offering assistance in these areas in the post-war years is not forgotten. In adult education the effects of the vigorous development of adult education programmes particularly in the British Zone are still quite evident today. Schleswig-Holstein, North Rhine-Westphalia, Hamburg and Lower Saxony are today still strongholds of adult education. The wide-ranging scope of the many suggestions made was reinforced most of all by a lively exchange programme; in the post-war years Britain was a sort of Mecca all those engaged in building up the adult education system were keen to visit.

While the stimulating effect of the British Occupation Forces' education policy in adult education can not be too highly praised, it must also be mentioned that with this strong stimulus certain unresolved problems of the British adult education system were also brought to Germany. The concept of 'liberal education', the clear rejection of vocational training modelled on the British system, became the basis for adult education work in German *Volkshochschulen,* and considerable effort has had to be expended in the following years to achieve—in contrast to this programme—recognition for the unity and interdependence of general and vocational education, to achieve some recognition for the OECD concept of 'recurrent education' and in particular in the form of certificate courses to introduce some measure of 'credit education' into adult Germany.

The British had also wished to see some sort of readiness on the part of the German universities to participate in adult education programmes, but this only occurred to a very modest extent indeed. It is not out of place to ask whether the crisis the universities were in left any scope for taking on further tasks of such magnitude. It seems to me to be very doubtful whether the adult education departments of English universities could be set up at all today, bearing in mind the overall situation of the universities today. The German imitation of the 'WEA', the *Arbeit und Leben* organisation, enjoyed only limited success. The trades unions did not bring the hoped-for masses of workers into popular education, and to the present day the *Volkshochschulen* and indeed further education in general have not succeeded in reaching the working class.

In the meantime various German universities have established Chairs of Adult Education. In spite of this, the centre of research and development in adult education is not the university, but the *Pädagogische Arbeitsstelle des Deutschen Volkshochschulverbandes* in Frankfurt. The programmatic and methodological stimulus emanating from this institute have a determining influence on the shape of adult education in Germany today. The future of further education in the Federal Republic seems to me to lie in the provision in all communities of a comprehensive course-programme in the *Volkshochschulen* at a local level, and in co-operation with vocational training institutions. Adult education in Germany has undergone many changes since acquaintance was first made with the British model, but our gratitude for the help given in the beginning must not be forgotten.

In the first years after the War I lived in the French Zone and not in the British Zone. I shall never forget the first time I was able to get through to Hanover in 1946, and in the still half-ruined and very dimly-lit city met Adolf Grimme, Erich Wende, Kurt Zierold and Otto Hase. Adolf Grimme had succeeded Carl Heinrich Becker as Prussian Minister of Education in 1930, i.e. shortly before the end of the Weimar Republic. He had been one of my father's colleagues. I had become acquainted with him in the 1920s, and now found a whole group of people from the Prussian Ministry of Education in the Weimar Republic gathered round him again. There was a will to continue the education policies of Weimar, and at the same time there was a feeling of gratitude towards the British who made it possible for the Germans to work in freedom. In 1944, shortly before his arrest, I came together with Adolph Reichwein, another colleague of my father's, later to be executed in connection with the events of the 20th July 1944; our discussion was filled with plans for a Germany that would undergo radical changes after the end of the War. In the year 1946 my father's colleagues were inspired not by Reichwein's vigorous Utopia, but by the necessity—as they saw it—of reconstructing a tried and tested order, and even for their very modest demands they failed to find enough support among their own countrymen. The Germans' state of exhaustion allied itself with the practical sense of the English, with their lack of resolve in educational matters, with their respect for the peculiarities and self-will of an occupied nation, to produce educational reconstruction lacking any concept of change. The real reforms had to be begun anew much later, under very much more difficult conditions, and they are a matter of dispute to this day.

NOTES

1. Saul B. Robinsohn and J. Caspar Kuhlmann: 'Two Decades of Non-Reform in West German Education' (1967) in: Saul B. Robinsohn: *Erziehung als Wissenschaft*, (Stuttgart, 1973).

2. With the exception of Berlin, cf M. Klewitz, *Berliner Einheits-schule 1945-51*, (Berlin, 1971).
3. The report by the delegation of the British Association of University Teachers went much further. Among the reporters were such outstanding scholars as E. R. Dodds, Lord Chorley, and Roy Pascal. But this report had only a very limited public distribution in Germany.
4. *Gutachten zur Hochschulreform, herausgegeben vom Studienausschuß für Hochschulreform*, (Hamburg, 1948).

Appendix I

Anglo-German conference on post-war Educational Reconstruction in the British Zone of Germany

St Edmund Hall, Oxford, 7-11 January 1975

Edited Record of the Discussions

At the conference a period was set aside for the discussion of each of the papers that were given. This account reshapes the record that was kept, drawing the various observations together under a number of headings in the hope that they may be of some help to those embarking on further research in this field.

Planning for the Occupation

The first theme concerned the planning which took place during the later stages of the hostilities. Here the discussions concentrated on the problems involved in formulating a policy which firstly would have to reconcile military and civil attitudes to the tasks confronting an occupying force and secondly would have to be acceptable to all the four powers involved.

T. H. Marshall referred to the training centre, set up at Wimbledon, which provided quite a long and detailed course of study for future civil affairs officers. This illustrated the potential tension between the military and civil approaches to the coming occupation. Denazification and demilitarisation were reasonably clear objectives; democratisation was another matter. Professor Marshall recalled that the work of the training centre had encouraged an approach which some members of the armed forces considered to be more appropriate to a mission than to a military occupation. It emerged from the discussions that the specific training of education officers took place at another base in the South-East of England; Donald Riddy recalled that in February of 1944 by agreement with 21 Army Group some twenty-five officers were seconded from their units and given up to two months' training in educational affairs.

In the subsequent discussions of the preparation for the administration of education an interesting consideration was the extent of Anglo-American co-operation. Professor Riddy recalled

that under the auspices of the Foreign Office in 1944 there had
been an Anglo-American committee under Sir Con O'Neill
concerned with the post-war reconstruction of German education. One of the main fruits of its work had been a remarkable
policy document, the draft Directive No. 8; R. H. Samuel had
been associated with the research for it. Though the French and
the Soviets had taken no part in the work of the committee it
had hoped that the document would be adopted for the guidance
of all Allied commanders at the end of the War. In the event
the most influential publication was the SHAEF *Technical
Manual for Education and Religious Affairs*. Riddy had been
brought in to collaborate with Major Taylor and Major Knappen
of the U.S. Army in this work which had been done at the time
of the German breakthrough in the Ardennes. In his view, the
manual signed by General Grasett, accurately conveyed the
spirit of policy in the early days.

One point in Donald Riddy's statement led to some interesting
comment. He mentioned that the draft Directive No. 8 had been
drawn up on the assumption that it would be possible to take
over the Reichsministerium in Berlin and make use of its existing
machinery to issue orders to all *Länder* and provinces. Though
as things turned out this was clearly a miscalculation it led
Arthur Hearnden to ask whether it suggested that there had in
fact been any intention to treat education as a centralised matter
rather than anticipate the very considerable regional differences
which in the event re-emerged. This stimulated comment on the
differing views about the future unity of Germany. Lothar
Kettenacker said that in the course of the pre-1945 planning all
Allied heads of government had been bent not merely on
regionalisation but on dismemberment. It was opposition within
the Foreign Office and the State Department which delayed the
decision by keeping the matter under study and then achieved
its abandonment. T. H. Marshall confirmed that among the
various views put forward at the time the one which favoured
permanent dismemberment based on regional differences was
never officially accepted. At the other extreme there was a legal
obstacle to centralisation in that an occupying power, unless it
annexed the country, was entitled only to administer, not to
govern, and administration had to be locally based. The prevailing view was that while neither scheme was acceptable, recon-

struction had to begin at the grass-roots. In this sense therefore the regional disparities were anticipated.

A. W. J. Edwards suggested that there was little evidence to explain all or even most of the achievements of Education Branch as the implementation of a clearly formulated strategy. In his experience the key factor had been the intuitive application of a consensus view in each locality. This did not mean that there had been no dissenting voices. He remembered that he himself had argued against a directive with his senior officer who concluded the discussion by telling him to 'go and do what is best for Germany'. In his view much of what Education Branch did was the result of tactical decisions by local officers guided by little more than a few very general principles. This naturally had a decentralising effect. Furthermore the regional differences which developed were very much in accordance with the aspirations of the Germans themselves. They were at this time extremely conscious of their cultural heritage and there was an atavistic desire to go back to a decentralised arrangement because it was under such conditions that Germany had held its most prominent place in the cultural life of Europe.

Another dimension to the preparations before the end of the War was provided by the early work that was done in the P.O.W. camps. Fritz Borinski recalled especially the activities at Camp No. 174, which had a link with the YMCA and where German educationists and theologians were given preparation for post-war reconstruction. The Swedish pastor, Birger Forell, was particularly involved in this. It was to put political education of this kind on a more permanent footing that Wilton Park had been established by Heinz Koeppler assisted by Waldemar von Knöringen and Borinski himself. There can be no doubt that Ernst Hessenauer was representing a view generally endorsed by those present when he emphasised the valuable part which Wilton Park had played in educational reconstruction and in promoting good Anglo-German relations. The many distinguished names that would appear in any list of 'graduates' was perhaps evidence enough. Two that were mentioned in particular were Professor Brundert who later became Mayor of Frankfurt and Professor Abendroth the Marburg political scientist.

Despite this agreement there was another view of the preparations for the occupation of Germany to be taken into account.

Willy Strzelewicz drew attention to the allegations sometimes
made by the younger generation that the purpose was to restore
not democracy but capitalism. If these criticisms were to be
analysed, questions had to be asked which went beyond the
pragmatism which had emerged as such a distinctive feature of
British policy. Lothar Kettenacker's view was that this had
been too early a stage for any deliberate decision to restore capitalism; this would have been to prejudge some far-reaching
political decisions. Arthur Hearnden pointed out that in educational affairs the British did not appear to have shown any
political partiality; the approach in North Rhine was for example
very different from the one adopted in Hamburg. Fritz Borinski,
too, stressed the pluralism of the approach in Wilton Park,
maintaining that there was never any attempt to exclude discussion of communism. Richard Löwenthal's book *Jenseits des
Kapitalismus* had been very influential.

It was however clear that a major preoccupation of the future
would lie in defining what was understood by 'restoration'.
Robin Cecil pointed out that the restoration of capitalism could
least of all be attributed to British policy which at the time was
formulated by a Labour government. Ronnie Wilson also spoke
of the climate of political change in the United Kingdom at the
time and in particular of the British desire to promote trade
union activity and welfare services; their aim had been to restore
an open society. This theme was further expanded in the discussion of British policy for adult education and is taken up later
in this account.

Conditions in Early Post-War Germany

It was clear from the discussions that at the risk of being
repetitive the difficult conditions of the time need to be constantly
re-emphasised. For Lady Flemming the most vivid memories were
of the profound impression which visits to England made on
those Germans who were fortunate enough to take part in them.
She spoke in particular of a conference in Folkestone in 1947
and of the first group of teacher training specialists to come
over in 1948. German visitors had stayed in their English hosts'
homes and this experience of normal daily life in England had
helped to bridge the gap between the two peoples. In reverse it

had had a profound effect on British people to visit Germany. She mentioned in particular a party which had attended a conference there in 1948 and seen at close quarters the destruction of Hanover.

This memory of appalling difficulties was reinforced at various stages in the discussions. Donald Riddy recalled the hardship of the first post-war winter when in 'Operation Stork' some 20,000 children were evacuated from Berlin. He also spoke of the unimaginable ruins; the University of Kiel could only reopen by using ships in the harbour as premises. In Hamburg the average student was found to be twenty per cent underweight and the rations were supplemented with soup. Indeed the problem of malnutrition had been a major one at all levels. Those officers who were concerned with food supply were in a key position. Berta Humphrey recalled that a team had been sent out from England to look at the problem and that a report had been written by a lecturer from Oxford University, Hugh Sinclair.

The provision of school meals was therefore a most important element in the educational work of the British authorities. During the discussions on the origins of this activity, Herbert Walker explained that in July 1945 he had become Regional Officer for Hamburg and Schleswig-Holstein. In the following month he wrote a report on the feeding of schoolchildren, recommending urgent action. The school meals service had then been planned at a meeting between himself, Donald Riddy and Frank Hollins, Director of Food and Agriculture Branch. Thereafter Ellen Wilkinson had taken a special interest as mentioned in the paper given by Edith Davies.

The hardship of the period was compounded by the problem of providing for the vast number of refugees who had fled to the West. In the discussion of Ken Walsh's paper Hans Alfken recalled from his own experience after being sent from Bremen to Hanover how vigorous the British involvement in youth work had been. He referred in particular to the valuable work of Joan Dunning. It had to be remembered just how many disoriented young people there were and the British authorities had shown a genuine responsibility for their welfare. He recalled the foundation of Vlotho in Westphalia and the remarkable co-operation of the newly-formed youth organisations. There were amicable relations between Western organisations and the FDJ among whose group leaders was Erich Honecker.

Berta Humphrey also spoke of the importance of Vlotho as a meeting place for young people. She was particularly appreciative of the work done by the Protestant Klaus von Bismarck, later Head of Cologne Radio, and the Catholic Hans Mertens on the German side, and by Nigel Spicer and Alan Andrews on the English. The Red Cross and the Salvation Army had also played an important part. Two particular issues in which the British authorities had featured prominently were the introduction of probation in cases of juvenile delinquency and the setting up of the first child guidance clinic in Hanover, staffed by a psychologist, a psychiatrist and a social worker. The latter was the direct outcome of one of the GER visits during which Hans Alfken had seen the Tavistock Clinic in London and the Child Guidance Clinic in Bristol. At his subsequent instigation the Hanover institution was set up. A linguistic illustration of the co-operation with the British authorities was the fact that this German foundation was known as the 'Child Guidance Klinik'.

The Reconstruction of the School System

In the discussion of the policy for schools Donald Riddy spoke about the question of denominational education which in the early days had taken up a great deal of time at main headquarters. The agreement on denominational education was one of the positive achievements of the Allied Education Committee in Berlin. This and other agreements had come about largely by virtue of the versatility of the word *demokratisch*. Despite the different meanings which the various factions attached to it, its use was a sure way of resolving disputes. Directive No. 54 of June 1947 was the culmination of two years of work and was an important document which still deserves attention. Sir Robert Birley agreed that judicious use of the word *demokratisch* was a valuable tactic in negotiations. He had found his Russian opposite number agreeable on a personal level and relatively uncritical of British policy. However, when Sir Robert attempted to get a Soviet Zone representative to serve on the university commission he was accused in immoderate terms of setting out to undermine Soviet policy and to divide Germany. It was his impression that the Allied Education Committee was in his time a much less effective body.

The importance of the question of religious education and the confessional schools was emphasised by Robin Cecil. In his view it reflected a feeling that religion had a significant part to play in arresting the decay in values and preventing extreme political reaction from manifesting itself. This policy was widespread outside Germany also. Ernst Hessenauer endorsed this view from the German side and Sir Robert Birley spoke of the differences between Berlin and the British Zone as a whole. Those in the Zone had taken little interest in the events in Berlin and Grimme had even referred to the city as a 'past life'. But there was one issue that did assume great importance, that of the private and confessional schools; their abolition would have given rise to angry reactions in the Rhineland. He agreed therefore that the urge to rebuild on Christian foundations had been very strong.

In more general terms Tom Creighton spoke of the atmosphere of improvisation and uncertainty in Berlin during the period dealt with in Marion Klewitz's paper. He had been given a free hand to implement policy as best he could and had found the school inspectors prepared to co-operate. Otto Winzer, later East German Foreign Minister, had been Head of the Education Department of the *Magistrat* and Ernst Wildangel had been his deputy as Head of the *Hauptschulamt*. Winzer's diplomatic skill had been formidable and he had done all he could to promote a sensible attitude to education at all levels. But since the three Western Allies were not in complete agreement about the aims of education policy in Berlin and their only means of applying whatever policies they had was through the Education Committee of the Kommandatura, there were many anomalies. Orders given by the committee had to be unanimous and were given to a Russian dominated *Magistrat* situated in the Russian sector.

There was then some discussion of the *Einheitsschule*. Trevor Davies who had been schools officer in Berlin recalled a lengthy talk given by Professor Klesse of the Pädagogische Hochschule in which he had set out the demands for the introduction of an *Einheitsschule* that went back to the Gotha programme of the SPD. Hans Alfken pointed out that to a remarkable extent the United States authorities had been in agreement with the SPD.

K

Fritz Karsen had been their adviser in Berlin where he had hoped to establish a complete *Einheitsschule* programme. In 1947 he told Grimme that he had failed and that he was returning to the United States a disappointed man. Arthur Hearnden remarked that an account of Karsen's work in Neukölln during the Weimar period would read like a compendium of contemporary innovations and illustrated how fertile a period this had been in Germany. He may have been disappointed in 1947 but many of the ideas he had pioneered had now come to fruition in a number of European countries. Here a comment made at the time by W. O. Lester Smith, Director of Education for Manchester, seemed apposite; what was being attempted was good but too ambitious and it would have been prudent to take things more slowly.

This was amplified by Willy Strzelewicz. Following the theme of the seminal thinking of the *Reform* movement he pointed out that many of the ideas behind the extensive changes in the Swedish school system since the War had originated in Germany. Political émigrés in Sweden had made a significant contribution to the debate about the *enhetsskola*. But there was strong political support for a radical initiative of this kind in Sweden. In postwar Germany, by comparison, it was advocated by isolated individuals only. It could only have been realised if there had been an organised movement behind it.

The Universities

Sir Robert Birley spoke of his experiences with the German universities particularly the difficulties that arose when Professor Konen was Rector of Bonn and Minister of Education at the same time. He recalled the move among some sections of the student population in Heidelberg to dissuade the U.S. Military Government from handing student corps premises back to the *Land* authorities. Lord Lindsay had played an important part in focusing attention on the problems.

One of the ideas associated with Lindsay as referred to in Harald Husemann's paper was discussed, namely, the *studium generale*. Fritz Borinski said that to his knowledge the idea had been put into practice at Tübingen on a residential basis and also at the *Technische Universität* of Berlin; it was a development which Grimme had been keen to encourage. Edith Davies made the point that the *studium generale* was less important in Germany where such a wide range of subjects was studied up to the *Abitur* (taken at the age of nineteen), than in England where there was a high degree of specialisation between the ages of sixteen and eighteen, often at the expense of general education.

T. H. Marshall recalled his own membership of the AUT delegation of 1947. He could not say that their investigation was very thorough as there were many factors working against this, not least the weather. However, they did have some good discussions. He had been in Cologne in 1937 and was in a position to compare his experience then with that of a decade later. In 1947 the shadow of oppression still hung heavily over the universities; there was an atmosphere of fear, particularly acute in the Humboldt University in Berlin. He had been impressed by the students he had met. Nazism had not penetrated very deeply. In 1947 they did not accept the idea of sovereign nation states, let alone nationalism. In consequence they were somewhat at a loss for something to which they could attach their loyalty.

In Werner Burmeister's view the need at that time was to encourage social cohesion. One of the great difficulties was the lack of a *Mittelbau* in the universities and this was not so much an administrative as a political issue. George Allen was interested in why there had been so little change of this kind until the 1960s. He thought it was perhaps because before that time there had been very little concern with structures in the education system. Fritz Borinski said that there had indeed been ideas but little action; he spoke of the isolated nature of the initiatives that had eventually led to the formation of the Deutscher Ausschuss. Much of what was being said in this context implied criticism of university professors for their reluctance to explore new ideas in the early post-war years. Donald Riddy pointed out, however, that all the material difficulties, which had been noted earlier as facing the students, applied also to the professors. They had the formidable task of coping with very large numbers, more than double the pre-war figure. The majority of them had not spared themselves in their efforts to get the universities working again.

One particular example of university work was quoted by Tom Creighton, the reopening of the *Technische Hochschule* as the *Technische Universität*. Situated in the British sector, it was solely a British responsibility but finance for it was controlled by the Assembly, supposedly under four-power control but actually dominated by the Russians. It was in the end reopened in the teeth of Russian opposition by the Military Governor's imaginative provision of funds from the British Zone. Professor Walter Kucharski and Professor Rudolf Wille on the German side and Hubert Middleton and Alex McDonald on the British devoted great energy to this task. It was, he thought, worth noting that the *Technische Universität* has not become, as the Russians expected, a renewed focus of German technological militarism.

Adult Education

The British effort to promote adult education had been centred on the *Volkshochschulen* and a number of aspects of their work were discussed. There was particular interest in the *Arbeit und Leben* movement in Celle, the result of an initiative that began in Hanover. Hans Alfken explained that its aim of bringing education to the working class had been realised very differently in the various *Länder*. Part of this aim had been to show people how to educate themselves. He quoted as examples the courses run by Dr Steinmetz at the residential *Volkshochschule* of Hustedt and the introduction of adult education at Göttingen. Among those who had attended such courses was Joachim Dikau who later became Professor of Education at the Free University of Berlin. Plessner, Weniger and Snell were all names that came to mind as supporters of the 'extra-mural' education movement. Following a conference at Oxford in December 1952 Professor Plessner and Professor Weniger had laid the foundations for an extra-mural establishment at Göttingen.

Criticism of the *Arbeit und Leben* movement came, however, from Johannes Weinberg; though it was designed to provide educational opportunities for the workers there was very little contact with them and he was surprised that this state of affairs could satisfy anyone who had been familiar with the relationship between the WEA and the universities in the United Kingdom. There were, of course, certain initiatives on the British side such as the *Kulturelle Bergarbeiterbetreuung* in the Ruhr. But this had met with very little co-operation on the part of the *Volkshochschulen*; it had in fact given rise to conflict. Indeed he wondered why the British had shown such a preference for the *Volkshochschulen* and not followed up other lines of approach such as the adult education provided by the local authorities in the United Kingdom.

Werner Burmeister explained that the kind of adult education provided by LEAs had been mainly vocational and professional courses, in shorthand and typing for example. This had not really been relevant to a situation involving social reconstruction. Those involved in adult education at that time saw their work as a continuation of the missionary tradition whereby a number of university teachers regarded it as their duty to make a contribution to education outside the enclosed world of the universities. There were humanist, socialist and Christian strands in this tradition. The greatest problem had been the shortage of people to do the work. In this connection the contribution of those involved in adult education was particularly important because of the reluctance of the German universities in this field. One element in the German university tradition was the almost mandatory use of esoteric theoretical language which impeded communication with the outside world. University professors were high priests of mysticism and this absence of any obligation to communicate with the lay public had been generally endorsed to the point where it was accepted that, to put it bluntly, if you understood a man, he was not much good. The difficulty of getting university teachers to participate in adult education was a continuing one. As to the question of the failure to promote education among working-class people, it had always been extraordinarily difficult to involve them. In the immediate post-war period it was important to sow seeds in the ground where the response was most spontaneous. Those concerned with adult education had always striven to reach the entire community, but it was a fact that the response had come largely from the middle classes. This was a common phenomenon, to be observed in the context of WEA and the Open University as much as in German *Volkshochschulen*.

Sir Robert Birley agreed that the work done had been enormously valuable. In 1947 there had been a move to bring the work of Education Branch to an end; the idea originated at a meeting of Foreign Office representatives in New York. General Robertson had not been consulted and instructed Sir Robert to

write a report on the subject. In the course of doing so, he consulted several leading German trades unionists all of whom were
adamant that the British education officers should not leave. Sir
Robert related how Ernest Bevin, after a very brief interview
with him, wrote across the report in pencil, 'This work must go
on. See the Treasury about it'.

Another theme was the distinction between control and help.
Johannes Weinberg pointed out that it was natural for the
Germans to interpret the intervention of the British as help but
he suspected that the element of control was greater than was
generally realised or admitted. For example, German educational
institutions had been obliged to send to the British authorities
monthly reports of their activities *(Tätigkeitsberichte)*; he
wanted to know whether these were read and if so what the
reaction to them had been.

In reply to this Ronnie Wilson recalled that often the reports
had led to action being taken, especially at the lower levels in
Education Branch. It needed to be remembered that as yet no
Landesverbände were in existence. Early on it had been recognised by the British staff that the *Volkshochschulen* were effectively the central agency for adult education. A further point
about the work in this field was that it was not seen exclusively in
Anglo-German terms, other nationals having been involved as a
result of British initiative through Education Branch. He quoted
the example of a summer school at Wadersloh in 1948, although
the budget had been too small to allow any great expansion of
this work. On the question of the comparison that had been
made between the *Volkshochschulen* and WEA he referred to a
conference on workers' education held in Berlin in 1952 at which
Heinz Küppers, Head of the Education Department at the
federal headquarters of the trade union movement spoke as
follows:

May I now, with our foreign friends especially in mind, say
something about the new departure known as *Arbeit und
Leben.* And here I concede that it is still too soon to reach a
mature judgement about it. When in 1947 English friends
from WEA came to Germany to discuss with us how to build
up an educational system for working people our reaction was
'We envy you your WEA. But we cannot establish it here for

we are not faced, as you were in 1903, with an inadequate adult education system. We have today a very well structured system of *Volkshochschulen* and it would be very difficult for us to set a special 'workers' education' alongside these *Volkshochschulen*. Furthermore it would probably not be a good thing to do. I believe that our English friends thoroughly understood these difficulties.

The speech as a whole, Ronnie Wilson explained, was largely a plea for the fashioning of a modern *Arbeitnehmerbildung* using the existing resources of the unions and the *Volkshochschulen*. Another quotation from the same speech was illuminating in that it linked the question of WEA with the problem of restoration which had been discussed earlier :

Finally there is the danger of restoration. There is not only a restoration from the right, there is another restoration which I mentioned at the beginning : you have a cherished ideology, you know that it is no longer quite what is needed but you have a certain compulsion to manipulate reality to fit the desired picture. And that is dangerous. Then you quote the experience of foreign friends, and mistakenly in this case, the experience of British friends. The WEA is not restorative in this sense but if we were to copy it there is no doubt that we would be taking a step backwards.

Ronnie Wilson pointed out that although Küppers was a controversial personality whose views and practices were not necessarily shared by his colleagues in other parts of Germany, it is hard to believe that on this occasion his text had not been cleared with his own branch, the DGB Vorstand, since it was being delivered to an international gathering, promoted largely with the support of the US High Commission and to a lesser degree British Cultural Relations.

In a further comment about the *Tätigkeitsberichte* Fritz Borinski confessed that he never wrote a report about his residential *Volkshochschule* in Göhrde. As for the reference to the British LEAs he pointed out that already at that time many *Volkshochschulen* had been financed and administered locally. He reiterated that in the *Arbeit und Leben* movement the regional differences had been considerable; for example the work of Heinz Küppers in Düsseldorf contrasted with the work in Lower Saxony. From the beginning, the residential *Volkshochschulen* had been important; he referred to the seminal influence of Sir Richard Livingstone in this connection. But it had always been difficult for working people to find the time to attend courses; block release remained a problem up to the present day. Some of the other problems and shortcomings in adult education in the period under consideration were due to mistakes in the appointment of staff. He also made the point that while there were affinities with earlier traditions there was no question of a return to them. Those who worked in adult education were convinced that they were involved in something new. He referred to an article published in the *Manchester Guardian* in which it was pointed out that in all three West German Zones no more than twenty people who had been involved in the pre-1933 *Volkshochschule* movement were active in adult education in the post-war period.

Several of these points were taken further. In the matter of the criteria for the appointment of German administrators and teachers Ernest Hessenauer said that in his experience the British officers had taken a more liberal view than their counterparts from the other powers; as a result there was a less anxious atmosphere in the British Zone. John Ryder mentioned the adult education institutions run by the Churches *(Evangelische* and *Katholische Akademien)*. Fritz Borinski said that their significance had lain partly in their promotion of residential courses, usually of up to fourteen days' duration and partly in their use as conference centres.

More recent developments in adult education were also discussed. S. P. Whitley had noted during an official visit in 1970 a growing tendency for *Volkshochschulen* to be taken over by local authorities and enquired about subsequent developments. Walter Ebbighausen said that North Rhine-Westphalia was the *Land* in which this development had started and that there were an increasing number of locally controlled *Volkshochschulen* in Lower Saxony. George Allen spoke of the change in the style of teaching and learning that had taken place within adult education in the post-war period. There had been a move away from 'chalk and talk' in the old style towards a greater intimacy of atmosphere and freedom of discussion. This had been pioneered in the residential *Volkshochschulen*; the main problem had been the lack of funds to provide appropriate facilities for work in small groups.

Shortage of funds also loomed large in the discussion of the role of the *Brücken* which had fulfilled a valuable function in promoting good Anglo-German relations. Robin Cecil explained that they were paid for out of Occupation costs till 1949 and thereafter from British funds. It was because the expense became too great that many had to be closed; the remainder were taken over by the British Council. The prevalent view at that stage was that the time for bricks and mortar was past and that it was more beneficial to deploy staff as widely as possible through contact with German educational administrators and teachers. Walter Ebbighausen and George Allen however both regretted the closing down of so many of the *Brücken*. For Professor Allen one of the most important features had been the provision of good open-access libraries and he had seen it as his task to slow down the closing of centres which offered this service. John Ryder remarked that fortunately the *Brücken* still exist in some places such as Düsseldorf in the form of a library supported by the British Council and by the Americans in conjunction with a lecture programme run by the *Volkshochschule* and the Deutsch-Englische Gesellschaft.

Kurt Jürgensen spoke of his own personal experiences with the *Brücken* while he was still at school. There were reasons for their success which were anchored in the period. They were heated and refreshments were provided, two important features at a time of cold and hunger. But this was not to belittle their achievement. They really were bridges, bridges to other people, other countries, other opinions, accessible through the variety of periodicals that were provided and this was, especially for young people, quite a new experience. Along with the visits and exchanges he thought that the *Brücken* aptly characterised the pragmatic nature of British policy.

Returning to the matter of the closing down of the *Brücken* Ken Walsh spoke in more general terms of the concern which the Germans had felt at the steady diminishment of the British presence from 1947 onwards. He described how a link was established between Arnsberg and the West Riding of Yorkshire which was a forerunner of the widespread practice of 'twinning'

K*

that has developed since. This work had thus arisen directly out
of the activities of the Education Branch, carrying on where the
Brücken had left off.

German Educational Reconstruction (GER)

Another strand in the thread running through the work of reconciliation was the activity of GER, the development of which was
outlined in Jane Anderson's paper. Hans Alfken said that the
significance of the organisation could be seen more clearly if the
comparison was drawn with the aftermath of the First World
War. Then it had not been till 1922 that the Holiday Fellowship
and the Society of Friends had taken positive steps to break down
the mutual antagonism between the British and the Germans. In
the case of GER, the work carried on before the end of the War
ensured that immediately after the cessation of hostilities a
process of reconciliation could begin; this was a remarkable
achievement.

The discussion brought some insight into the kind of difficulties experienced by a voluntary organisation and recollections
of the personalities involved. Karl Mannheim, for example, had
expected greater recognition for the work of GER and Fritz
Borinski suspected that it was official indifference which had discouraged him from taking a very active part even though he had
been on the Board till his death; this was understandable in view
of his particular interest in planning for social reconstruction. By
comparison, the political émigré Fritz Burchardt of the Institute
of Statistics at Oxford had played a more significant role. The
presence of both of these men on the Board rather than the
Executive Committee which was the body made up of émigrés
was explained by the fact that both held established posts in
England. Prominent among the personalities mentioned was,
naturally enough, S. H. Wood. George Allen spoke of his remarkable ability to inspire; while he might have shown some
prickliness over points of protocol, the abiding memory of him
was one of passionate commitment.

Fritz Borinski spoke also about the terminology of GER. The
phrase 'educational reconstruction' had been consciously used to
contrast with the term 're-education'; it was deliberately intended
that it should relate to the reformist conception of social recon-

struction. Whatever the inference of the comment by Charlotte
Lütkens, mentioned in Jane Anderson's paper, 're-education'
was not really the intention. The work of educational reconstruction was seen as essentially a German task. GER was no
Stabsquartier for émigrés but a gathering of people who were
determined to return to Germany after the War. With regard
to the comment about political rigidity, the political complexion
of GER could be described as 'leftish' but it was not static. A
certain rivalry developed with the communist-controlled Free
German organisations, for example in the sphere of youth
activity where co-operation with the FDJ was quietly discouraged. The security question precluded any very strong orientation towards the far left. As to the influence of GER, Professor
Borinski thought that it was helpful to consider the state of mind
of the people concerned. Before the formation of GER they were
disoriented. GER contributed the sense of purpose that was
needed by giving them a practical aim; in this lay the key to its
significance. Initially those concerned with it concentrated their
efforts on giving material assistance. And it was through this
medium that eventually they became aware of their democratic
beliefs, a progression from the practical to the theoretical. The
practical emphasis was appropriate at a time of severe austerity
but the true significance lay far in the future. Nor was it to be
understood in any narrowly political sense.

Following this Werner Burmeister indicated three salient points
about GER. Firstly, its fundamental principle was that the way
to achieve its aim was to work through personal relationships.
Secondly, the task of reconstruction was considered to be one for
the Germans themselves; there was no element of paternalism.
Thirdly, the Board was drawn from a great variety of walks of
life so that educational reconstruction was interpreted in the
very widest sense. As to the influence of GER, he thought that
this could not be quantified. What was important was the bond
of humanity. GER made it possible for leading figures in British
public life to talk to their counterparts from Germany as
colleagues. Mr Burmeister mentioned in particular the role which
Otto Kahn-Freund had played in building up the network of
Anglo-German contacts.

One particular aspect of the work of GER to be discussed was
its involvement in the textbook question. Kathleen Davis em-

phasised that what had happened had been caused by the need
to observe priorities since the practical difficulties had been
enormous, in particular the shortage of paper. The Germans
themselves were deeply involved in the selection of books and
publishers had an important say. The only 'banning' that took
place was of Nazi texts. If some classic works of literature were
withheld it was either because of the harsh need to make choices
or because the editions concerned had been dubiously annotated
during the National Socialist period. As regards *English Journey*,
J. B. Priestley himself recommended that it should not be used.
Donald Riddy confirmed that there was little question of rejecting any suggestions from outside, for example from GER, on any
grounds other than the shortage of paper.

Recalling earlier comments about Wilton Park Jane Anderson
mentioned the indications in the documents that GER was out
of sympathy with what it was doing. In Fritz Borinski's view
this really concerned the attitude of Erich Hirsch who considered
that the work of Wilton Park had too strong an element of
propaganda in it. In more general terms Borinski spoke of the
range of GER contacts. The network extended to the USA and
Sweden and the organisation had been heard of in Germany as
early as 1944.

At a number of points the discussion touched on the matter of
evaluating the influence of GER. Johannes Weinberg thought
that it was not out of the question to attempt a precise assessment. From his own experience as a schoolboy at a time when
books were scarce he could point very specifically to the ones
that had exercised the greatest influence on him. It was potentially fruitful to relate recollections of this kind to the books that
were made available to schools. He was suggesting some kind of
empirical analysis of the text book programme and its effect. The
more general view was that there could be no exact measure-
ment. It was nonetheless, as Donald Riddy pointed out, worth
remembering that many matters of policy were first raised in
discussions between officials of Education Branch and members
of GER. And indeed as Sir Robert Birley added, it was sometimes difficult to distinguish between the two.

                                                                    A.H.

Appendix II

Diary, 1944-1955

1944

Easter Recruitment of Education Branch staff begins.

Spring/Summer First training courses in civil affairs for Military Government officers.

Summer/Autumn Policy directives, technical manuals, handbooks, etc., compiled, printed and distributed. Policy laid down before the end of the War was based on the assumption that Allied control of German education would be indirect, i.e. the Germans would carry out the policy directives of Military Government under their control and surveillance. Education Branch was therefore recruited and organised with a view to supervision rather than direct administration. In the event, conditions in Germany at the end of the War were such that Military Government had to assume a much more executive role than had been anticipated in the planning period.

1945

Spring Recruitment, research and training continue. Preparations for move to Germany.

July Education Branch Headquarters move to Germany (to Bünde in Westphalia) and assume control over German education in the British Zone and the British Sector of Berlin, acting through Military Government units already active in the field.

August Potsdam Agreement signed : 'German education shall be so controlled as completely to eliminate Nazi and militarist doctrines and to make possible the successful development of democratic ideas'.

August First schools reopen. By the end of the month about 3,000 schools were operating either full-time or part-time with around half a million pupils. The figures at the end of the year were about 11,250 and 2,250,000 respectively.

September Göttingen University reopens all its faculties. By mid-December all six universities in the British Zone were operating in whole or in part.

Winter By the turn of the year several educational bodies had been organised at Zonal level and had begun to function, e.g. the university rectors' conference, the school administrators' conference, the Allied Education Committee (in Berlin), the Zonal Education Advisory Committee, the Zonal Textbook Committee, etc. Centre for Visual Aids restarted in Hamburg, operating on a Zonal basis.

School meals schemes started, mainly on a local basis.

School broadcasting begun from Hamburg (November), relayed throughout the British Zone.

Operation Stork—25,000 Berlin children evacuated to the Zone.

1946

January/February School meal schemes extended to include country areas and older age-groups, foodstuffs being donated by international relief organisations and by British and foreign governments. When food was available, fuel and footwear often were not and many schools had to be closed according to the vagaries of the weather.

Easter Twenty-eight teacher training colleges functioning with a total of about 4,000 students.

May Fifty-five Adult Education Colleges open.

June Eighteen Reading Rooms/Information Centres open to the public. By the end of the year the number had risen to forty.

Summer First sponsored visits to and from the United Kingdom. Visitors to the UK included Herr Grimme, Prussian Minister of Education until 1932 and Herr Landahl, Senator for Education in Hamburg. Towards the end of the year the Wilton Park conferences were attended by Germans resident in the British Zone. Over the year there were 150 visitors to the UK and about 100 to the British Zone.

November Education Branch moves to Berlin.

December End of the period during which Education Branch controlled German education in the British Zone (1945-1946).

1947

January One of the longest and coldest winters in memory. Ordinance No. 57 came into force and responsibility for education was handed over to the legislatures and the governments of the *Länder*. It marked the beginning of the end of the 'bricks and mortar' chapter and of denazification and demilitarisation and ushered in a more congenial and rewarding period of constructive reform and re-organisation. The hand-over also meant the end of direct control and its replacement by the forces of advice and persuasion reinforced by the spirit of friendship and goodwill that had grown up between British and German educationists since 1945. Taken together, these forces were to prove arguably more effective than direct control in the realisation of the long-term reforms that now lay ahead.

January Visit to the British Zone of an eight-man delegation from the Association of University Teachers.

April *Land* parliaments elected. They assume responsibilities, including education.

May Mr Robert Birley appointed Educational Adviser to the Military Governor and Commander-in-Chief. This new post arose naturally out of the new relationship between British and Germans in the field of Education, as determined by Ordinance No. 57.

June Control Council Directive No. 54 issued, giving guidance on the basic principles for the democratisation of German Education.

July Sixty-three Information Centres operating under ISD.

Sponsored visits in 1947 amounted to 2,140 (to the UK) and 870 (to the British Zone). These included participants in Summer Schools and Vacation Courses which were to become regular features of Education Branch's annual programme of visits. The 1947 programme also included the first visits between British and German local authorities, e.g. between Hanover and Bristol, a link which led to the foundation of the Bristol-Hanover Society.

The appointment of an Educational Adviser reflected the new relationship between British and Germans in education and complemented the new advisory role of Education Branch whose work he had to supervise. His main terms of reference were 'the initiation and co-ordination of policy for bringing influence to bear upon the German mind and outlook so that Germany may become a truly democratic nation ready and fit to take her place in the community of peace-loving nations'. The main aim of

British effort would therefore be political as well as social and would entail presenting to the Germans the best in modern Western civilisation so that they could choose whatever pattern of democratic living best suited their nature and their needs.

1948

This was perhaps the most eventful, the most decisive year, politically, if not educationally. It was the year when compromise ran dry and East and West decided to go their separate ways. In March, the Russians left the Allied Control Council, thus facilitating agreement among the Western Allies that Western Germany should be governed on a federal basis. In June, the reform of the currency in the Western Zones and Sectors of Berlin saw the virtual end of the black market and the re-appearance of goods for sale in the shops. When the announcement was made that the new West German currency was to be introduced into the three Western Sectors of Berlin, the Russian reply was the blockade—the severance of the road and rail links between West Berlin and the Western Zones and the cutting of fuel and food supplies for West Berlin. A matter of days later the Allies countered with the Berlin airlift.

July   The Russian delegates walk out of the Berlin Kommandatura.

September   £105 million of Marshall Aid allocated to West Germany.

September   Parliamentary Council meets in Bonn to draft a constitution. As far as education was concerned, 1948 was in some ways the peak year. British staff remained at the 1947 level of 250 with the addition of about 200 youth officers. Visits to the UK reached their peak at 2,350 as did visits from the UK at just over 1,000. The British Council made a valuable contribution by arranging courses for German teachers in the UK and by awarding, for the first time after the War, scholarships and fellowships tenable by Germans at British universities.

November/December   Relations between the Soviets and the Allies continued to worsen throughout the summer and autumn until at the end of November the inevitable split finally came. The City Assembly and the Magistrat, including most of the educational administration, escaped to the West, accompanied by most of the staff and students of the Berlin teacher training college.

Three days later, on 3 December, elections were held for a new City Assembly in West Berlin and the Russians set up a new puppet government in the Eastern Sector of the city. Thereafter, East and West went their separate ways.

But the educational highlight of the year was without doubt the *Report* of the University Commission that was set up in April by the Military Governor to report on the condition of the universities and make recommendations for their reform. The Commission, which comprised twelve members, ten German, one Swiss and one British (Lord Lindsay, then Master of Balliol) published a unanimous report with a large number of recommendations relating to internal organisation, staffing relations with the State, responsibilities towards the community and towards education, especially adult education and teacher training. The Commission also recommended the wider introduction of the *studium generale* as a counterweight to excessive specialisation and greater opportunity for the students' viewpoint to be heard in the counsels of the universities. The *Report* was published in October.

In April, the offices of the Educational Adviser and of Education Branch moved back from Berlin to the Zone (Bad Rothenfelde), taking with them an indelible memory of the fortitude of the Berliners in their beleaguered city. They were to face even greater tests of deprivation and endurance during the ten months of the blockade but, thanks to the close co-operation and mutual respect that the airlift engendered between the Allies and the Germans, both emerged firmly ranged on the same side against the new menace from the East. The old enemy Nazism gave way to the threat of Communism. To counter it would demand more intense action in the world of ideas but the weapons would be those used to nullify Nazism—the dissemination of the spirit and the institutions of Western democracy as well as the supply of the necessities for survival. Only this time an ever-increasing number of right-minded Germans supported the West's cause and lent their weight to the task of convincing the remainder. To this end it was decided that the work of Education Branch should be based on the British centres so as to reach the widest possible circles of local population where German public opinion is traditionally formed.

1949

This year proved to be, if anything, even more 'political' than its predecessor. The work already begun on the Basic Law by the Parliamentary Council continued until May when it was promulgated. The year was otherwise marked by the growing activity of the political parties in preparation for the federal elections in August. The opening of the federal parliament in Bonn on 7 September was closely followed by the election of a President and a Chancellor and the formation of the federal government. Military Government came to an end and the residue of its functions was assumed by the Allied Control Authority (now tripartite). The respective powers and responsibilities of the German government and the Allied Control Authority were defined in the Occupation Statute which came into force in September. The year was also marked by the opening of the Zone and West Berlin to tourists, businessmen and other private visitors on the German economy (they had hitherto been treated as temporary members of Military Government) and the way was again open for trade and commerce with the outside world. This resulted in a decrease in the number of official visitors sponsored by Education Branch—just under 2,000 Germans went to the U.K. whilst the number of British visitors to Berlin and the Zone was around 1,000.

The Berlin blockade ended in May but the Allied airlift continued until the beginning of October, by which time Anglo-German co-operation on this arduous and vital operation had ripened into mutual understanding and respect and ranged West Berlin firmly and finally on the side of the Western Allies. This political *rapprochement* spread to the field of education. Assured of German support Education Branch could now commit itself to further plans and policies in the certitude that they were on the right lines. During the autumn several of the more important centres were moved to new and bigger premises with the assistance of the local German authorities, who were also quick to remonstrate when it became necessary to close down a centre.

In August Mr Birley relinquished the post of Educational Adviser and was succeeded by Professor Marshall, who inherited a staff of 178.

This first year of German independence also marked the beginning of a gradual reduction in Education Branch's operations, including the number of British staff, the number of sponsored visitors and the number of centres. Until the end of the year the centres were managed by Information Services Division.

1950

1950 was the natural sequel to the developments decided upon in the previous year. The British centres (now numbering fifty-one) were transferred from Information Services Division to the Office of the Educational Adviser and ceased to be charged to 'Occupation Costs'. Three months later, in April, the costs of Education Branch were also removed from 'Occupation Costs' and debited to H.M. Treasury. This meant a stricter overall control of expenditure and consequent reductions in staff (to 155), sponsored visitors (to the UK—just over 1,000 and from the UK—about 350) and British centres (from fifty-one to thirty-five, although the policy of creating larger centres continued unabated).

The British Council had already been of great assistance to Education Branch in previous years in arranging visits and courses in the UK and the British Zone. In April they opened an office in Düsseldorf and from there initiated their normal scheme of activities including the award of scholarships and fellowships tenable by Germans at British universities as well as shorter visits and exchanges for academics and educationists of both nationalities. At the end of the year they also took over responsibility for books, music and theatre from the Educational Adviser who had taken it from Information Services Division two years previously.

The creation of the West German Federation in 1949 meant that as far as Allied cultural operations were concerned there were no longer any Zonal boundaries. While the French and Americans spread their activities into the British Zone, Education Branch sent representatives to open centres in the most important towns of the French and American Zones—Munich, Stuttgart, Freiburg, Mainz, etc.—and operate from them throughout southern Germany. The British Council followed suit by including the whole of West Germany in its activities.

1951

In January a long-due change of title took place—Education Branch became Cultural Relations Division, confirming at last that the Educational Adviser's brief went far beyond the field of formal education. His original title was retained when, in February, the post was taken by Mr George Allen, himself an educationist.

It had been agreed by the Foreign Office in the previous year that the work of the Division should be prolonged at its existing level for the three years up to the end of 1953. In the first year of this period there was actually an increase in the number of sponsored visitors but an unfortunately sharp cut-back in staff (to 116) and in the number of centres (to twenty-four). The decrease in funds was largely restored the following year, but it was most unfortunate that the cuts in funds and staff should have come when a new network of British centres was being developed in southern Germany to act as focal points for activities which depended for their success on close and personal contacts with the Germans.

Pressure for further economies persisted throughout the year, however, and in the end it was decided that, if the service was to be maintained at a level satisfactory to Germans and British alike, the Germans would have to be invited to share the management and the running costs of the twenty-four centres that were still operating at the end of the year.

1951 and 1952 saw the brunt of the battle for German youth —waged between East and West with weapons differing characteristically one from the other but calculated to achieve the same ends in the hearts and minds of the coming generation. The largest single manifestation was undoubtedly the Communist Youth Festival held in the East Sector of Berlin from 5-19 August 1951. This followed hard upon an International Youth Camp held under German and Allied auspices at the Lorelei from 22 July to 6 September, and attended by about 7,500 young people from fourteen nations.

But the real Allied/German campaign to assist German youth goes back to December 1950, when the Federal Government made fifty-three million Deutsche Marks available for youth work under a Federal Youth Plan. The measures taken to counteract the influence of the Free German Youth movement were solid, constructive and, above all, capable of absorbing and supplementing much of the work already begun with too few means by *Land* and local authorities. Centres were opened for the training of youth leaders, homes and jobs were provided for homeless youth, schemes were introduced to ease unemployment among school-leavers. On the welfare side, the first of a series of child guidance clinics was opened in Hanover in February 1951 and shortly afterwards the foundation of a probation system was laid. A large number of exchange visits was arranged between Germany and the UK enabling students to study at universities and colleges, youth leaders to meet their opposite numbers and young teachers to attend courses or summer schools. In 1952 alone about 10,000 young people took part in exchange schemes either of a purely educational nature or in the broader context of the town-to-town and area-to-area exchanges that had by now been developed on a large scale.

1952

This year brought a welcome increase in the amount of money available for activities sponsored by Cultural Relations Division, thanks to generous contributions from the German authorities, estimated at about two million Deutsche Marks. These were used largely to support the Division's course and conference work. The number of visitors to the UK was maintained at about 1,000 but the total of British lecturers fell sharply to 200. Cuts in British staff reduced the total to 109.

Much of the year was devoted to negotiations with the German authorities at federal *Land* and local level with a view to winning German support for the activities and the maintenance of the centres.

March Foundation meeting of the Anglo-German Association in London under the chairmanship of Lord Pakenham. Membership about 200.

Special schemes for the treatment of youth problems were continued. A federal youth week was organised in September and was attended by some 200 young people from the United Kingdom. The cost of the travel entailed in these schemes was considerably eased in July when the British and West German governments agreed to waive the fees for visas for young people from either country.

October A typical 'British Week' held in Stuttgart, largely financed by the local German authorities with contributions from Cultural Relations Division, Information Services Division and the British Council.

November Title of 'Educational Adviser' changed to 'Cultural Relations Adviser'.

December Course and conference activities carried on as before. An Anglo-German conference was held at Oxford to follow up one of the most important recommendations of the University Commission—the role of the university in adult education. At the request of the Commander of the Federal Frontier Police a series of lectures on current affairs was arranged, with American assistance, for the officers and men under his command. The cuts in specialists and the continuing pressure of activities both inside and outside the centres brought in their train even closer collaboration between the specialists and the staff based on the centres.

1953

This collaboration developed throughout 1953 and led eventually to further economies in manpower and the harshest cut of all—from 109 to sixty-three by the end of the year. The number of sponsored visitors to the United Kingdom was nevertheless maintained at about 1,000 while the volume of visits in the opposite direction actually increased and included a large proportion of eminent specialists for the course and conference work of the Division.

March Completion of negotiations with the German authorities on the future of the centres. Of the twenty-four still operating, two were to be closed, four were to remain British and the remaining eighteen were to become Anglo-German centres, jointly managed and financed from British and German resources.

1954

A year of further economies in manpower and money, made unavoidable by the imminence of German sovereignty and the consequent need to reduce resources to the scale normal for an embassy.

1955

May The Contractural Agreements between Germany and the Allies were finally ratified and the Occupation came to an end. The British High Commissioner became the British Ambassador and Cultural Relations Division became the Cultural Department of the Embassy with Professor Potter as Cultural Attaché.

G.M.

The Contributors

Jane Anderson is a Research Officer in the Department of Comparative Education at London University Institute of Education.

Hellmut Becker was formerly President of the Deutscher Volkshochschulverband and Deputy Chairman of the Deutscher Bildungsrat. He is a Professor of the Free University and Director of the Max Planck Institut für Bildungsforschung in Berlin.

Geoffrey Bird was with Education Branch of the Control Commission for Germany from 1945 to 1951 and thereafter became Warden of Stephenson Hall of Residence and Honorary Lecturer in German at the University of Sheffield.

Sir Robert Birley, KCMG, was formerly Headmaster of Charterhouse and of Eton and a Professor at the University of the Witwatersrand and the City University, London. He was Educational Adviser to the Military Governor, Control Commission for Germany from 1947 to 1949.

Fritz Borinski was involved in the foundation of Wilton Park and of 'German Educational Reconstruction' (GER). He was a member of the Deutscher Ausschuss für das Erziehungs- und Bildungswesen and is Professor Emeritus of the Free University of Berlin.

Werner Burmeister was involved in the foundation of GER of which he was Chairman from 1950 to 1953. He was with Education Branch (in 1955 it became the Cultural Relations Department of the Foreign Office) from 1953 to 1956, on secondment from the University of London where he later became Director of the Department of Extra-Mural Studies.

Edith Davies, MBE, taught German at Maidstone Girls' Grammar School before serving with Education Branch from 1945 to 1955. Thereafter she was successively British Vice-Consul (Cultural) in Kiel and, from 1959 to 1969, Education Officer at British Council Headquarters in Cologne.

Trevor Davies was with Education Branch from 1946 to 1957 and Lecturer in English at the Pädagogische Hochschule, Berlin, from 1957 to 1962. Since then he has taught French and German at Thomas Bennett School, Crawley and at Brighton College where he is Head of General Studies.

Kathleen Southwell Davis taught French and German at Oxford High School before serving with Education Branch from 1946 to 1949. Thereafter she became Head of Languages at Mid-Herts College of Further Education.

A. W. J. Edwards was with Education Branch from 1946 to 1957 and later became Inspector for Technical and Further Education with the Kent Education Committee.

Arthur Hearnden is Secretary of the Standing Conference on University Entrance and an Honorary Research Associate of the Department of Comparative Education at London University Institute of Education.

Harald Husemann, a former Leverhulme Fellow at the University of Keele, is Professor of English at the University of Osnabrück.

Marion Klewitz is a lecturer in History at the Pädagogische Hochschule, Berlin.

George Murray, MBE, was with Education Branch from 1944 to 1956 when he was transferred to the Foreign and Commonwealth Office in London.

Ken Walsh, OBE, was with Education Branch from 1945 to 1959 and was subsequently at the London Headquarters of the British Council. He is now doing voluntary work for the Christian Community in the United Kingdom and Germany.

Conference Membership

United Kingdom

Professor G. Allen
Miss L. J. Anderson
Sir Robert Birley
Mr W. Burmeister
Mr R. Cecil
Mr T. R. M. Creighton
Miss E. Davies
Mr D. T. Davies
Mrs K. S. Davis
Mr A. W. J. Edwards
Lady V. Flemming
Dr A. Hearnden
Mrs B. Humphrey
Mr F. W. Jessup
Mr P. Macdonald
Professor T. H. Marshall
Mr G. Murray
Professor D. C. Riddy
Dr A. J. Ryder
Mr H. Walker
Mr K. R. Walsh
Miss M. Wane
Mr S. P. Whitley
Mr R. H. Wilson

Federal Republic

Herr H. Alfken
Professor F. Borinski
Herr W. Ebbighausen
Dr J. Grutzner
Dr E. Hessenauer
Professor H. Husemann
Professor K. Jürgensen
Dr L. Kettenacker
Dr M. Klewitz
Professor W. Mertineit
Professor J. Olbrich
Dr K. Schulz
Professor W. Strzelewicz
Professor J. Weinberg
Herr P. H. Weitkamp
Dr L. Wernecke

Glossary of German Terms

Abitur: leaving certificate of the *Gymnasium*

Abwicklungsstelle: department responsible for the winding up of educational administration in Westphalia after the fusion of that province with North Rhine to form *Land* North Rhine-Westphalia

Adventskranz: advent decoration

Allgemeiner Studentenausschuss (ASTA): students' union

Arbeit: work

Arbeitnehmerbildung: workers' education

Aufbaugymnasium: Gymnasium with shortened course for late beginners

Ausland: a general term for foreign countries, *im Ausland =* abroad

Auslandsdeutscher: a German living outside Germany

Austauschdienst: exchange service

Bergarbeiterbetreuung: provision of (cultural) facilities for mine-workers

Berufsschule: vocational school for part-time study, usually in conjunction with apprenticeship

Bezirk: administrative district

Bildungsdurchstoss: educational breakthrough

Bildungsgesamtplan: all-embracing plan for education

Bildungsweg: educational route

Brikett: briquette of pressed coal

Brücke: bridge

Bund Entschiedener Schulreformer: League of Radical School Reformers

Bundesschule: residential college of the trade union movement

Bündische Jugend: branch of the Youth Movement

Bürgermeister: mayor

Christlich Demokratische Union (CDU): Christian Democratic (Conservative) Party

Denkschrift: consultative document

Deutsche Demokratische Republik (DDR): German Democratic Republic; 'East Germany'

Deutsche Forschungsgemeinschaft: German Research Association

Deutscher Ausschuss für das Erziehungswesen: German Committee for Education

Deutscher Bildungsrat: German Education Council

Deutsche Oberschule: type of secondary school created in the 1920s, later much favoured by the Nazis

Deutscher Gewerkschaftsbund (DGB): German counterpart of the Trades Union Congress

Deutscher Wissenschaftsrat: German Higher Education Council

Einheit: unity

Einheitsschule: general term for comprehensive school or comprehensive school system. It is now used only in East Germany; the West German term for comprehensive school is *Gesamtschule*

Einrichtung von Schulversuchen mit Gesamtschulen: Establishment of experimental comprehensive schools

evangelisch: Protestant

Fachschulreife: certificate of maturity to attend college of technology

Fahneneid: oath of allegiance

Falken: falcons, a Social Democrat youth organisation

Fragebogen: questionnaire

Freie Deutsche Jugend (FDJ): Free German Youth, the East German youth organisation

Gebildeter, Gebildete: educated man, woman

Geschäftsführer: chairman, managing director

Gesellschaft: society

Gilde: guild

Grundschule: primary school

Gruppenführer: group leader

Gutachten: report

Gymnasialverein: association of grammar school teachers

Gymnasium: grammar school

Heimvolkshochschule: residential institution of adult education

heisses Eisen: 'hot iron', issue of topical interest

Hochburg: stronghold

Hochdeutsch: high German, standard German

Hochschule: institution of higher education

Hochschulkonferenz: conference on higher education

Höhere Fachschule: college of technology

Humanistisches Gymnasium: grammar school specialising in classical languages

jenseits: beyond

Jugendpfleger: youth officer

Jugendplan: plan for youth

Kampf: struggle

katholisch: Catholic

Klärung: clarification

Kommunistische Partei Deutschlands (KPD): German Communist Party

Konfessionelle Schule: confessional/ denominational school

Kreis: smaller administrative district

Kulturbolschewismus: cultural bolshevism

kulturell: cultural

Kultusministerium: Ministry of Education

Land, plural *Länder:* constituent State of the Federal Republic of Germany

Landesverband: regional association (of adult education institutions)

Landtag: Land parliament

Leben: life

Lehrbuchprüfungsstelle: department responsible for the scrutiny of textbooks

Lehrer: teacher

Lehrerbildungsanstalt: institution for the training of teachers

Lehrergewerkschaft: teachers' union

Lehrerzeitung: teachers' newspaper

Lehrfreiheit: freedom to teach

Lernfreiheit: freedom to learn

Lesebogen: emergency substitute for textbooks

Liberal-Demokratische Partei (LDP): Liberal Party in Berlin and East Germany

Liebeserziehung: education in love (physical education is *Leibeserziehung*)

Luftbrücke: airlift

Lyzeum: secondary school for girls

Mädchengymnasium: girls' grammar school

Magistrat: City Administration

Ministerialrat, Ministerialrätin: senior civil servant

Mitbestimmung: power sharing, worker participation

Mittelbau: intermediate level of established university teaching posts

Mittelschule: intermediate school

Nachwuchsförderung: nurturing of the younger generation

Nationalpolitische Erziehungsanstalt ('Napola'): National Socialist Party School

Neubau: new building in the course of erection; reconstruction

Niedersachsen: Lower Saxony

Nordwestdeutscher Plan: North West German Plan

Oberprima: final year of the *Gymnasium*

Oberschule: Secondary school

Oberschulrat, Oberschulrätin: inspector of secondary schools

offen: open

Pädagogische Arbeitsstelle: Centre for educational research

Pädagogische Hochschule: college of education

Philosophikum: name given to a new kind of transitional stage between school and university, the introduction of which was mooted in Lower Saxony

Realschule: intermediate school

Referendar: trainee grammar school teacher

Referendariat: induction period for grammar school teachers

Reformpädagogik: educational theories of the pre-Nazi reform movement

Regierung: government

Regierungsbezirk: see *Bezirk*

Rektorenkonferenz: German counterpart of the Committee of Vice-Chancellors and Principals

Richtinien: guidelines

Sammlung: collection

Schule: school

Schülermitverwaltung: pupil participation

Schulhelfer: unqualified teacher

Schulreferententagung: conference of educational administrators

Schulverwaltung: administration of schools

Schulwesen: school system

Simultanschule: multi-denominational school

Sozialdemokratische Partei Deutschlands (SPD): Social Democratic Party (West Germany)

Sozialistische Einheitspartei Deutschlands (SED). Socialist Unity Party (East Germany)

Sportverein: sports club

Stabsquartier: headquarters

Strukturplan: structural plan for the educational system put forward by the Bildungsrat in 1970

Studienrat, Studienrätin: grammar school teacher

Tätigkeitsbericht: report on activities

Turnverein: gymnastics club

Verband: association

Volkshochschule: institution for adult education

Volksschule: elementary school

Vorbereitung: preparation

Walpurgisnacht: Walpurgis night (of witches' revelling)

Wehrmacht: armed forces

Welt: world

Wissenschaft: learning, scholarship

Zonenerziehungsrat (ZER): Zonal Education Council

Zonenstudentenrat: Zonal Student Council

Zug: stream, as in the educational term 'streaming'

zweiter Bildungsweg: alternative route to higher education via vocational training and part-time study

L

Index